PRAISE FOR *Intelligence in Danger of Death*:

De Corte is one of the greatest contemporary Catholic philosophers. It was above all in studying Aristotle that he became convinced that [Aristotle and Aquinas] used identical intellectual processes, and that they were, and are, among the best philosophers in history. This was enough for De Corte to oppose modern ideologies with the perennial relevance of classical philosophy.
—DANILO CASTELLANO, author of *L'aristotelismo cristiano di Marcel De Corte*, 1975

"I have loved justice and hated iniquity; that is why I die in exile." These are said to have been the last words of Pope St. Gregory VII. Those of Marcel de Corte could have been analogous: "I have seen through the grotesque intellectual frauds around me; I have made due distinctions; but I lived in times when the difficult judgments men must make regarding complex issues has been used to block the knowledge of my work; therefore I die unappreciated." This translation will go a long way towards awakening thinking English-speaking Catholics to the recognition he so deserves.
—JOHN C. RAO

De Corte's analyses of the way in which a whole society can be made to believe a made-up story useful only to those who govern have been vindicated time and again since 1969; consider recent events such as a man-made virus and its made-up cure(s), made-up sexual categories, made-up universes in electronic media, transhumanism, and so on. De Corte could not have known of these, but the principles he outlines make sense of them, and his reliance on a vast body of philosophical, political, and literary markers from the eighteenth to the twentieth century show the near-irresistible momentum that has led us to this point. This book is an essential read for whoever wishes to understand the road that has led to the current epistemological crisis and its underpinnings; it is a red-pill time capsule. For the solution is precisely to see reality *as it is*, and to abandon the sophistries and fairy-tales that are imposed upon us.
—PETER A. KWASNIEWSKI

## BOOKS BY THE SAME AUTHOR:

*La Liberté de l'Esprit dans l'Expérience mystique* (Paris, Éd. de la Nouvelle Équipe, 1933)

*La doctrine de l'intelligence chez Aristote, essai d'exégèse* (préface d'Étienne Gilson, de l'Académie française. Paris, Vrin, 1934)

*Le Commentaire de Jean Philopon sur le Troisième Livre du « Traité de l'Âme » d'Aristote* (Liège, Fac. de Philosophie et Lettres; Paris, Droz, 1934)

*Aristote et Plotin. Études d'histoire de la philosophie ancienne* (Paris, Desclée De Brouwer, 1935)

*La Philosophie de Gabriel Marcel* (Paris, Téqui, 1938)

*L'Essence de la poésie. Étude philosophique de l'acte poétique* (Bruxelles, Cahier des Poètes Catholiques, 1942)

*Incarnation de l'homme. Psychologie des mœurs contemporaines* (Paris, Libraire de Médicis, 1942; réédition anastatique: Bruxelles, Éd. Universitaires, 1944)

*Philosophie des mœurs contemporaines* (Bruxelles, Éd. Universitaires, 1944)

*Du fond de l'abîme. Essai sur la situation morale de notre pays au lendemain de la Libération* (Bruges, Desclée De Brouwer, 1945)

*Essai sur la fin d'une civilisation* (Bruxelles, Éd. Universitaires; Paris Libraire de Médicis, 1949)

*Mon pays où vas-tu? Philosophie et histoire de la crise belge de 1950* (Paris-Bruxelles, Éd. Universitaires 1951), translations in Spanish and German.

(Coécrit avec Marie de Corte, son épouse) *Deviens ce que tu es: Léon, notre fils, 1937–1955...*, édité en 1956 et préfacé par Gustave Thibon (Paris, Éd. Universitaires, 1956; réédition: Paris, Nouvelles Éditions Latines, 1969)

*J'aime le Canada français* (Québec, Presses Universitaires Laval, 1960)

*L'homme contre lui-même* (Paris, Nouvelles Éditions Latines, 1962)

*L'intelligence en péril de mort* (Paris, Club de la Culture française, 1969)

*De la Justice* (Jarzé, Dominique Martin Morin, 1973)

*De la prudence. La plus humaine des vertus* (Jarzé, Dominique Martin Morin, 1974)

*De la force* (S.l. Dominique Martin Morin, 1980)

*De la tempérance* (S.l. Dominique Martin Morin, 1982)

*Descartes, philosophe de la Modernité* (préface d'Arnaud Jaÿr), Paris, L'Homme Nouveau, coll. « Hora Decima », 2022

# INTELLIGENCE IN DANGER OF DEATH

# Intelligence in Danger of Death

## L'intelligence en péril de mort

MARCEL DE CORTE
*Translated by Brian Welter*
*Introduction by Miguel Ayuso, Ph.D.*

This English edition is based on the French edition published by Éditions de l'Homme Nouveau in 2017 which also includes the explanatory notes of Jean-Claude Absil. The book was originally published in 1969 by Club de la Culture française in Paris and then reissued in 1987 by Dismas with a new preface by the author. We have included additional footnotes to provide more context for English-speaking readers. Subheadings included by the translator.

Copyright © Arouca Press 2023
Translation © Brian Welter
Revised by John Pepino, Ph.D.

All rights reserved:
No part of this book may be reproduced or transmitted, in any form or by any means, without permission

ISBN: 978-1-990685-55-2 (pbk)
ISBN: 978-1-990685-56-9 (hc)

Cover image by Hoach Le Dinh
Courtesy of Unsplash
Cover design by Julian Kwasniewski

Arouca Press
PO Box 55003
Bridgeport PO
Waterloo, ON N2J 3G0
Canada
www.aroucapress.com
Send inquiries to info@aroucapress.com

PUBLISHER'S NOTE: Every effort has been made to locate the original copyright holder for this book. We publish this English edition in good faith and will gladly cooperate with the copyright holder upon notification. We believe Marcel De Corte's works deserve to be known in the English-speaking world due to the deep philosophical insights he had into modernity.

## CONTENTS

Publisher's Note   vii
Translator's Foreword   xi
Introduction, Miguel Ayuso, Ph.D.   xix
Preface for the First Edition (1969)   xxxv
Preface for the Second Edition (1987)   xlvi

1 Intellectuals and Utopia   3
2 The Romanticism of Science   67
3 Information that Deforms   146

Conclusion   216
Index of Names   245
About the Author   249

# Translator's Foreword

BRIAN WELTER

The thoughts of Belgian Thomist philosopher Marcel De Corte (1905–1994) in *Intelligence in Danger of Death* are powerfully relevant in 2023 despite the original publication year of 1969. This timeliness—or timelessness—stems from the author's concern with eternal things. He evaluates the propaganda, narcissism, subjectivism, and emotionalism of his day through the lens of Thomistic realism. His concerns speak to us today, particularly the way information is contorted to fit a predetermined image and to advance an unspoken agenda behind the image. The reader will frequently forget that De Corte wrote this in the late 1960s, given how much of it applies to our current situation.

Bolstering the analysis is the realist assertion that the world and the truth exist independently of our subjective perception. Such an assumption has been completely rejected by the society that De Corte analyzes and that we are a part of today. Society now rejects realism even more than it did in his era while enthusiastically embracing the propaganda, emotionalism, and subjectivity that feeds the mindset of the perpetual adolescent who is fiercely protective of his feelings and opinions.

The subjectivism that De Corte saw all around him was not, in his view, innocent or naive, even if many of its followers might have been. This subjectivism is very deliberate in what it wants. Its purveyors deliberately move the individual and society towards something which is ultimately sinister. This is why De Corte argues that information is not simply data. Newsworthy events are given biased coverage and the images bombarding us intend to alter our perceptions in intentional ways. Information, stories, and images have a purpose to them, particularly in how they are timed, framed, and spun.

When De Corte reveals the falsity of information, news reporting, and images, he arouses in the reader questions such as, "Why are we being shown *this* image at *this* time? What is the agenda behind the image or the news story? What do the purveyors of this image want me to think and to feel? What is their agenda? How do the desired thoughts and feelings that they want to evoke in me serve their purpose?" The purpose of this deception is to take us away from the realist perspective that all humans naturally have, and instead wrap a cocoon of subjectivity and make-believe around us. This deception takes us ever further from the truth.

Information is never neutral. It is *in-formation*, as De Corte often spells the world. It forms us into something. It educates us to be a certain type of person for a certain type of society, without our awareness. It takes us away from our true selves. He asks us, "How can man know his natural end if he is ignorant of the place that he occupies in the universe and the fundamental relationship of his intelligence to the real and to the Principle of reality?" Information is deceptive and devious because the informer is deceptive and devious. Information is always taking us somewhere without our full consent or awareness. De Corte sheds light on how misinformation and propaganda develop, grow, spread, become accepted, and, ultimately, deform the person and all of society.

Why has this deception become such a problem here and now? De Corte shows how falsehood can grow quite easily in certain societies, particularly in those that have no defense against falsehood after their rejection of metaphysics, the truth, and a realist perspective. Falsehood grows in such defenseless societies just as the common cold spreads more easily among individuals with vitamin deficiencies or other vulnerabilities. When society is made up of the spiritually and psychologically weak and sick, falsehood can spread because its very existence depends on its ability to convince us of things that are not true and have no basis in reality. A strong mind will not put up with such nonsense.

Where is this information taking us? If the reader is to believe De Corte, this whole process is diabolical, and we are caught up in a spiritual war. But it takes an understanding of metaphysics, of ultimate things, to perceive this. When the human intelligence is switched off, or trained to follow imagery, which is ultimately the work of the imagination in place of realist metaphysics, it cannot even perceive this spiritual war. The overly-manipulated intelligence lets its guard down or becomes confused. The intelligence found in the typical modern human is not vigilant, but slothful and easily distracted. This is the same dynamic as what led to the Fall. Humans are being sold a pack of lies once again. It is rebellion against the truth and against God. We are being led away from God, and from the real world that He created for us. We are led into the world of deception. This is a world where the intelligence follows the imagination instead of the imagination following the authority of the intelligence. The tail wags the dog.

De Corte argues that the imagination is powerful. It is so powerful that it is almost Godlike, at least from the human perspective. Unsurprisingly, its potential for deception and deviousness can make it diabolical. It is not innocent. We are worse off than the pagans, De Corte observes, because they were realists at least. Now, we are not even living in the real world. We are living in the world of image, deception, and propaganda. Yet miracles still happen: "When one thinks of the generations that were educated, or miseducated, for almost two centuries, at all levels of teaching, in an atmosphere that was oversaturated with idealist haze and smoke, one marvels when noticing that there still exist a few reserves of good sense in humanity."

A non-realist perception of the world is nihilist. This perception strives for the image, which is nothing. In the present, we build little that is real or that is based on the real. This failure leaves us isolated, depressed, unhappy, and unfulfilled. We would rebel against this deception and regain our right minds if we really saw what was happening to us. Therefore, the informer must trick us into projecting our need for community, joy, and fulfillment into the future. This is why the modern western world keeps generating utopias. The non-realist world of the imagination is *tomorrow country*. The utopian promises never arrive, and never will. To assuage our unhappiness and disappointment, a new utopia will always be generated. This is why the information and the image are so crucial for the non-realist. They provide escapes from the hell on earth that is created when we turn from reality and therefore from God.

If De Corte could see all that in the late 1960s, what would he say of our world today? A camera in every hand, on every street corner, mounted on every car, all producing millions of images every day, which are quickly uploaded to be viewed and commented on—a virtual world, a simulacra. De Corte tells the story of two women enjoying a cute baby, with the mother declaring, "This is nothing. You should see the pictures!" Our trip to the Leaning Tower of Pisa or Notre Dame Cathedral is only valid if we have uploaded a picture of ourselves standing in front of it. The image validates reality.

Reading De Corte may remind readers of two other Catholic thinkers of the mid-twentieth century, Marshall

McLuhan and Augusto Del Noce. The latter saw perpetual revolution as the dominant feature of modernity. De Corte notes this ceaseless revolution even within the Church: "The 'pastoral' has become or tends to become constantly revolutionary, subversive, and, in so far as it projects its imaginary forms into reality, as a deceiver." Del Noce describes modernity as revolutionary in its very nature. Wolf-like modernity seeks its prey. This target is anything related to custom or tradition, which is to say, anything that ties the modern individual down, restricts him, and reminds him of his duties. Such things are to be stamped out as *phobias* or a cause of inequality and injustice. The utopian vision (at least the one of 2023) causes us to see custom and tradition as inequality and injustice. As for McLuhan, he famously saw the power of the modern media. The media surpasses in importance and power the information that it conveys. In selecting and shaping information and images, it creates its own world, one which is radically different from the world perceived by the realist. De Corte sees the same thing: The more powerful the media is, the more powerful the deception can be, and the further we are taken from the real world.

If there is any doubt among some conservative thinkers about the viability of Thomism, Marcel De Corte's *Intelligence in Danger of Death* will quickly put that error to rest. His Thomist-based analysis cuts through the facade of the modern mentality. This mentality is the harmful outgrowth of the Enlightenment and Revolution of 1789. He demonstrates the type of stance a conservative or traditional mentality should adopt. The Thomist cannot come to terms with the modern world in any way because this world is anti-human: "Perfect ignorance and absolute ignorance reveal themselves in the rejection of the human condition."

De Corte's insights are sometimes unparalleled in their brilliant perception of the true nature of the modern state and society: "Democracy and information go together.

They are symmetrically unreal." Evolution, the great fetish of modern man, is perpetual revolution, and therefore has a spiritual or metaphysical force to it. Novelty is continuously sought, and is usually imposed by utopian thinkers, to be eagerly embraced by the brainwashed masses as they huff and puff away on their treadmills. Nothing organic is allowed to develop in human society even though organic development is what makes society so human. Everything is imposed from above, from bureaucrats and the ivory tower and from people who are removed from anything natural. Such thoughts remind us of Roger Scruton, who spoke so convincingly against modern architecture and its ugliness, as he lamented how architects with a Ph.D. were coming up with monstrosities to replace the beautiful built-environment of a mostly illiterate medieval and early-modern culture.

How does De Corte define realism, the philosophical orientation that would right the wrongs of this world of image, propaganda, and delusion? "Man knows, as of his birth and because of it, that he is inserted into a physical and metaphysical universe that he did not make, into an order that is not at his mercy, into a hierarchy of beings whose distribution he cannot alter without doing damage to himself. Whatever he does, man recognizes that he cannot become other than what he is by nature, vocation, or grace. No one can run away from his own being." We cannot run away from ourselves, and whenever we try to, we end up deceiving ourselves and building false worlds from deceptive information and images. De Corte argues that people become mentally and spiritually weak when they are uprooted and no longer part of an organic society. This is why he moves from his analysis of information as propaganda, and its psychological effects on the individual, to an analysis of society.

Sadly, in some sense he comes to agree with Margaret Thatcher's famous observation, "There is no society."

## Translator's Foreword

Modern materialist capitalism and democracy, which make up part of the facade for the idealist mindset that rejects realism, undermines all organic bonds among men. De Corte observes the impact of the loss of the sense of the real: "In a society such as ours, which is a society in name only, and whose true label should be *dissociety*, the French Revolution did not only ravage natural communities. *It constructed in their place collectivities that are rigorously and strictly imaginary, whose fictional existence grants every freedom to unleash its own impulses to dominate.*"

Perhaps surprisingly, De Corte is not a pessimist, despite all of this. *Intelligence in Danger of Death* is deeply optimistic. The author offers a simple remedy: stop believing in the image and return to realism, which is a deep part of human nature. What is unnatural is the utopian vision, supported by the constant propaganda that we are sold every day. This cannot last because it is so deceptive and unnatural, so out of alignment with the real world. Anyone who bothers to read Marcel De Corte already knows this. What such a reader gains from this book is a more accurate awareness of the metaphysical meaning of this subjective society that is built on the image. The media is metaphysically significant because of the hold it has over us. The same goes with the scientistic mentality that reduces everything to the quantifiable. The answer is therefore to live more in the real world of faith, family, and local community, and to switch off the phony world of lies.

Let us end with wise words on this topic from Pope Leo XIII in *Aeterni patris*:

> We know that there are some who, in their overestimate of the human faculties, maintain that as soon as man's intellect becomes subject to divine authority it falls from its native dignity, and hampered by the yoke of this species of slavery, is much retarded and hindered in its progress toward the supreme truth and

excellence. Such an idea is most false and deceptive, and its sole tendency is to induce foolish and ungrateful men wilfully to repudiate the most sublime truths, and reject the divine gift of faith, from which the fountains of all good things flow out upon civil society. For the human mind, being confined within certain limits, and those narrow enough, is exposed to many errors and is ignorant of many things; whereas the Christian faith, reposing on the authority of God, is the unfailing mistress of truth, whom whoso followeth he will be neither enmeshed in the snares of error nor tossed hither and thither on the waves of fluctuating opinion. Those, therefore, who to the study of philosophy unite obedience to the Christian faith, are philosophizing in the best possible way; for the splendor of the divine truths, received into the mind, helps the understanding, and not only detracts in nowise from its dignity, but adds greatly to its nobility, keenness, and stability.

# Introduction

**MIGUEL AYUSO, PH.D.**
*Professor of Political Science and Constitutional Law,
Comillas Pontifical University in Madrid*

The Belgian philosopher, Marcel De Corte, is one of the most notable figures in traditional Catholic thought writing in the French language in the second half of the 20th century. After an early period in which he distinguished himself through a series of valuable historical and theoretical books of an Aristotelian nature, his fame—once installed as "ordinary professor" in 1940—was due in good measure to the commitment to the criticism of "modern civilization" by a Catholic intelligence. And, specifically to his analysis of the epistemological inversion of modernity, of the unhinging of the "rational man" which it has carried out, of the unsolvable crisis of its civilization, of the corrupting character of a polity founded upon the "religion of democracy" and of the crisis of the (post) conciliar Church.

After a general characterization of him as a philosophical realist, we develop each one of these aspects, metaphysical, ethical and religious.

\* \* \*

When in 1985, having reached his eightieth year, the Italian journal, *Filosofía oggi* asked him for a presentation of his philosophy, his first words were that as far as he knew he had no personal philosophy, and hence, it was impossible to respond to such a request. "I have not philosophized except via my reading of Aristotle and St. Thomas Aquinas, followed by meditations sometimes quite long, over what they meant—or better mean—for me, simply the *truth*. In addition I have tried to pick out in my abundant reading of modern and contemporary philosophy the elements of truth—in my judgment exceedingly rare—which they transmit and which can agree with the *eternal truth* of the great masters of the past from which I daily drink and of which it can be said, with total justice, that it was the philosophy of *common sense*. Hence—not even for them—*their philosophy* but rather the philosophy which every man in this world receives in the intimacy of his conscience when he opens himself to what is real and what is outside of his own mind." I think, he continued his confession, "that every man normally constituted and who responds to the definition of an animal who reasons, in which the two characteristics—the first generic and the second specific—communicate between themselves and nourish themselves reciprocally, is gifted with this common sense which sustains philosophy and the investigation of the universal causes and objectives of *that which is, of being*, as much in its essence as in its existence, and which concerns, in the final analysis, all the beings which we know."

This recognition, however, is not an assumption, that is, the principle of a system, but is a truth which establishes the relation of agreement of the mind with the object. In this sense, one can affirm that the philosopher does not differ from the man of common sense, of man himself, inasmuch as truly a man, but one who searches solely, *in the measure of what is possible*, to reach this characteristic of his perfection: "The philosopher of peasant origin, which I am, cannot but adhere with all his strength to the philosophy of common sense: all the activities of a farmer revolve around the objective reality which is revealed to his senses and his intelligence, under pain of being eliminated from existence and from his occupation and even from sheer existence.... The profound crisis which we suffer at present and which invades the entire world is the result of a lack of reality which has filled with its chimeras the intelligence of a good number of our contemporaries and which has cast aside all the healthy nourishment and the stimulating energy which introduce into them the philosophy, more or less living, but still their own, of common sense." Yet another reason, tied powerfully to the previous, hinders him from speaking of his philosophy: "It is that temperamentally, idiosyncratically, I am the least 'reflective' that I could be. I do not practice that turning of thought upon itself of which a great number of contemporary philosophers are artists and propagandists. I open my eyes and ears to the world and to men. My intelligence nourishes itself from the data which the senses supply. This is enough for me and more. Moreover, I do not practice the turning to my past. I march continually without returning to what I have written, always in the same direction, despite certain contrary appearances. I will confess here that I have not ever returned to reread certain of the books which I have published. I look toward other books, other articles, through an impulse to continue and surpass them."

The Italian philosopher Augusto Del Noce has written concerning the radical disjuncture which at all times threatens those who embark in the ships of thought: on the one hand, the way of the classical-Christian philosopher, who situates himself "over an uncreated order of values, apprehended by an intellectual intuition and not dependent on any decision, even the divine;" on the other, the road of the modern philosopher who does not recognize anything beyond that which he creates and realizes, so that permanent values cannot exist for those who incline toward an act of recognition because the 'positive' is neither natural nor real, but a creature of human intelligence, however much subordinated in this *poiética* or creative activity to the human will. De Corte, confronted with the same situation, and having unavoidably to choose, will choose the first, and reject with all his strength the second. Indeed the negation of an uncreated order of values opens the door to modernism—theological, philosophical, moral or political—marking the end of the value of tradition, and, finally, of morality and religion. Hence we must pass immediately.

To this intellectual attitude, unsurpassable as we have said, is added in our subject, however, another of a decisive and chronological nature. As he himself explains— and as Danilo Castellano has developed magnificently in the first two chapters of his book on our author, *L'aristotelismo cristiano di Marcel de Corte*, dedicated to situate the author in the culture and the philosophy of his time— he takes the intellectual field in a moment in which the "dispute over Christian philosophy" is still living, in which Gilson and Maritain are powerfully revealing their teaching or in which Bergson completes the arc which leads from *L'évolution créatrice* to *Les deux sources de la morale et de la religion*. De Corte, who will never be a Bergsonian—contrary to Maritain—and who will be considered without reason and superficially a disciple of him in his first period, will, on the other hand, always read Gilson with profit, he who—as he prefaced his doctoral thesis on *La doctrine de l'intelligence chez Aristote*—declares having been captivated by his interpretation and that as a result he had been definitively fixed in making Saint Thomas a direct heir of Aristotle.

Saint Thomas the Aristotelian, in as much as Aristotle—following Plato—impeded the development of Neoplatonism and the idealistic dialectic. Saint Thomas the Aristotelian, representing Greek thought in its purity and in its separation from the emanations that characterize oriental thought.

*Introduction*

\* \* \*

The philosophical realism professed by De Corte harmonizes perfectly with his antimodernism. We have seen how the denial of the uncreated order of values leads to modernism and concludes with a denial of tradition, religion and morality. "Esse est coesse," to exist is to exist with, he repeated incessantly. Being, for man, is being with, and includes therefore a familiarity, an agreement, a sharing with other beings and with things. That which characterizes modernity, however, is the rupture of the fundamental relation of man toward the other, the universe and the Principle of being. Thus, it tries to rule the world with criteria antithetical to those which led to the civilized life, to culture, to law. The questions burst forth in a cascade: What does it mean to be able to have, in light of these reflections, the modernist vision of "creation"? To what is religion reduced except to which immanence assumes the position of a false transcendence, the projection of atheism in the religious dimension? What does morality become except an abstract rule, an imposition and finally hypocrisy? What meaning can the political, an instrument at the service of utopia, put on in the best hypothesis? What value remains to the conscience which would not be able to decipher images and structures imposed through another in order to transpose the plane of the subjective to the objective? What meaning, distinct from repression, and hence always lagging behind with respect to the social affirmation, does the law acquire? Finally, where do we leave man, reduced to an instrument to support the "movement of history"? Castellano responds that "the negation of all these realities which man and society require, comes first substituted, and afterwards imposed despotically, since man continues existing side by side with them.

The answer formulated by the Belgian philosopher is that which Jean Madiran has called "the Christian answer to the modern world," which Augusto Del Noce has pointed out as "a Catholic form of the answer." It is the calling into question of the whole modern world, understanding that its intellectual methods—and in the end, its practical consequences—are foreign and contrary to the supernatural order, and not in the mere sense of a natural order which is ignorant of grace, but in the more radical sense of what are so foreign both to nature as to grace. And so, it is a matter of a critical understanding of everything, as previously we have had occasion to outline and now we must develop more in detail.

In the moral sphere, understood on the firm foundation of anthropology, he undertakes the criticism of contemporary man and his customs from the tradition which begins with Aristotle and Theophrastus, put into the language of today, and in which a concrete analysis of customs appears always sustained by an ontological conception of "the everlasting man"—to follow the happy formula of Chesterton, of whom our author was so fond. His concerns begin with the profound moral crisis which preceded the Second World War, and which has not ceased to worsen up to our own time, its profound cause masked by a whole series of secondary phenomena. He affirms that the present moral crisis cannot be explained better than through the essential unfaithfulness of man to his nature as a rational animal, made to subsist in the only and true substance which unites spirt and life, body and soul. It results from the rupture of a previous state of harmony, as if from the separation and the conflict of the two elements made in order to unite and complete themselves in man. Contemporary man—he writes—is a *homo duplex*, a *Platonic man*, torn apart by a dualism in which the intelligence offers itself up to idolize great devouring idols: Science, Progress, Liberty, the Nation, Work, etc., so much so that it uproots itself from everything which is organic in it: family, fatherland, profession, faith, which—abandoned to their fate—become merely useful reflections in order to embody the hollow and empty ideas in existence. In this atmosphere the unitive and tranquil energy of daily duties disappears and the essence of man is shaken in its physical and metaphysical foundations: "Man identifies himself with one or other of his functions: *homo rationalis, homo politicus, homo economicus, homo ethnicus, homo sexualis*, etc. each one governed by disincarnate ideologies. We enter into a major crisis of civilization in which the hypertrophy of one part imitates the fullness of the whole, something which was unknown in any previous crisis. Disincarnate 'morality' seeks to eliminate one or the other for the benefit of one alone of these which will submit to its dominion the political, the social and the individual, as is seen perfectly in communism. Hence, the crisis of civilization which he analyzed at the beginning of his career, when nothing portended that it would swell and reached the amplitude which we know today, is unknown in history" (*Autobiographie philosophique*). He had reasons—he opined—which our ancestors did not know.

As well in the epistemological field. Before we read his confession that he lacked a philosophy of his own and his protestation of realism. Equally let us follow him in the affirmation that the human being is constituted in a fundamental relationship, prior to all knowledge and all activity: it arises in the physical, metaphysical, social, political and religious world, which he did not make, and with which he enters into immediate contact from the moment of his birth and in the course of his whole life. It is therefore impossible not to recall the pages and pages of our author, unsurpassable in their description of that vital interaction which modern philosophy has disintegrated and crushed: "Similar to a vigorous tree—he writes referring to the generation of his parents—they sunk their roots in the fertile earth of the real, where they sought nourishment.... Their roots absorbed the sap from the earth. The chlorophyll of the human tree drank the light of the heavens. A tacit nuptial agreement was sealed between man and the universe. Tempests and cataclysms succeeded one another, but they resisted them: reserves from the watery world below and from the world above accumulated in its sap.... The man of today has broken the agreement...." And so, devoid of all relation between the genuine man who is in solidarity with the genuine world, our liberty has been inexorably condemned to construct a new world which becomes appropriate for him and which substitutes itself for the human world progressively being annihilated" (*L'homme contre lui-même*).

And it is the chief function of intelligence to recognize and to discover the order which underlies this fundamental relation, conforming itself to it and placing man appropriately in the universe. The modern epoch, however, broke this relation and turned its gaze toward man: "Man has turned his back to the universe in order to rest from the outset on himself as the unique and only reality: *cogito ergo sum*. In this way man has set himself as the center of the world because of his unique faculty that, due to its spirituality, he is capable in itself of reflecting on himself: through his intelligence." From this rupture the intelligence reigns, not indeed over reality—from which he has been freed as someone who has abandoned an intolerable weight—but rather over his dreams: "Indeed man cannot live without a world around him. His decision to break the cords which unite him to the world and to its Principle oblige him to a work always immense, always forced to begin again: to construct a new world, a new man, a new society and undoubtedly new gods, starting solely from the demands of human reason. The intelligence no longer conforms to reality, it is reality which has to conform itself to the intelligence, and it can do this only if the intelligence recasts it, remodels it, re-creates it in order to make it correspond to the perfect model of the world which it forged in its bosom" (*L'éducation politique*).

*Introduction*

The origin of this sickness of the human intelligence, which attacks man at the juncture of soul and body, beyond which is the precisely and specifically human, was investigated with great detail in his *L'intelligence en péril de mort* published here for the first time in English. If the Western philosophical tradition starts off by distinguishing adequately between theory, praxis and *poiesis*, modernity has gone on to invert them. *Homo faber* has eliminated almost totally *homo sapiens* and man dedicated to others, that is, *homo politicus*: "Once the attracting and penetrating primacy of attraction of the speculative intelligence over the other two has been eliminated, there remains nothing in man more than animality, which expands through his whole being, as contemporary morals demonstrate and the prohibition—there is no other word—which the technical intelligence throws over the metaphysical and political intelligence, expelling them. Everywhere the *homo oeconomicus* reigns despotically. There are no more problems for the man of today which are not economic. And once the material problems have been resolved a new paradise will open before the divinized man" (*Autobiographie philosophique*).

Behold how the human type of the "intellectual" appears, hoisted up to the summit as an incomparable model of this our age, the being capable of dominating the new activity of the intelligence. He is believed to be clothed with an august mission: reforming morals, changing ideas and tastes, proposing and imposing a new concept of man, of society and of the world. Hence, he is able to change himself into the "technocrat," into the "functionary" or into the "reporter." The phenomenon of the "disinformation," magisterially analyzed as well by De Corte, fits in exactly at this point of the explanation. Let us see. Each collapse of the system which deprives man of his specific difference compensates with an improvement in the art of deception, as the parasite sees itself obliged, in order to prolong its existence, to multiply and perfect its artifices. From the political discourse before the multitude to the mass media of today, the continuity is uninterrupted: "It is a matter of always giving a pseudo-social form to that which does not have a form and cannot have one; a matter always of informing, of clothing human beings in a manner that instills into them the illusion of communication. More exactly, it is a matter of thinking, if that word can still be used in its place, and of inserting the appearance of a collective opinion, when the manipulators of the system act upon a conditioned reflex which has overcome them and which they have obtained technically to be the only masters.

\* \* \*

Disinformation, charged with creating and sustaining artificially the so-called public opinion, presents a close connection with the sociology of the democratic phenomenon: it is the sociology of this system in which is combined the real power of a minority and the imaginary power of the majority, which explains the phenomenon of disinformation. Thus we are in conditions of penetrating entirely into the recesses of his political thought which, in this point as well, correspond admirably with his core developments. Marcel De Corte sees as the most characteristic feature of our epic the destruction of the social and its reabsorption by the collective. *The social*, at least, shows itself as something real: there are natural societies (family, city, parish, region, etc.). It exists, then, in the measure in which it is organic, in which it unites concrete human beings, bound by mutual interactions—in this sense egalitarianism is always the death of the social, since it destroys the possibility of that interaction—the ties of blood and spirit. *The collective*, on the other hand, does not exist except in the imagination, it has no other existence than that of the image, which resides in the mind.

Where the social relation is weakening, collectivism arises automatically with a means of representation destined to serve as a guide in the chaos of monads without cohesion, in which interactions are reduced to a minimum (*Essai sur la fin d'une civilisation*).

Chiefly in *L' homme contre lui-même* he analyzed in detail the diverse phases through which the pathology of liberty has passed: the crisis of good sense; the crisis of the elites; the decay of the notion of happiness and of reality; the Machiavellianism of deed which—camouflaged under a Rousseauism of law—contemporary politics displays in order to embody in its existence the myth of Progress, etc. The result is that we do not live in a society, in a *nouveau régime* which has been substituted for the *ancien* régime: we find ourselves in a genuine "dissociety," on its way toward a "nest of termites."

Democracy is nothing but the concrete political incarnation of the entire conglomeration of individualism, egalitarianism and utopianism which we have discerned. When all is said and done Maurrasism cannot cease to regard itself as a "religion." What is the end of modern democracy? De Corte does not hesitate: "It is the construction of a new 'society' where each individual enjoys the most complete liberty, where his behavior carries neither obligation nor sanction, where each Ego constitutes its own absolute. Democracy, as a result, is never complete; always we need more democracy. It is not sufficient to have a system which guarantees freedom, it is necessary—by means of a permanent questioning of all ties, natural, semi-natural and institutional which unite individuals among themselves— to create from all its pieces a "new world," extended to all the planet and where each one depends on nothing except his own autonomous conscience. As long as there are in the world people subject to others, however that may be, there is no true democracy, because it is not possible for each one to manifest himself according to his free choice and in equality of conditions with others" (*De la justice*). In light of these words, the slogans which insist with so much frequency on the necessity of "a deepening of democracy" acquire a new aspect, beyond the merely verbal. Democracy devotes itself without ceasing to substitute for the natural authorities, which do not cease to sprout forth. One cannot ignore with impunity the nature of things and always remain a trunk of a tree, although at moments one cannot distinguish them, covered as by ivy.

The consequences are, for one part, the vanishing of the common good and, on the other, the tendency toward totalitarianism. The purpose of civil society is nothing other than the common good, consisting in "an order, a mutual ordering of the parts among themselves which permits its own interchanges, its mutual help, his complementarity." Everything which favors this mutual relation pertains to the common good. The common good, he writes, is hence *everything which unites these, the middle term* which integrates people within itself, the relations of every kind which link the successive generations, the unmeasurable realities which knead together its life in society and which perpetuate themselves beyond their brief existence. A paradox results, but the realistic approximation underlines "the distinctive" in the society, in order to end up in "the union," without which the social and political order disintegrates. On the other hand, modern democracy, aggressively unifying, receives its foundation in a disintegrative pluralism, in the radical "differentiation."

Without leaving the French context, to be sure Spanish Carlist thought has explained this a thousand times, Maurras had already observed that "liberalism" kills "liberty." And Madiran added that, equally, "pluralism" destroys "plurality." Marcel De Corte does not move in another sphere. Modern democracy, then, based on the "differentiation," renders it impossible to attain the common good, characterized precisely by the "union." In as much as an idea, a being of reason—which does not exist except in the thought which thinks it, a type of subjective representation—comes to constitute a type of ideological form in which the individuals swim, a myth which envelopes them in a secret cult that each one professes for himself. The common good in democracy, De Corte insists, if it is possible to speak in this way, can be nothing except democracy itself, which does not unite people except in the imagination.

The propensity to totalitarianism was also firmly asserted in the work of the Belgian philosopher. And, again, as in previous occasions, not through having been set forth in the "counterrevolutionary" school, it fails to emphasize the rigor and the subtlety of De Corte in developing it. It would begin by upholding that for the contemporary State and its manipulators, "democracy is not only a masquerade, a facemask, a decoration intended to deceive the last devotees of a religion which already has expired and which has entered into its customary phase of ritualistic rigidity." What is given to discover, in our age, under this caparison of the State? The *dissociety*, the society of the masses, a "society"—as we have previously sketched—which owes nothing to the original impulses of the social nature of man, defined by the simple juxtaposition of its devitalized and homogeneous members. This occurs because, placed before a collectivity where now there are no natural communities but only individuals, the State acquires an unlimited reach. A State which crowns a *dissociety* will fatally end up being the only entity, the whole of society, and assume all the social functions which nature has conceded to man:

> It becomes obvious that the growth of the totalitarian State is correlative to the decline of the political education which has its seat in the natural communities. In these are articulated the complementarity of the reason and the will with the impulses of nature and

they acquire habits, typical ways of behavior, conduct submitted to well-known norms which bring about that the acts of each one of its members are able to be foreseen by the others and that there reigns among them a certain permanent form of order, while the social relations are established in such manner that they do not deceive each other.... The more lasting and rooted are the uses and ways of behavior, so is the norm in the mutual relations where nature possesses the initiative, the sovereign power is less able to launch itself in a projector toward absolutism, which is characteristic of it when it abandons its own proper role. (*L'éducation politique*)

If the essence of totalitarianism lies in the omnipresence of the state, there is no difficulty in asserting a totalitarian character to democracy. De Corte expressed it in this way:

Each State constructed over a natural community and over the education which they spread about, sees its power reduced to a just measure; and each power is seldom felt as an exterior force by the citizens. On the contrary, each State without a society is automatically a coercive police State, armed with an arsenal of laws and regulations with which it is charged to give meaning to the unforeseeable and aberrant conduct of individuals. Its tendency to totalitarianism is in direct proportion to the weakness of the natural communities, decay of customs, the destruction of education. In the end, the "big animal" of which Plato speaks, the terrifying social Leviathan which we know, substitutes for the moderate authority which imprudently has been eliminated through a Constitution or stupid legislation.

Hence, Professor Marcel De Corte follows out the ultimate consequences of his Catholic philosophy, in the manner that the moralist of the classic tradition and the Aristotelian-Thomistic philosopher makes himself a counterrevolutionary sociologist and a Maurrasian expert in politics. The anti-modern metaphysical, epistemological and moral anti-modernism is also a social and political anti-modernism. And not only much more lasting than he who made the saying famous, but also much more refined and wise. Thus Marcel De Corte has enrolled himself in the school of Maurras, and, as an outstanding student, is capable of resolving the *aporias*, the paradoxes, which surround the thought of the master, overcoming the difficulties, integrating the weaknesses and extracting at each moment its richest veins. Avoiding also the risk in which more than once the school of Maurrasian verbiage has fallen victim—the discernment, unsurpassable, is again that of Jean Madiran—of following in an inverse sense the road of Maurras, that is, instead of going, as he, to the conversion of the *politique d'abord*, making Catholics to recede from the living faith in Jesus Christ as far as the *politique d'abord*.

\* \* \*

In the last point, as well, which I will not leave without noting, since an adequate treatment would require a greater length than that which I have, De Corte is a militant traditionalist in the French intellectual orbit. With Madiran and with [Louis] Salleron. With [Gustave] Thibon and with Michel de Saint-Pierre. And with so many others who suffered in their flesh—without any metaphorical meaning, indeed in truth who was in a sorrow which reached even to the depth of the soul—the crisis called forth by the Second Vatican Council. As with those, he had to follow the road of resistance as much as that of faithfulness, and to suffer the epithet of "integrist." As did they, he confronted the "heresy of the 20th century:" he defended the Traditional Mass, criticized the catechetical paralysis, faced up against the "cult of man," combated the ecumenical tendencies and sustained the traditional doctrine against the failure of religious liberty.

In the Hispanic world, with the necessary difference of emphasis, we discover the pure Carlist movement, with great personalities, not only in the Iberian peninsula, but also abroad. Names such as Rafael Gambra or Francisco Elías de Tejada, but also the Chilean Osvaldo Lira, the Argentine Rubén Calderón Bouchet, the Brazilian José Pedro Galvão de Sousa and Frederick D. Wilhelmsen himself.

But that is another story...

*Translated by Thomas Storck.*

# Preface to the First Edition (1969)

To Henri de Lovinfosse
With my deep friendship,
M. D. C.
In memory of our philosophical
conversations at Waasmunster

The work that we present as *Intelligence in Danger of Death* is part of a series of works that we have dedicated to the crisis of contemporary civilization: *Incarnation de l'homme, Philosophie des moeurs contemporaines, Essai sur la fin d'une civilisation, L'homme contre lui-même*. Our diagnosis has become more and more precise throughout the course of this long meditation. This work represents the final stage.

We have ventured as close as possible to the origin of this strange ailment that affects man in the second half of the twentieth century. It infects him at the point of union between body and soul, which is to say, at the point where he is specifically man. We believe we have found the cause in man's soul itself, at the very summit of his being, in his specific distinctiveness, which is his *intelligence*.

Contemporary man, hurtling down the mountain slope under the thrust of the man of the eighteenth century and the Revolution, has increasingly sacrificed his *speculative intelligence* (which endeavors to correspond to the reality of beings and objects) and his *practical intelligence* (which attempts to provide the means that are used for the ultimate end of human life, to which this intelligence is attracted) to its *working intelligence*. This latter is the maker of a world, society, and type of man that are all artificial. Instead of coming before *homo sapiens*, as still occurred in the old evolutionary mythologies that we were taught in my youth, *homo faber* now follows him.

We are in the last stage of this development, of this "mutation." It is deadly, as are all biological mutations, as in the case of a five-legged sheep. In this mutation, the true and the good that are grasped by the speculative intelligence and the practical intelligence are sacrificed for the benefit of *man's will to power, which from then on is intellectually and morally blind.* This will spread its power over the world, including over the human race itself.

Let's not be mistaken here. This power to transform everything with which man is blessed is only contained within its just limits, and only functions *normally*, when regulated by the lights of speculative and practical intelligence. As soon as man turns his back on these, he sinks into the darkness of idolizing himself. This idolatry is more certainly destructive of his being and specific difference than the worst ignorance and moral perversion. Perfect ignorance and absolute immorality reveal themselves in the rejection of the human condition. Armed with all the technological possibilities for renunciation and the construction of a "new world" that justifies this "mutation," man kills in himself the intelligence that tirelessly reproaches him for having crossed the limits of the real.

We enter the imaginary when we exceed the boundaries of the real. We are more and more in the world of contrivance, in a utopian society, before phantoms that take form and then vanish right before our eyes according to the relentless "march of history." We are in the last stage of this ailment. With the death of man's intelligence, nothing remains in him except animality, "the perfect and definitive hive of activity" about which Valéry spoke.[1]

---

[1] "A certain confusion still reigns, but some time after that everything will become clear. We will finally witness the miracle of

*Preface to the First Edition (1969)*

This is the monstrous specter of Leviathan evoked by Pius XII.[2]

Two *graffiti* scrawlings and some "theses" that rebellious students[3] recently left in the Sorbonne shows us the three steps of this collapse: 1) "Dream ["rêve"] + Evolution = Revolution"; 2) "Let's imagine new sexual perversions"; 3) "No more professors will be appointed after today. The crisis in the recruitment of professors has been resolved since every student will make an equal effort, with mentoring and teaching, on academic subjects." Everyone mentors and teaches everyone else, just as the world mentors and teaches each individual in the new prison that has been baptized "new Eden."

Particularly in Catholic milieux where this cancer has invaded, one is criticized for employing an "obviously outdated" Aristotelian classification of the activities of the mind.[4] We simply ask our opponents to present us with another classification scheme *that is objective* and that is based *on the very nature* of beings and objects with which the human mind can enter into a relationship. We are sure that the "dialogue" will go no further than it does with Aristotle.

---

an animal society, a perfect and definitive hive of activity." Paul Valéry, *La crise de l'esprit, première lettre*, in *Essais quasi politiques*, Oeuvres, tome 1, Paris, Bibliothèque de la Pléiade, 1975, 994.

2 "We need to stop the person and the family from letting themselves be led to the abyss, as tends to happen when one is socialized in everything. At the end of this socialization, the terrifying image of Leviathan will become a horrible reality. It is with this last energy that the Church will give battle. At stake in this battle will be the highest values, which are the dignity of man and the eternal salvation of souls." Pius XII, Radio Message to the Congress of Austrian Catholics in Vienna, September 14, 1952, in A. F. Utz, J. F. Grosser, A. Savignat, *Relations humaines et société contemporaine. Synthèse chrétienne. Directives de Pie XII*, Editions Saint-Paul, Tome 1, Fribourg/Paris, 1956, Section 710, 307.

3 During the Revolution of May 1968 in Paris and elsewhere in France.

4 Aristotle, *Metaphysics* and *Topics*.

In our case, we will go further. Without fear of falling into error, let us affirm that every substitution of an activity of the mind for another immediately provokes a disorder, an organic disruption in man's soul. When man abandoned this classification and replaced speculative and practical activities of the mind with *poetic* activity (that which makes, fabricates, builds, etc.), he lost his natural equilibrium and went astray. The true or the good cannot be reached by the same paths as those taken to build something, achieve a piece of work, or introduce a specific form onto matter. Our analysis will prove it, and be confirmed by the experience of disasters produced by such a confusion.

This classification corresponds to reality and to this "natural metaphysics of human intelligence" so neatly that Bergson himself did not fail to discover it in Greek philosophy, much to his amazement.[5] Greek philosophy is the philosophy of common sense, realism, and human intelligence that is faithful to its essence. In brief, it is man's higher health. Every time we repudiate it, we pay a price.

We will provide only one example, and it is a big one.

Christianity, particularly Catholicism, is not connected to Greek philosophy by simple historical chance. The connection comes from the force of faith in search of intelligence, of *fides quaerens intellectum*, and of a *universal* conception of the mind, just as the message of the gospel

---

[5] "We did not have the pretension [of Greek philosophy] to reconstruct metaphysics *a priori*. It [metaphysics] has multiple origins. It is attached by invisible threads to all the fibers of the ancient soul. Attempting to infer it from a simple principle would be in vain. But if we eliminate everything that comes from poetry, religion, social life, as well as from a still-rudimentary physics and biology, if we set aside the brittle materials that are included in the construction of this immense edifice, a solid structure remains. This structure sketches out the great lines of a metaphysics that, we believe, is the natural metaphysics of human intelligence." Henri Bergson, *L'Evolution créatrice* (Paris, P. U. F., 1948), 325.

itself was *universal*. The Greek concept of intelligence, a faculty of the real where all men meet and come to agreement among themselves, guaranteed this *universality*.

This solidarity between the supernatural realism of the faith and natural realism of human intelligence lasted roughly two millennia and, with diverse adventures, it constituted the axis of Christendom and the pivot of the Church that was the depository and vigilant guardian of the faith, of intelligence, and of custom. This was broken during Vatican II.

The consequences of this catastrophe for the Church and for humanity, provoked by a gang of conciliar Fathers with a disoriented intelligence, will never be measured. It is known that all of the preparation of the Council, following the orders of John XXIII, was carried out according to traditional norms and filled with scholastic vocabulary. This vocabulary, an evolved form of language, is conducive to "the natural metaphysics of human intelligence." The majority of the Council, led by its "organized" minority, rejected this method of presentation and declared itself in support of a formulation that was allegedly more accessible to the modern mind and to the *aggiornamento* required by the Pope. It appeared to be a simple change in the presentation of the Gospel message and of dogma. The prescribed return to the Biblical speech even appeared to be required, at least in certain sectors and notably in that of preaching, by the Fathers who were the most attached to the tradition of the Church. In this way, the Girondins of the Council retained a good conscience at little cost and got their way, as if they were sending a letter via the post.[6] It was a loaded letter, filled with explosives. We have begun to feel the first shocks set off by its explosion.

---

6  In the French Revolution, the Girondins, or Girondists, formed a part of the Jacobins. The Girondins had second thoughts when revolutionary violence spun out of control. Many Girondins were executed in 1793.

One cannot change his language as he does his clothes. Undoubtedly, every language is established by convention. Language is originally a system of verbal expression of thought made up of artificial signs invented by man. But in its effort to create these signs, human intelligence is powerfully aided by its very nature, which orders it to the reality to which its act must correspond in order to be true. The human art is added here as it is everywhere, at the risk of degenerating into a pure arbitrariness that is lacking in every signification other than that of a subjective will and that is accountable to no one but itself. Language *participates* therefore in the dynamism of the intellectual nature that seeks the truth. The more this nature is developed, the more the language is weighed down by objective signification. This is the case with Greek, the language of the most intelligent people in the world. Throughout all the upheavals of history, this language conveyed "the natural metaphysics of human intelligence." This is the case with scholastic Latin, which is the heir of the achievements of the Greeks.

The natural effort of the human mind that was focused on the search for truth had reached an unequaled point of perfection in scholastic language. The Council's refusal to use this scholastic language led to losing the realism that the Church had always overseen until then. Instead of pouring new wine into the empty flask, the flask received the wind of all the storms of human subjectivity. We look on with stupefied horror at the ravages carried out by this subjectivity in the Church and Christian civilization. In repudiating the language, the sign of concepts, we repudiated things, and in repudiating things, we suddenly entered into permanent subversion and revolution to the great astonishment of the Fathers themselves, or the majority of them.

There was an attempt to stop this collapse, timidly called "the post-conciliar mentality," that even the least-informed minds could have foreseen. Lacking unity at the

## Preface to the First Edition (1969)

level of truth, which is the object of contemplative intelligence, the Fathers pivoted the Council towards "action" because disagreements fade when everyone pursues the same intention. That is why this Council wanted to be strictly *pastoral*, unlike all previous councils.[7] It did not proclaim any dogma. It could not have done so without articulating its definitions of traditional dogmas. It would have thereby demonstrated its ineffectiveness in providing definitions, adjusting itself to essences, and utilizing as an instrument, *sicut ancilla*, the only philosophy that can agree with the faith and which the history of the Church has shown to be fruitful.

But this attempt to limit the Council to the "pastoral" was bound to fail, as anyone can see. "Pastoral" means nothing other than the collection of rules of conduct that have as their objective directing man towards his supernatural end. The pastors of the flock are given the task of applying these rules. But how can man be led to his supernatural end if he has no knowledge of his natural end?[8] Strategy assumes knowledge of the terrain, which

---

[7] "The human values of the council have diverted the attention of the Church in council to the trend of modern culture, centered on humanity. We would say not diverted but rather directed. Any careful observer of the council's prevailing interest for human and temporal values cannot deny that it is from the pastoral character that the council has virtually made its program." Pope Paul VI, Address during the last general meeting of the Second Vatican Council, Rome, December 7, 1965.

"The truth is that this particular Council defined no dogma at all, and deliberately chose to remain on a modest level, as a merely pastoral council; and yet many treat it as though it had made itself into a sort of 'super-dogma' which takes away the importance of all the rest." Cardinal Ratzinger Addresses Chilean and Colombian Bishops in Colombia, July 13, 1988.

[8] On the distinction between the two ends of the human being, one natural and "proportional to human nature," and the other supernatural and freely given, see St. Thomas Aquinas, *QD Veritate*, q. 14, a.2, resp. A, 1, a and b (Marietti, 283); *ibid.* Q. 27, a.2, resp. (Marietti, 514); *Sum. Theol.*, Ia, q.23, a.1, resp.

in this case is man in the world. Grace does not abolish nor replace nature. How can man know his natural end if he is ignorant of the place that he occupies in the universe and of the fundamental relationship of his intelligence to the real and to the Principle of reality? The "pastoral" orientation cannot ignore practical or speculative philosophy. How can we return to this knowledge when the feature of our time, to which many want to attach Christianity at all costs, is to ignore these philosophies and replace them with the single poetic activity of the mind?

The Council's "pastoral" orientation did not permit any choice. This orientation has had to become the *poetic* activity of the mind, maker of a new world and new society, and creator of a new man! The "pastoral" has become, or is constantly becoming, revolutionary, subversive, and deceptive in so far as it projects its imaginary forms onto reality. It has equally become the alibi and the mask of the progressive will to power and of a theocracy that dares not speak its name, and thereby conceals the worst of its tyrannies. Chesterton spoke of this latter tyranny as playing on the soul with the keyboard of "love."

Occurring right before our eyes is this extraordinary phenomenon of the destruction of the Church from within and thereby of civilization by those very people who in the past saved it from disaster. The following pages will shed light on this without being soft on anything.

The Church (at least that part of it which holds the high ground, monopolizes the information, and frolics in the mess of the *aggiornamento*) embraced fiction at full speed. It did so in shamelessly displaying its indifference and scorn for the value of the truth of intellectual concepts, and of the formulas that these concepts express. It did so by cutting the two millennial-old umbilical cord that linked Aristotelian philosophy to common sense. The example of the *New Catechism*, approved by the entirety of the Dutch episcopate, demonstrates this. The commission that examined it found no less than eighteen major points, including conception and wording, that did not correspond to the realities of the faith. More numerous are the minor infringements on dogma and on the supernatural. The authors of this catechism do not hide the fact that they wanted deliberately to undo "outmoded" Aristotelianism and Thomism.

What seems normal in the contemporary Church, however, is the primacy of the *poetic* activity of the mind, and, consequently, of the will to power. This is true even with as many exceptions as one would like, as these special cases are scattered and isolated, lack major channels of diffusion, and are sometimes reduced to silence. There is a desire everywhere to "*do* something," to *transform* everything. Nothing escapes the zeal of the new *reformers*, who impose their conceit on everyone. Such a Church is therefore pushed to compete with the social and political systems that are in the grip of the same affliction, and even to take over for them. Like these systems, the Church puts an artificial stamp on the intellectual and moral behaviors (whether supernatural or secular) of the faithful under its authority, though this stamp is prefabricated by the literary set.

This new form, according to which the "pastoral" henceforth shapes souls, as the sculptor shapes clay, is "the Kingdom of God" *here below*, the very inversion of the Ascension. It is the exaltation of the fall, the *yes* spoken to the Tempter who grants all powers on earth to whoever *falls* in adoration before him. One can now understand the significance of the words of Bishop Schmitt ("Socialism is a grace"[9]) and innumerable parallel declarations

---

[9] Bishop Paul Joseph Schmitt (1911–1987), bishop of Metz from 1958–1987: "Socialism is not only an inescapable fact of history. It is a grace." In *Bulletin officiel de l'évêché de Metz*, number 134, September 1, 1967, 4. Cited and commented on by Jean Madiran, *L'Hérésie du XXe siècle*, Paris, N. E. L., 1968; seconde édition (avec epilogue), 1987, 155.

of so many clergymen who, according to Dietrich von Hildebrand's wonderful expression, bring "the Trojan horse into the City of God"[10] when they draw parallels between communism and Christianity.

This "mutation" of the Church will not of course come to pass without the "mutation" of modern man. We will analyze this latter phenomenon in this book.

Three cuts, as it were, have been made into the organic tissue of suffering humanity.

It would be very surprising if we spoke only in passing of art and its current breakdown. It is just that its case is so clear. Contemporary art (and literature) wants to escape from the order of the universe. It is in permanent revolt against the human condition. It has nothing left, at the end of its "liberation," than its poetic activity emptied of its spiritual, intellectual, and moral substance. This poetic activity is nothing more than a raw power that produces an unformed form, if one can call it that, in any formless matter. What the contemporary artist executes on paper, canvas, clay, bronze, and so on is exactly what the "intellectuals," "geniuses," and "informers of opinion," whom we will discuss in the chapters devoted to them, want to do to the world and to man. This is a world that is but the work of man, a man who is the work of none but himself.

We have carefully studied three sectors of contemporary society that are among the most affected. The three great fetishes of our era are the *intelligentsia* and its utopias, the "miracles" of Science with a capital S, and the *Mass Media of Communication*.[11] These three transmit the forces that work the most at the disintegration of the world and of man in traditional civilization. These three work at the kneading and modeling of the "new world"

---

10  Dietrich von Hildebrand's book, *Trojan Horse in the City of God* was published in English in 1967 and then again in 1993.
11  *Mass Media of Communication* is written in English and italicized in the original.

## Preface to the First Edition (1969)

and "new man." They extend out to the rest to make a single gigantic mechanism that is similar to the enormous presses that stamp the factory line of identical car bodies. This twisted and generalized information is to be very soon replaced by psycho-social data processing information. Huxley's *Brave New World* and George Orwell's *1984* described the extraordinary power of transformation for us ahead of time.

Intelligence is in danger of dying.

*Tilff-sur-Ourthe, on the eve of the Assumption, 1968*

# Preface to the Second Edition (1987)

IN MEMORY OF HENRI DE LOVINFOSSE

Dismas Editions, directed by Mr. Alain Aelberts and Mr. Jean-Jacques Auquier, have kindly asked me to publish once again this book, which has been sold out for a few years. They think it could shed light on the great crisis that all of humanity has been encountering in our era and that doesn't seem to have an end at this point in the twentieth century.

Despite my advanced age, I happily agreed to their request, not only to please them, but also and above all because I consider that the diagnosis of our malaise and upheavals that have already been raging for almost two decades since its publication, has undeniably grown today according to the major lines of analysis and predictions that I made then. I am like a doctor who sees his patient once again after a certain number of years and who observes that the semiology that he had proposed at that time, the ailments that were then suffered from, are still valid, more than ever, today. We therefore republish this book after having made a few indispensable changes.

As the reader will understand now more than before, the three sections that we made in this diagnosis and that converge towards unity, can be reiterated in our current time. In the first chapter, we said that a certain type of man—contrary to all the other types of men that preceded him and that flourished with the same human nature that was present from humanity's origins—was henceforth hoisted up to the summit as an incomparable model. This was the *intellectual*. This is not someone who exercises his intelligence to comprehend the external world and to submit himself to *what it essentially is*, but someone who makes up from nothing a new world that obeys his utopias and the images that he thinks it must wrap itself in.

In this way a previously unheard of earthly paradise is to be constructed, whose new man will be the irremovable center according to the vow expressed by these thinkers—or the majority of them—who inaugurated the modern era in which we live and that will be the work of human intelligence *alone*, divinized somehow. Man is no longer an intelligent being who lives in a world that does not depend on him and on the divine Principle of this world. Man is now a sovereign being that continually transforms the world in order, at the end of the day, to submit it to his so-called rational domination.

The current crisis whose ravages we are experiencing, has barely started. Its pace has quickened since then, as it possesses a power never seen in previous civilizations. This power could inaugurate, I think, the first phase of what can be called the decadence of "man" (who was defined by the ancients as the reasonable animal living in a society) and his replacement by a maker of utopias condemned to ultimate failure. If a reaction does not emerge, this will be the very end of humanity properly speaking. Contemporary man is increasingly reduced by those who claim to manage him to the single mission of transforming the world according to his most materialistic desires camouflaged as "humanism." He finds himself facing a collapse that becomes more apparent by the day. His transformative intelligence, fabricator of a new world, his *poetic* intelligence (from the Greek, ποιεῖν, to make) as the ancients said, predominates in an almost exclusive way.

The crisis from which we could die if we do not revitalize our morals, above all our intellectual morals, is hardly mentioned by the scientists who brought it about and who built out of nothing an increasingly artificial world around us and even in us. On the contrary, when they concern themselves with this problem, it is to propose re-taking an ailment and continuing with the same abstract and utopian plan that failed in previous attempts. I recently read that a group of scientists had met and proposed, as a remedy for the contagion that is currently spreading across the planet, new and specialized machines that expert, seasoned technicians set in motion. These machines are already at work. The evil from which we suffer reaches all areas of human life. According to these intellectuals, we must put our confidence in the reinforcement of every type of mechanism that brought about this evil in the first place. The mechanism will therefore further exclude what is vital, make the concrete abstract, and make the real utopian.

One hardly hears talk of the real anymore. There is an attempt to make current pseudo-society function without rites or ceremonies (especially without religious ceremonies) and without reference to patriotic faith or the nation. One is to think only of industry (which will see the already immense number of jobless people increase) and commerce. The latter will increasingly rid itself of small businesses to definitively establish a few giant businesses, if not to usher in the universal socialist state, which is the unique master of this ultimate novelty. Rational language will shrink to a technical vocabulary that is only accessible to the initiated. Normal language will become a pure jargon of "things, machines, and stuff" because it will no longer communicate the real. Producing and consuming will be the unique law of men according to the suggestions conveyed by the *media*. Being a citizen will mean being a laborer (if work can be found), technician, creator of strictly material goods, and buyer of these goods, in an endless circle.

Everywhere the endlessly renewed utopia will have replaced social reality, with only the new style "intellectuals"

## Preface to the Second Edition (1987)

benefitting. This will provoke an even graver crisis that will make it impossible to distinguish pre-made fiction from the reality that will still survive. The unified Europe that the blind politicians propose in place of our homeland, this vast continent where no one will really know anyone else, is the utopia of this utopia.

Industrial and commercial technicians, bankers (who too often weakly submit), and states who have become mere handlers of money are all divorced from social reality. Add to this all the sycophants of the "new world" who thrive despite the crises that affect this world and, in fact, the majority of other men today. These are no longer men who are open to the multifaceted reality that surrounds them and to its supreme Cause who governs us today. Except for rare exceptions, they are the feudal lords of our pseudo-democracy (a democracy in name only). This is to say, they are union leaders (not the unions themselves) and the apparent and real leaders of parties (not of the parties themselves, and less still of the electorate of these parties). Because they are no longer incarnated in authentic social realities, such as family, region, and nation, because they no longer communicate with those who until recently lived in the real world, because they only have relationships with anonymous individuals who are on the path to disincarnation just as they are, they only have language at their disposal. This is just like the romantics of the last century. Or they have actual or hidden violence under laws that will supposedly save us. They do this in order to extend their will to dominate.

The specialist of the word and the leaders of the masses are the real rulers. This is increasingly visible in the terrible crisis that extends over all the planet. This is what we have already called the renewal of *romanticism* under the mask of science. More precisely, it is the new conception of the world. This conception is built under the sole perspective that is imposed by the builders of the new society. These builders are technology and the so-called poetic activity. The romanticism of science, reduced to the single disincarnated idea, has invaded all of the pseudo-civilization that affects us under two very visible forms today. The first is the dry, burnt, and emaciated romanticism of the so-called pioneers of science (in the sense that they are ceaselessly digging up novelty) who offer a radiant, truly scientific future of the universe for those who obey them. The second is the verbal, gossipy, and prolix romanticism of those who use the transformations that the former have proposed in order to raise themselves to the highest point in the society that they build.

Both cases present us with anthropocentric worlds clothed in a divine character that humanity had always recognized as the realities that transcended and ruled it. Today, in 1987, men turn less than ever towards the great, authentically social successes of the past or towards God who derived them from human nature. They direct themselves towards a world that they have themselves constructed according to their disincarnated reason. They therefore find themselves deprived of transcendence, which has been upgraded to an integral "humanization." Romantic rationalism—these two words do not go together—is hostile to all metaphysics and morality. It is based solely on instrumental reason, which will supposedly get us out of the crisis and build a well-measured new world from this time on. Romantic reason once more corresponds to the primacy of the *poetic* imagination, to the primacy of "making" and "building" in place of reality, which is an obstacle. Despite the crisis, or because of it, we have more and more confidence in this world that we make out of nothing and over which we aspire to be the masters even while it submits us to the harshest slavery. The romantic-idealist temptation has not stopped its destruction. Instead, it has strengthened it.

The proof is in the credulity that never stops in this Democracy with a capital "D." "Liberals" and

## Preface to the Second Edition (1987)

contemporary "socialist-communists" still get intoxicated from this Democracy every day even though it exists in words only. The majority of humans believe Democracy to be the transcendent and unsurpassable political regime. It is even, for certain individuals, "the voice of God." Pius XII showed very well in several encyclicals and speeches [1] that democracy is a valid regime but that this validity depends on the restricted and real field where it carries out its projects. But it is of total and universal democracy that more and more men dream today. One only has to read the newspapers to be convinced of this. It cannot be otherwise. When political systems founded on family, land, trades, and nation disappear, as we have increasingly observed since the first edition of this book, what remains are *individuals who are separated from each other* (they "vote in the polling booth,"[2] where they are isolated from others, as this word indicates so well!) and their disembodied conceptions of pseudo-reality that they desire to see. How can such disembodied individuals, who have broken with the true social realities that are written in their human nature, be *united*, if not in the deceitful promises of a perfect future, with unreal abstractions and words?

This is the source of the increasingly extraordinary propositions regarding this verbal democracy in all of contemporary literature—or in what claims to be literature. The crisis stems from not having enough "democracy"! Universal democracy will save us from the stagnation into which we are sinking! The smallest state that is born today must be "democratic" in order not to incur the most vehement criticism from all sides. This is what is printed every

---

1 Pius XII, "Radio-Message au monde entier": 24 décembre 1944; "Message de Noël": 23 décembre 1956.
2 De Corte uses the word *isoloir* for "polling booth," and wants to highlight the connection of this word with "isolation." His point is that our current democracies, even in the act of voting, promote the isolated individual. [Translator's note]

day in the late twentieth century. This is what the mass media says at every instant, under the influence of a new romanticism that is distilled like a Science with a capital "S." This romanticism is disembodied and placed within the reach of every Tom, Dick, and Harry. It requires no effort besides "fighting" to satisfy only his personal needs, owed to society—or what remains of it. We are dying under the romantic influence of an abstract Democracy that has turned its back on social reality ever since the French Revolution. And the publicity that we are increasingly drowning under uproots us from the real world by offering us the same, though impossible, Eden as the new Democracy, but not without demanding money from us in return.

The enormous deficit of *social security*, that overwhelms the majority of the countries of the world, stems from the same evil. A lavish bureaucratic apparatus is constructed, like a gigantic bureaucratic *abstraction* that is destined to definitively provide for *individuals* who are capable of still working, whatever the reason may be. As the crisis implacably increases their numbers, the machine turns out to be ineffective. This apparatus is all for the benefit of a romantic abstraction instead of having individuals' insurance guaranteed by the workers themselves in associations they would watch over! As for the individual, this very definition (being constituted of a distinct unity and *separated* from other, similar units) tells us that he is incapable of this simple management which he would have control over. What effectively reconnects him to the other? *Social security* literally eats up the contemporary socialist state to the point of emptying it of its substance.

Our third chapter, dedicated to the *Deforming information*, has finally become a reality that is glaringly obvious at the slightest attentive look. We only very briefly speak here of sacred and contemporary art. The analysis of their degradation would take a long chapter. If there is a single aspect of *dissociety* today that corroborates all of our analysis, it is art. Art has become abstruse, incommunicable, and incomprehensible, because it has become founded on the *individual author separated* from other humans and the universe. As we showed in our book *L'essence de la poésie*, art is not founded on the individual as author, but on what needs to be called *being with* the artist. This artist *lives with* all the beings who surround him. The artist's creativity therefore permits the communication with the other that his work normally attracts, if the other rediscovers by himself his own *being with*, instead of withdrawing into his individuality which is closed up in itself, as the current world invites him to do.

In addition, aside from a few exceptions, contemporary art *informs* the other in perpetually attempting to *deform* him. The individuality of the artist vainly attempts to reach the other, even though it is incapable of this by definition. This individuality can only startle, astonish, and surprise the other and, at the end of the day, far from making a reconnection, makes the other withdraw into himself and into his own silent incomprehension that rapidly turns away from the artist. It is not an exaggeration to say that, for the first time in history in periods of decadence, art is in the process of disappearing in its human form. As was to be expected, the majority of literary and art critics have not discerned this dangerous ailment and have even presented it as an undeniable renewal of the intellectual health of the man of today. The nearly-total disappearance of a poetry that responds to its name and fuses the poet and his reader with the poetic universe is the blatant proof. We can go beyond these points and provide examples at length in this preface, but we leave it to the reader to do this when he has read the third chapter of our book. Poetry, under its contemporary deforming form, is no more.

It is the same with the formative mission that is attributed to the modern state. It has become deforming. It has been calculated that thirty percent of the young can neither read nor write nor calculate on leaving primary school except by muddling through. And still! Contemporary pedagogy does not care about this. It continues its path towards the instauration of the worst intellectual disorder by inventing new machines for writing and counting which will replace the human brain and bring it to perfection! I have observed this with certain of my grandchildren, who are given over to those methods. Their parents must review orthography and mathematics day after day. Since the first edition of our book came out, this pedagogical dictatorship has harshly progressed in impressing its deformation on poor, obedient heads. The state is not worried about this. It is increasingly focused *solely* on the economic crisis that overwhelms it and that it makes worse in many cases. In certain schools, the notion of the homeland, for example, is ridiculed and equated with xenophobia and racism. In Belgium, linguistic regions have taken the place of the homeland and language, which is one means at our disposal for expressing thought. This substitution has thereby deformed the reality to which thought needs to submit.

How can we not see that today's youth, cut off from their natural relationship with the real world that surrounds them and from this world's transcendent Principle, withdraw into themselves and succumb to drugs? These further encourage this withdrawal of the individual into his isolated individuality that is separated from everyone else. This deforming "information," with a pathological style, is situated on the horizon of youth. There is nothing more for this poor youth except the *ego*, which is emptied of its relationship with what is not himself and filled instead with dreams. He is sealed up in himself. Left only to the economic life, only to production and the *consumption* of things, to food, drink, clothing, medication, and leisure, he is continually incited to digest the deforming information that assails him. In a dissociety that is increasingly oriented towards the isolated individual, deprived of all spiritual and

## Preface to the Second Edition (1987)

physical rapport with his colleagues, it is understandable that carnal pleasure first of all, followed by the cerebral pleasure of the dream, takes an increasingly preponderant place because such pleasure is indistinguishable from the ego and closes man in on himself.

But it is above all in the Catholic Church itself that the deforming information, cut off from its constitutive relationship with the revealed supernatural, is most noticeable, with its immediate consequence. This consequence is the rupture of the nature of man and of society where he lives from birth. Nature and the supernatural go together. One does not go without the other. Into what would the supernatural become incarnate, if not into that which is natural to man—his intelligence, will, and very flesh? Into what would the natural reach the fullness of its being, if not into the supernatural that is grafted onto him to help him achieve his entire fullness with a solid foundation? From the highest to the lowest, the notions of nature and the supernatural have, with rare exceptions, totally disappeared from the vocabulary of clergymen today. How then can we restore the *nature* of man who has been denatured by the economic basis alone, where political leaders have placed him? How can we solidly incarnate the supernatural there? Clerical *verbalism* always attempts to replace divine transcendent *realities*. The prolix information of this verbalism inevitably turns to the deformation of the theological virtues that are nevertheless essential. In the majority of cases, current theologians, and contemporary clergy that blindly obeys their leaders, no longer speak of this.

The Benedictine monk Dom Gerard[3] has recently assured us that "I have maintained that for thirty years now divine transcendence has entered the season of mist and

---

[3] Dom Gérard Calvet (1927–2008), founder and first abbot of the Abbey of Sainte-Madeleine du Barroux. The community was canonically established in 1989 after much difficulty due to their adherence to the traditional Roman Liturgy.

that those who are not concerned about this have abdicated the pride of the son who is jealous of the Father's honor."[4] The situation of the Church since Vatican II shows us that the contemporary heresy, that puts into parentheses the essential theological truths, increasingly saps all supernatural belief, without eliciting the concern of the clergy perched high above. An abstract Christianity, uprooted from its basic and existential orientation towards the God of Revelation, is finalized in man in general and in the temporal goods with which he must henceforth be provided. It is no longer a matter of man as a member of a family, region, and homeland. Because of the *duties* that these words involve and the real relationships that they form, they have almost disappeared from the ecclesiastical mind. Instead, we have the conceptual Man that comes from the French Revolution, communism, and Freemasonry, all the themes of which are taken up to make an *effective* alliance with their deforming information. In certain cases, these points are never criticized by the Hierarchy.

The current Church no longer has any of the barriers against arbitrariness. These barriers were *laws* to be dutifully obeyed. Now, anarchy reigns. Above all in France, this anarchy is crowned by the dictatorship of the higher clergy that firmly sided with democratic Man and who, similar to politicians of all kinds, address themselves to the individual separated from his eternal social conditions. They manipulate him and introduce him to pseudo-religious information that warps things. They make this information the new master. The excommunication issued by Mgr. Boucheix against the traditional monastery of Sainte-Madeleine du Barroux, and the one against the parish community of Port-Marly,[5] with the aid of the

---

4 Les Amis du Monastère, no 35, 26 avril 1987, Abbaye Sainte-Madeleine, 1201, chemin des Rabassieres, 84330 Le Barroux.
5 See Peter Kwasniewski, "French traditionalists show us how to take back our churches when closed by bishops," LifeSiteNews,

civil police, where the priest was violently pulled away from the altar while celebrating the holy Mass, show us that the clergy in France is dominated by a communizing "fascism" that dares not speak its name. These measures of *force* are approved by the cardinal and primate of the Gauls, Mgr. Decourtray. Information that twists things is henceforth official in the French clergy.

This deceptive information has become official in the universal Catholic clergy under the cross of the current pope whose philosophy and underlying theology on the primacy of the individual camouflaged as "person" opposes the Augustinian and Thomistic traditions of the traditional Church. John Paul II is surely a pious priest, but his piety is above all an *individual sentiment* that carries the strong risk of transforming the teaching of the Gospel if it is not nourished by philosophical and theological *realism*, as demonstrated by Vatican II, the massive introduction of the new Mass, and the weakening (if not the disappearance) of the abyssal differences that separate Catholic from Protestant ritual.

The Pope very silently supports the interdiction of the traditional Mass issued by the bishops, above all the French ones.[6] He supports with the same silence the interdict launched by the heterodox clergy on the *Catechism of the Council of Trent* and the *Catechism of Saint Pius X*.

---

November 24, 2020. The community of Port Marly was eventually entrusted to the Institute of Christ the King Sovereign Priest.
6  In 1988, Pope John Paul II extended wider use of the Traditional Latin Mass with his Apostolic Letter *Ecclesia Dei* in reaction to the Episcopal Consecrations of Archbishop Marcel Lefebvre. While this extension did create more opportunities for priests to celebrate the traditional liturgy, many bishops still presented obstacles for priests wishing to celebrate this liturgy. In 2007, Pope Benedict XVI with his own Apostolic Letter *Summorum Pontificum* gave even greater freedom for priests to celebrate the traditional liturgy. However, in 2021 Pope Francis sought to curtail these freedoms with the Apostolic Letter *Traditionis Custodes*.

He supports everything that Jean Madiran[7] reproaches of this clergy: "its embrace of socialism and approval of the C. C. F. D,[8] its senseless claim of the immigrants' right to vote, its public pact of unity with the left-wing followers of Freemasonry." These acts have ruined its moral and religious authority. This has led to the emptying and closure of many churches, seminaries, and monasteries. Yet again, distorting information, the negation of the supernatural, human (too human) pseudo-creationism, and unhealthy clericalism triumphed without an official fight on the part of the papacy to hold back their ravages.

The fact that we lack a saint such as Pius X to reinvigorate the Catholic Church and re-establish it on the solid foundation of Tradition is proven by the example of the ecumenical reunion of Assisi instigated by John Paul II. Qualified representatives from diverse Christian and pagan religions gathered together to say, as we always knew, that belief in God is a normal phenomenon in the life of humanity and that it is necessary to restore it. Such a "council" empties the Catholic religion of the supernatural character that was *revealed to it alone*. The information that this "synod" spreads is, certainly, a marginalization *of the historic fact* that the Catholic Church alone possesses divine truth. It informs and deforms at the same time with all of the authority that still remains with current popes since Paul VI.

We never tire of repeating it: It is necessary to resist and to maintain in ourselves the integral human nature that we possess and the Supernatural that was revealed to us. Let us never tire of praying.

*Tilff-sur-Ourthe, April 1987*

---

7 Jean Arfel (1920–2013), French traditional Catholic thinker, and founder of the magazine, *Itinéraires*.
8 Comité Catholique contre la Faim et pour le Développement.

# Intelligence in Danger of Death

## L'intelligence en péril de mort

# I

# Intellectuals and Utopia

REALITY AND CIVILIZATION

Every society revolves around a certain type of man who embodies for its members a chance of some success. This man is considered, consciously or unconsciously, to be their model. Greece had the καλὸς κἀγαθός, the handsome and good man who aims at excellence in the physical and moral order. Rome had its *bonus civis dicendi peritus*,[1] the Middle Ages its knight, Spain its *hidalgo*, the French seventeenth century its *honnête homme*, and the Anglo-Saxon countries the *gentleman*. This moral and social elite ceaselessly renewed itself from out of a multi-millenarian peasantry or by a regular relationship with it. Gathered together in two classes, the higher of which could generally be called the nobility and clergy, society sank its roots into a life that was constantly lived in contact with the external world, with nature, with the experience of beings and things that were accumulated by the generations and, confusedly, with the Principle of being. This elite endeavored, with a certain amount of happiness, through innumerable attempts, with innumerable failures, to orient human conduct towards the True, the Good, and the Beautiful.

---

1 "*Orator est, Marce fili, vir bonus dicendi peritus.*" This definition of a Roman speaker, due to Cato the Elder, was part of a sort of encyclopedia of practical knowledge that he wrote for his son, entitled *Praecepta ad filium*. It is reported, notably, by Seneca the Rhetoritician in his *Controversia* (1.9).

This triple end towards which the activities of man are directed is not arbitrarily defined and chosen. Man's real nature, and the very nature of reality with which man is in relationship, imposes this end on every human being. To be in the truth means, for man, to conform his intelligence to a reality that his intelligence neither built nor dreamed of. This reality imposes itself on his intelligence. To do good is to avoid abandoning himself to his instincts, affective impulses, and own will, and to order and subordinate his activities to the laws that are prescribed by nature and by Divinity and that the intelligence discovers in its untiring quest for happiness. To compose a beautiful piece of art is not to project whatever idea onto whatever material nor to construct any sort of world that depends only on the creative act of the artist. It means to obey the law of perfection proper to the work that is undertaken and that reveals itself, in the very inventive act, in the generative activity of the artist.

In brief, and without fear of being wrong, it can be stated that all the energies of a civilization that we have labeled as *Greco-Latin*, *Christian*, or *traditional*, are characterized by the submission of intelligence to reality and by the rejection of subjectivity in every domain. It is not an exaggeration to claim that no member of the elite of traditional civilization had the audacity to proclaim that man is the measure of all things, either by his personal reason, or by an impersonal reason that is common to all men. The only exception to this was the open break in the culture by *sophistry*, a break that was sealed off by the pivotal reaction of every human being against the ravages that it announced. On the contrary, man from his earliest years knows that because of his birth he is inserted into a physical and metaphysical universe that he did not make, into an order that is not at his mercy, into a hierarchy of beings whose distribution he cannot alter without doing damage to himself. Whatever he does, man recognizes that he cannot become other than what he is by nature, vocation, or grace. No one can run away from his own being. To surpass oneself in some way, to add a cubit to one's height, to be more is to exclude man from the universe and from order. The Christian conception of sin as a rupture of the law imposed by God on each of his creatures corresponds with the Greek conception of ὕβρις, of immoderacy, according to which each man who exceeds his limits is immediately punished for his temerity by the very breakup of his incontinent being. In obeying reality in all its operations, intelligence therefore teaches man to become what he is, to "do man well" according to Montaigne's admirable formula,[2] taken from Aristotle, and to bring it to completion. The hero, the genius, and the saint do this to perfection. They are the elite of the elite.

Even with so many failures, falls, collapses, parodies, and falsifications experienced by this second-hand and second-rate elite, regardless of how decrepit its social façade may be, the fact remains that this elite never renounced the agreement that united it to its prototypes and to all those who, being fully realist, humbly directed intelligence towards the very heart of beings and things instead of directing it towards itself in order to marvel at itself and its accomplishments. They modestly employed this intelligence as a receptacle which welcomed the influxes of the universe and its Principle. They regulated its activities in all their fields of operation and the injunctions that came from the realities thus contemplated.

There is only truth if the intelligence is in agreement with the real. Nothing is beautiful except the truth. Only the truth is lovable. The primacy of being over intelligence, the subordination of intelligence to reality, and the docility of intelligence to the order which shines forth from all that exists are the hallmarks of the actions of the man of traditional civilization when he aims for excellence.

---

2  "There is nothing so beautiful and legitimate as to do man well and duly." Montaigne, *Les Essais*, L. III, ch. 13 (Paris, Bibliothèque de la Pléiade, 2007) 1160.

Intelligence obeys its nature as intelligence. This is to conform to the real. It is obedient to the nature of man. It is obedient to the nature of things. It is obedient to God, the source of all nature and reality. Its characteristics are adhering to that which is and rejecting that which is not.

### THE NEW INTELLECTUALS

To this elite of the past, our era substituted a new ruling class, one with no historical precedent. We can assign a very precise date to this change: the eighteenth century. That was when this ailment of the intelligence began, what Paul Hazard called "the crisis of the European conscience." At this moment, a new aristocracy, the *philosophes*, took charge of the conduct of human life. They never ceased to be reborn under various forms: the *intellectual party*, as Péguy said, the *intelligentsia* in the Russian sense, *the mandarins* of Simone de Beauvoir. These are men of literature, artists, scientists, and other thinkers, all those whom Thibaudet[3] brought together in his *République des Professeurs* and that today he would place in the class of technocrats and specialists of "practical reason," of politics, information, social relations, the economy, and even religion since the recent Council—everyone, or almost everyone, who gives contemporary men their messages, pastoral letters, instructions, directives, and instructions. They see themselves invested in the mission of reforming behavior, changing ideas and preferences, proposing and imposing a new conception of the world, bringing out of the alchemy of evolution or the magic of the Revolution a "new man" and a "new society." From the eighteenth century to the present, the most general system under which humanity, if we can call it that, lived and still lives under *the dictatorship of intelligence* as how it has become

---

[3] Albert Thibeaudet (1874–1936), French literary critic and political theorist. His book, *La république des professeurs*, was published in 1927.

since it was monopolized by developed, under-developed, or still-developing intellectuals. There is no era in history in which humanity deliberately recognized in the well-read this formidable and exorbitant privilege of leading it towards a new terrestrial paradise, better tomorrows, an omega point, a planetary fraternity, a universal communism, a worldwide democracy, an ecumenical fusion of all the theisms, atheisms, monotheisms, and polytheisms—in brief, towards utopia. From one pole to the other of this circular machine, the most authorized voices, like the braying of asses, cry out their desire like the romantic poet:

> Your reign has arrived, PURE SPIRIT, king of the world.[4]

In spite of the sparkling denials radiating out from our experience of the last quarter millennium, our incurably retrograde era has kept to the vision of man and the world of the *Encyclopédie*.[5] The young Clémenceau[6] still expressed its outlook at the sad dawn of this century, which was promised to two world wars and a holocaust of three or four million offered to the Molochs of fixed and obsessional ideas: "The sovereignty of brutal force is on the way to disappearing. We are walking, though not smoothly, towards the sovereignty of intelligence."[7]

Charles Maurras described for us in *L'Avenir de l'Intelligence* the ascension of the class of these intellectuals and sovereign creators of opinion with their written and

---

4  The author capitalizes PUR ESPRIT in the original, p. 21, and provides the following footnote: Alfred de Vigny, *L'esprit pur*, in *Oeuvres complètes, I* (Paris, Bibliothèque de la Pléiade, 1986), 167.
5  The *Encyclopédie* was the great work of the Enlightenment to give their interpretation to all things. Denis Diderot and Jean le Rond D'Alembert were the editors.
6  Georges Benjamin Clémenceau (1841–1929), Prime Minister of France from 1906 to 1909, and 1917 to 1920.
7  Cited by Charles Maurras, *L'Avenir de l'intelligence* in *Romantisme et Révolution*, édition définitive (Paris, Nouvelle librairie Nationale, MCMXXV), 40.

spoken words and their Merovingian-like degradation to the benefit of the Mayors of the Palace who, holding gold and power, worked the levers of the world. We could say, without paradox, that this is where Maurras meets Marx, for whom intellectual power is nothing but the reflection of material power, and "the superstructure" the reflection of "the infrastructure." The difference is that for Maurras, this is not a universal law that regulates the relation of these two orders of power, but intelligence as it has become in those who would save it but who have altered it.

The current era has done nothing but confirm this analysis of the enslavement of intelligence to all the anonymous forces that rule on Earth. This is a state without a head, or with a head that is separated from its body, its finances equally scatterbrained, the Church in the grip of the myth of the Kingdom of God on Earth. Behind these realities hides the will to power of Caesars who are both visible and invisible, mediocre or puffed up, and drunk on power. They are tyrants who are camouflaged as liberators who put humanity under submission by deafening it to the promise of its apotheosis.

The extraordinary enslavement of the clergy, laity, and episcopacy to ideological propaganda, commercial publicity, and noisy marketing, which the ancients derisively referred to as "the world's theater"; the hunt for scientists, to which the modern exploitative state surrenders what it scornfully calls "gray matter"; the patronage of experts, the credentialed, and the competent whose will to power seeks qualifications to build itself up and dominate; the monopoly that they claim more than ever in intellectual and spiritual matters are the rather sinister testimonies to the fall of Icarus. The balloon of intelligence has cut its rope and sees itself floating in rule over the land of men, even while it is swept away by the cyclones and anticyclones of an atmosphere that is stronger than the short-lived noble gasses which have filled it. Maurras noted, "We should not conceal that by doing this we run the risk of seeing man himself die out—the politician, the rationalist, the artist, and the singer. Whoever lengthens the double romantic and revolutionary tendency opens the Spirit to the ample freedom to die."[8] Utopia is the death of man.

## TRUTH AND FALSEHOOD

In the following pages, I would like to extend, if not possibly deepen, the diagnosis that Maurras provides on the future of intelligence and, *vox clamantis in deserto*, in fearlessly putting up with the smiles and laughter of the specialists of "gray matter" and the technicians of the brain. In the following pages, I would like to denounce the mortal danger faced by the human mind in our age of darkness.

Lacking a philosophy that might reveal anything to him except in the brief flashes of a poem, Maurras' diagnosis remains admittedly rather short. *Explaining* the cause of this ostentation and presumption of intellectuals requires more than discovering the cause in history, noting the devastation, and concluding that "It's the fault of Voltaire. It's the fault of Rousseau." The moral reasons by themselves, however high or acute that they are, fail to explain more clearly the dismemberment of the empire of the Spirit that happened so quickly. Pride and vanity, which are referred to so frequently, are the imitation diadems with which the reasoning animal crowns himself in order to mask the injury that he has inflicted upon himself. They are the exterior and glossy signs of a more basic disorder. The truth is that the intelligence is a terribly ambivalent faculty in us and, in the language of Aesop, is the best and worst of things.

The simplest or slightest experience that we can have shows us that our intelligence can sometimes set itself the task of apprehending the *presence* of beings and things and their natures. These are taken according to

---

8   *Ibid.*, 24.

the representation that we have and that we declare to be conforming to their realities. At other times, we make this *representation* however we wish, and make reality conform to it. Either the reality that I have conforms to the real, or the real conforms to the idea that I create. Either the reality that I have of man is adequate to his reality, or I force man's reality to conform to the idea that I create of him. How many times have I been tempted to substitute for the reality of Tom, Dick, or Harry the seductive or repulsive representation, which I can make pretty or ugly? In any case, such writing is fake or deceptive.

Joubert (1754–1824) admirably described this double attitude of thought that discriminates between the true and false spirit: "False spirits do not have the sense of the truth, but they have definitions. They stay inside their heads instead of looking at what's in front of them. In their debates, they look at the ideas that are connected to things, and don't look at the things themselves."[9]

The world of theater and the political scene overflow with these ghosts or puppets that the human intellect mass produces to the extent that it loses control of itself when it places itself at the service of the instincts and the passions that secretly oversee it. Modern society has long passed the stage of the individual artisan who makes his own idol or figurine. Real factories have been built and filled with specialized teams. They have been instructed on all the mechanisms of the human puppets and impulses of subjectivity that are produced and released onto the market according to the demands of the current masters. They have been instructed on all the representations of events, effigies of individuals, images of objects, and conceptions of the world whose function is to supplant reality itself and to prevent man from entering into lived relation with it. Today, there exists an *industry of utopia* which uses

---

9 Joseph Joubert, *Pensées, Essais, Maximes et correspondance*, tome premier (Paris, Librairie Ve Le Normant), 169.

the modern means of communication to offer its products. The university is the recognized provider of these products.

## THE EXHAUSTED INTELLIGENCE

The fundamental ambiguity of the intelligence comes from the nature of its structure. It is a fact that, in order to know the present reality that it welcomes and fertilizes, the intelligence produces a "representation" of the object which it uses in order to seize reality. This representation is what we call a *concept*. Every concept is a means of knowing reality. To know a thing is "to make an idea" of this thing. Thanks to the idea, we know the thing in question. All knowledge is made by generating, in the heart of thought, a system of signs by which the intelligence expresses to itself the reality that it knows. The concept that is thereby produced is essential to intelligence. Without the concept, the intelligence would not know how to say to itself what reality is. But however essential this is, it is not what the intelligence grasps. It is the means by which the intelligence grasps reality. When I come up with an idea of a thing, it is not this idea that I contemplate, but the thing by this idea.

For there to be a concept requires conception. The concept is the child of the marriage of the intelligence and the real. The birth of this offspring requires that the intelligence has commerce with reality. It is obvious that the vigor of the child depends on the health of the father and the mother and on the vigor of their union. The intensity, extent, depth, richness, and quality of the rapport formed by the generative elements that stamp the concept with their seal communicate to it the imprint of the real.

It is impossible to probe this mysterious moment when the intelligence and the real consummate their union. The intelligence cannot turn towards itself at the moment at which it turns towards the real and at which it offers itself to it in order to be fertilized. This primary relation of the intelligence to reality is purely and simply lived. The conception is a vital and instantaneous experience, including as well long anterior preparation, that can only be described in metaphors. *But it is conception that supports the entire edifice of knowledge.* The concepts that are elaborated by the intelligence are worth only what the original conception is worth. The original conception is the essential act where the intelligence and the real embrace. The concepts are the expression or the fruit of this embrace.

This is where the drama of the intelligence is formed. The uniqueness of an expression is the power to separate itself from the reality that is imprinted in the soul and to which it is correlative, just as the uniqueness of fruit is the power to detach itself from the tree. Every expression can set up an independent entity. Every concept can isolate itself from the conception. Every sign can detach itself from the signified.

*It is enough for the intelligence to divert its gaze from the beings and things that the concept signifies, in order to set it exclusively upon the concept itself, on the fruit of its entrails, that is to say, on itself and its own creative subjectivity. The supply current that goes from reality as conceived to the concept is therefore broken at the same time that the current that returns from the expression to the expressed reality is also broken. The living experience of the real no longer nourishes the concept. Knowledge degenerates into the construction of scaffolding and the architecture of formulas. Abstractions replace the energy and vigor of the organic conjugation of the intelligence and reality.* Instead of springing forth from the experience of beings and things, and thereby being ceaselessly refueled in a type of living circuit, the concept becomes a mold that is manufactured by mechanical processes in the laboratory of the brain. Instead of marrying reality in a transparent way, the concept encloses itself behind an

## Intellectuals and Utopia

opaque partition wall.

Man in the grip of this deviation closes himself in a mental world whose reality becomes exhausted to the benefit of anemic appearances. Reality is transformed for him into combinations of signs, symbols, numbers, and even words substituting for beings and things. Man no longer even perceives the existence or the nature of beings and things. Utopian knowledge is the creator and organizer of this network it draws out of itself and its subjectivity. Utopian knowledge exiles real intelligence, which is conformed to the object, to inactivity. The natural movement of the intellect, which is to become attuned to the real, inverts itself. Henceforth, it is reality that must adapt to the abstractions that are fabricated by the intelligence. Reality becomes the specific object of human intelligence.

The first result is that the world is no longer understood. It is seized, fixed, and enclosed in constructions and forms that take it from the outside, define and frame it, and that impose on reality its own configuration, essence, and even being. This table on which I write is no longer a plank of colored and hard wood, supported by four legs. It is a cloud of electrons which are regulated by a system of subtle equations. The intelligence itself generates the object that it seizes. Far from being measured by the real, the real is measured by the intelligence. By so measuring it, the intelligence creates it. The world is no longer the creation of God, but of man and his knowledge.

The result is that reality no longer has anything essential to communicate to the intelligence, in particular the being that reality possesses. This being belongs to itself independently of the mind that knows it. This being is, in other words, reality's stable, unvarying, and unalterable nature that makes reality specifically what it is, and not something else. Reality is no longer known by its intemporal and necessary qualities. In order for the mind to stamp reality with its own imprint and project onto it its own premade categories, it is necessary for reality to be nothing other than pure nothingness. In other words, it is necessary for reality never to be this or that, and to be always changing. In this way, the world turns to some sort of liquid, a flowing and continually changing mass. In order to avoid losing this perpetually-flowing matter, the intelligence multiplies the forms and formulas that it uses to intercept reality. The mental structures that the intelligence invents for this objective are superimposed one upon the other, and become more and more numerous and complex. The world is transformed into the history of the world and thought into the history of thought. In a nutshell, nothing is. All is becoming, all becomes. And it is utopian intelligence, intelligence as the midwife of forms, concepts, and ideas, that depends only on itself, that confers a sense of what is becoming by capturing this becoming.

The final result is that the intelligence deprived of its natural nutrition declines to the point of sustaining itself on poor, tasteless, and unappealing nutrition. The intelligence dries out, hardens, and becomes exhausted. *It then requires the extra contribution of the imagination, sentiment, passion, and instincts, that is to say, all the inferior animal faculties that it no longer controls, that it arouses and that give it a fake vitality.* Not being rooted in experience and the transmitted experience that comprises tradition, abstract thought always extends itself in a destructive fury of the present reality which its chimerical character runs up against. It extends outward in a compensatory mirage of a fabulous future. It thus persuades itself of its incomparable productivity. Because the real world ceaselessly inflicts on abstract thought the most scathing rejections, this thought must appeal to hostile forces, such as resentment and hate, that can destroy this real world. It cannot achieve its promises and dreams. It is congenitally unable to bring them about in the present, when they are always refuted by the very force of things. Therefore, abstract thought has to appeal to the powers of the appetite, desire, and concupiscence to support the logic of its dreams and project them onto the future. All modern ideologies, whether political, social, economic, esthetic, or religious, are, *without distinction*, sterile. But they are all equally affected by an imaginary pregnancy that never comes to term—and for good reason!—that commences with each failure—and for another good reason! This pregnancy leads humanity into a gripping race where nothing is set and where reality flows like a river, if not a torrent, where the truth is converted into its contrary at every instant, where everything becomes relative, and where nothing remains in the wreckage of the universe but the specter of man in the grip of the delirium of permanent revolution and eternal evolution.

## THE INTELLIGENCE AND IDEALISM

If we refer to idealism as a system of thought that proclaims the *primacy of the intelligence over reality*, the world in which we live today is an idealist world. It is built by intellectuals with tremendous reinforcements of abstractions, and it is superimposed on the world of experience which is constantly put in doubt.

Our twentieth century world is so minimally materialist that it is a construction of the mind, from one side to the other, right down to its moral turpitude and its eroticism. Despite its pretensions and bluster, Marxism is not in any way materialist. It is an *idea* projected onto society in order to destroy it, knead it into dust, blend it into a mushy and obedient paste, and impose on it a form that is matured for a long time in a mind that is sequestered into itself, far from reality. It is all a lie, right down to the terms that it decks itself out in, "dialectical materialism" or "scientific materialism." Its idealism bursts out in its hate of all divine and human reality, in its desire to subjugate nature to its will to power, and in the extraordinary waste of material resources in which it engages to maintain its ideological orthodoxy in the countries where it has installed itself. Our world, in the so-called free democracies, is no longer materialist. It underwent transformations in its innermost depths brought about by the mind of modern man. Matter no longer appeared as its own reality. It is always transformed there by human contrivance.

"The illustrious prelate," whose conversation with one of his disciples is recounted by Maurras, says it well:

> "Young man, you believe that materialism is the great error of the moment. False! It's idealism."
> "Why?"
> "It lies the most. Materialists are rightfully looked down upon. Because they are swine. But we can see them as such. We do not always see what social or political idealists are: Fellows who let everyone see their hearts, which are huge, and who pound their own chests while making a lot of noise, in order to put the world to flames in order to make it better."

With its sublime false airs, its pharisaism, its blissful elevation of thought and heart, and its hypocrisy, which is so deep that it is not self-aware, the idealism, for which modern intelligence is dying, is without doubt the greatest sin of the mind.

Its gravity is all the more harmful that it is *contagious*. It has not been noted enough that idealism—and its aftermath—*is learned* whereas realism and its active receptivity by all the voices of the real—*is not learned*. Idealism is learned because it is a mechanism of ideas contrived by the mind. It is always possible to teach such an art of manufacturing, along with all sorts of processes and formulas. Idealism is a technique that aims to imprison reality in preconceived forms. The characteristic of every technique is that it is communicable. Ideas, representations, and knowledge are easily transmitted from mind to mind as soon as their textures and plans are laid bare. But the very act of knowing, which is the synthesis of the intelligence and of the real, does not pass from one individual to another *because it is a lived act.* Every man must accomplish it for his own benefit. Every man must personally feel the presence of reality and its intelligible content. Every man must conceive it by himself.

The intelligence does not have license to hide behind the myth of a universal Reason that suggests, provokes, and enthrones the faculty with which ideas pour out from one reason into another. It was idealism that introduced this universal Reason into all spheres of teaching. It is the convergence of *personal* acts of knowledge and lived conceptions *towards the same known reality* that underpins communication among men. Some go more deeply and further than others, but they all progress in the same direction. It is the real that gathers together the diversity of intelligences, not a common system of technologically-elaborated knowledge. Said another way, it is the finality of intelligences reaching out to the same reality to be known. This is the source of agreement, not the identity of intellectual mechanisms or methods, nor the inundations of "dialogue." All roads lead to Rome. There is no unique road. There is no collective thought or conscience. There are intelligences—in the plural!—that lead the most vigorous intelligence towards the common goal by their own paths.

It needs to be ceaselessly repeated that this is why no spiritual, intellectual, and moral tradition of humanity can exist without saints, geniuses, and heroes. There is no such tradition without their examples, without their magnetism arousing in every generation an elan that is similar to the movement towards the True, the Beautiful, the Good, towards the reality that we must know, towards the reality that we must make shine in a work and that we must love. Their intelligence obeyed with perfect rectitude the law that regulates it and that compels it to submit itself to order—in the double sense of the word—of reality and of the Principle of reality. Their intelligence respected the original agreement that unites it to the universe and its Cause without ever betraying this agreement. The intelligence also subsequently traces a long stream of light in its wake. This stream orients the attempts at experimentation for all those who obey the law that orders the intelligence to conform to the real according to the capacities granted to them at their levels.

If knowledge results from the fertilization of the intelligence by the real, this is because man's *being* itself, whose specific mark is its intelligence, is in constitutive relation with, or in other words, in prior connivance with, *the being* of all reality. The intelligence can never open itself to the presence of beings and things if the human being, the seat of that intelligence, is separated from the totality of being. Our being is fundamentally in relationship with universal being, and knowledge is in some way merely the discovery of this connection. Intelligence can *become all things* according to Aristotle's prodigious statement,[10] because the being of man, as soon as he exists, is articulated by total being, including in its Principle. In all of its operations, the intelligence reaches its being, its sufficient object, because the entire universe and its transcendent source are *co-present in the human being*. It is essential to the being of man, as it is for every being except the One who is sufficient in Himself, to be *with* all the other beings. The intelligence exercises its influence in the background or, more precisely, at the axis of the co-presence of universal reality. Without this, it could only grasp being from outside and never in itself. It could only achieve the

---

10   Marcel De Corte was undoubtedly referring to the following passage: "We once again state that the soul is, in a sense, all beings... in repeating that the soul is, in a certain way, the totality of realities." Aristotle, *De Anima*, III, 8, 431 b21.

appearance or the phenomenal state, and not the essence. It could only grasp appearances, not what is.

But this connection, which is fundamental and prior to knowledge, is in some way embedded in us, though it is not noted as a cause. The capital function of the intelligence is to reveal this connection, conform to it, know it, and, thus adequately situate man in the universe. This is why the conception of the *cosmos*, or the act by which the intelligence submits itself to the universal order and understands that order, is of an inestimable importance. Without this conception, life is nothing but "a tale told by an idiot, full of sound and fury, signifying nothing."[11] A world which lacks a conception of the world that is adequate for its reality descends into every sort of disorder.

This is our present situation. We wander in a "broken world" or, more precisely, we have been ejected from the real world. We sail aimlessly in a world of appearances which is ceaselessly made and unmade. This stems from modern man's refusal to accept the place which is allotted to him in the unity of nature and from his intelligence not accepting to function according to its nature as intelligence. Instead of submitting to things, it claims to bring the universe to submission. Man is therefore no longer a *being in the world*, but a *being outside of the world* who has lost his substance and his characteristics as an intelligent animal. He searches desperately for who he is because he has chosen to no longer be a *being with the world and with his Principle*. The consequence is inescapable: Modern man is whatever one wants, except intelligent. He is delivered over to a formal intelligence that works less and less with the real and more and more with signs. His intelligence becomes byzantine to the extreme and, to conceal this disaster, hides behind the claimed requirements of a "universal reason" or a

---

11  Shakespeare, *Macbeth*, Act 5, Scene 5.

"universal conscience." These are meeting places of all sorts of alarming subjectivities. Man is no longer anywhere. He is in full *utopia*. This is why he is no longer himself. He is no longer man. He wishes to be a "new man" in a "new world."

### THE RUPTURE WITH REALITY

We have stated that the rupture of the relationship between the intelligence of the real and the man of the universe was consummated in the eighteenth century. All historians agree on this. But why did this come about in this era? Why did the traditional and realist conception of the world, from Athens to Rome, and from Jerusalem to Rome again, which had been the conception of thinking and acting Europe, collapse in the eighteenth century?

The reason is simple. A conception of the world does not float, disincarnated, in inaccessible ether. It becomes incorporated into the life of men and, because their life is communal, it becomes incorporated into the institutions of human communities. In the case that the elites who express this conception of the world (and whose influence on daily life is immense) turn from it, renounce living their lives by it, replace it with something less austere but brighter and more complimentary, then the accredited world becomes shaky. Only a few critically-located cracks suffice for the edifice to collapse in body and soul. When the high clergy enjoys denying God and exalting man in the Lodges and when the aristocracy joins the school of rhetoricians and intellectual dilettantes, however talented they are, we can state the brutal truth that it is the end. "Small causes, huge effects," as the proverb goes. And, as Auguste Comte assures us with remarkable acuity, "in this matter, it is a general rule that there is never proportion between effect and cause. The effect is always huge in relation to the cause." A woman enters the life of a CEO, and suddenly the factory goes downhill. Cleopatra's nose is eternal.[12]

It would be superfluous here to reiterate the analyses of de Tocqueville, Taine,[13] or Augustin Cochin[14], and to recall the fascination of eighteenth century thinkers for the aristocracy and clergy. It would be superfluous to recall their critique of traditional civilization, deification of reason, will to destroy a society that did not grant them the place that they felt was their due, yearning for equality, denunciation of privileges, and above all, prodigious ability to transform their felt passions into unchanging principles. They wanted to resolve all human problems with debates, writings, worldly conversation, colloquia, or, as we say today, universal "dialogue," at salons, churches, circles, literary sets, or assemblies.

But this unexpected and spectacular ascension of specialists of the word, the quill, the manipulation of ideas, or mental representations and the words that express these representations, is nothing but the sociological aspect of a much deeper change. What we see with the eighteenth century—and the adventure has not yet come to a close— is a *mutation of the human mind*. We can say this with precision, now that it has reached its height, if not yet its terminal point.

Indeed, until the eighteenth century, the events that marked human history, such as wars, technological inventions, geographical discoveries, the establishment of cities, kingdoms, and empires, the arrival of saints, geniuses, heroes, or transformations of religious ideas, affected the

---

12  This is an allusion to Pascal, "Le nez de Cléopâtre s'il eut été plus court, toute la face de la Terre aurait changée." "Had Cleopatra's nose been shorter, all of world history would have been different."
13  Hippolyte Adolphe Taine (1828–1893), French historian, critic, and philosopher.
14  Augustin Cochin (1876–1916), French historian of the French revolution.

human being *in his very life*. None of these events or individuals were purely intellectual at their origin—not even the invention of logic by Aristotle. The least we can say about this logic is that it gave to the human mind its definitive position. They were not purely intellectual at their origin because the art of reasoning is not at all the work of reason, but of man himself, in flesh and blood, who uses his reason. According to the Stagirite's profound observation, it is not the thought that thinks, but man by his thought.

None of these occasions were able to achieve intelligence in itself. Whatever happiness and unhappiness these occasions provoked, they did not destroy the vision that man's intelligence is the faculty that knows and conforms to the real. In no case was the primacy of the very activity of intelligence, the contemplation of the truth, questioned. The *first* function of the human mind did not cease to be the function of knowing, the θεωρία. Virgil transmitted to us the secret of the highest type of life, the contemplative life: *Felix qui potuit rerum cognoscere causas*.[15] This type of life has always been considered as the summit of wisdom and happiness. This absolute priority of the intelligence that is submitted to the object was never contested, whatever some may say, by Christianity. Love did not supplant intelligence, because if God is love, it was necessary that He make itself known as such to men and that He teach the Good News.

There is an essential condition that the intelligence is ordered to follow and that it has always observed, no matter what the conditions were. This is the at least implicit recognition of its dependence on reality and on its transcendent principle. The is the confession of the nuptial link of the intelligence that unites man's being to universal being and to its cause. If the intelligence in its first act does not turn towards extra-mental activity, if it instead returns

---

15 "Happy is the man who knows the causes of things." Virgil, *Les Géorgiques*, L. II, v.490, in *Oeuvres*, Paris, Librairie Hachette, 1945.

towards itself and projects on itself a nocturnal glance of complacence, in other words (and according to the ancient formula), if it refuses to be measured by the things by their own measurement, then the intelligence no longer knows things. It repudiates its own function in rejecting the law.

Before the eighteenth century, knowledge was linked by its power of communion with the universe and its cause, and therefore to its power of consent, acceptance, and docility. This original pact was broken after the eighteenth century. Intelligence began to consider itself to be a sovereign that governs, exercises a regency over, dominates, and tyrannizes reality. It projects from the height of its transcendence *only its light* on the world, and orders the world according to its own requirements. Reason considers itself to be a creative force that is deployed, developed, and advanced throughout all of humanity and the universe in order to *make* a true humanity and an authentic universe. The universe no longer receives its law from the real, but is *the supreme legislator* that imposes its norms on reality.

The *Philosophes* of the eighteenth century keenly perceived the reversal that they were making in intellectual activity. By their own admission, the *Encyclopédie* was created "to change the common way of thinking." It was in fact an inversion, if not even a complete subversion, of the act of knowing. Intelligence no longer exists in order to contemplate the order of the universe and to know it, but to construct an order based on rules that it discovered and knew from itself and that it then imposed on reality. Henceforth, to understand was to dominate. Descartes formulated once and for all and in every sense the new charter of reason, according to which the knowledge that reason has from itself and from its method of knowing makes man "master and possessor of nature."

## SYNTHETIC KNOWLEDGE

This empire of reason and of reason's illumination is practiced in two rather authoritarian ways, which are given the seemingly harmless labels of "analysis" and "synthesis." The first breaks down the real into simple elements. The second rebuilds the real from these same elements according to the order of reason. With these two phases, reason manifests its omnipotence by its work of dissolution and reconstruction which is carried out according to the norms that it dictates. Reason henceforth knows the real not because it received the imprint of the real, but, on the contrary, because it imprints the real with its own contrived stamp. Therefore, for the spirit of the eighteenth century, truly knowing something requires *redesigning* the object and *producing* it with its own *fabrication*. Then, and only then, is understanding without mystery. A reality that cannot be entirely created by the mind remains obscure to the mind, whereas a being that is constructed by the mind is entirely transparent to it. It is luminous right through. One knows what one makes. Knowledge is making. Every act of understanding is a constructive activity. The *poetic* activity of the mind completely supplants the *speculative* activity. Today the former has radically eliminated the latter.

Kantian philosophy systematized this new attitude of human thought. It can be reduced to three positions: First, the intelligence is incapable of grasping the intelligible, which is present in the sensible. The "noumenal" order entirely escapes the intelligence. Second, the function of the intelligence is to organize the multiplicity of sensations and images that appear to it into a coherent whole. Instead of the intelligence being generated by the real world, it is the intelligence that begets the world of phenomena and confers sense on it. Third, man is no longer a being who is in a fundamental relation with the fullness of being. He is a reason, which is present in an identical way in all human beings, who themselves contrive a system of relations. The framework of this system is then projected onto the diversity of the sensible world that is linked to reason.

Adriano Tilgher (1887–1941), a historian of work in western civilization, formulated in a remarkable way modern man's inversion of intellectual activity:

> Kant is the first to conceive of knowledge ... as a synthetic and unifying force that, from the chaos of sensory input, derives the cosmos, the world that is ordered by nature, by proceeding according to the immanent laws of the mind. The mind therefore appears as an activity that creates order and harmony from its own depth. Knowing is making, acting, producing. It produces unity and harmony. The idea of productive action became implanted in the heart of speculative philosophy and did not leave it. All history of modern philosophy in its living and significant streams, from the criticism of Kant to the latest forms of pragmatism, is the history of the deepening of this idea of the mind that is conceived as synthetic activity, as a productive faculty, as demiurgic creation. One does not truly understand what one does. But what does man really make? Certainly not the latest sensory input. This input seems to him to be imposed from outside. It is *in* him, though it is not *of* him. But thanks to his work, he can combine in different ways this latest input in a way that makes them obedient to his needs, will, and caprice. Bit by bit, he substitutes for real nature, "natural nature," a nature of the laboratory and the factory. He knows this nature because he made it. This is clear to him because it is his work. There is a practical solution to the problem of knowledge. The technique practically resolves the problem of knowledge.[16]

---

16  Adriano Tilgher, *Homo faber*, Roma, 1929. French translation by Elena Boubee and René Maublanc, *Le travail dans les mœurs et*

## IDEALISM, THE INTELLIGENCE, AND THE PLASTIC WORLD

This is a matter of a full-fledged *mutation* of human intelligence and, from this fact, of man. This cannot be in doubt. Kant was perfectly aware of this. He was convinced that he had brought about in philosophy a genuine *Copernican* revolution. Instead of the mind orbiting things, it is henceforth things that orbit the mind, like the planets around the sun.[17] Marx only had to pinpoint the consequence of this reversal: "Criticism of religion liberates man so that he thinks, he acts, *he forges his reality* as liberated man and *returns to reason, so that he revolves around himself, which is to say, around his true sun*. Religion is nothing but the illusory sun that orbits around man *as long as man does not orbit around himself.*"[18] Man has nothing more to know of a Creation such as the Creator made it. He henceforth refuses to *alienate himself* in the illusion of a world that is independent of himself and suspended in a transcendent Principle. Marx goes on to say that man henceforth knows that "human conscience is the highest divinity" and that he has as his task to create a "new man" and a "new world," which will be the "real" man and world.

Already before Marx, Feuerbach had defined this mutation and subversion of intelligence whose echoes rumble in the souls of today's men: "The object with which a subject is in an *essential and necessary* rapport is nothing other than this subject's *own* but *objective* essence."[19] Stated another way, the object of the human intelligence is the intelligence itself that seizes itself in its creative

---

*dans les doctrines*, Paris: Librairie Félix Alcan, 1931,70, 71, and 74.

[17] Emmanuel Kant, *Critique de la raison pure*, "Préface de la seconde édition (1787)," Paris, P. U. F., 1971, 18 sq.

[18] Karl Marx, *Pour une contribution à la critique de la philosophie du droit de Hegel*, Oeuvres III, Philosophie, Paris, Bibliothèque de la Pléiade, 1982, 383. The italics are from Marcel De Corte.

[19] Ludwig Feuerbach, *L'essence du christianisme*, Paris, Gallimard, collections "Tel," 2011, 120.

impulse which the intelligence joins as a principle of itself and of the world. The intelligence is Narcissus, but not a Narcissus who is frozen in the contemplation of himself. It is a Narcissus who, in front of his own mirror, creates himself in creating the world. He progresses, never stopping, towards his own apotheosis. "*Absolute being, the God of man, is his own essence,*" Feuerbach notes.

Such is the infallible consequence of the mutation of intelligence. It is pushed into deification. In effect, if the mind is a productive faculty, if knowledge is a productive work, if knowing something is nothing more than "to become the other as the other," then knowing is to act on beings and things in order to make them intelligible in substituting for them the idea that one has of them and transforming them into that representation. Henceforth, one no longer knows what one is doing. The world is only the world insofar as it is constructed by man's intelligence. Undoubtedly, man does not create his sensations. He still receives them from the exterior. But this exterior world, which he appears to depend on, is not, properly speaking, known. It is a kind of plastic matter in which the human intelligence imprints its form.

Thanks to this work by the intelligence on sensory input, man can transform the exterior world in a way that makes it obedient to his own desires, to what he considers useful or necessary for all the necessities of his individual and social life. The exterior world no longer resists man. With the fusion of the atom, its last redoubt was pried open. The world is therefore transformable at will. There is no longer anything mysterious or sacred. *Caeli et terra NON enarrant gloriam Dei.*[20] There are no longer *realities* that are external to man and to which man must submit himself. There are no longer *events* that are foreign to the human will and to which man must submit. Everything is *made* by man and for man. The world becomes that

---

20 "Heaven and earth NOT depicting the glory of God."

which man wants it to become. Man rules over the world like a god or demiurge. The more he highlights his hold over the world, the more he erects himself as an absolute, substitutes himself for the Creator, and establishes himself as a being who has no need for God. He is sufficient in himself, with total independence and liberty.

This immense aspiration for aseity[21] and deity, this prodigious self-sufficiency and idolatry of oneself, inaugurated by the Cartesian *cogito* and enthroned by Kantian reason, brought to the pinnacle by the Hegelian mind, magnified in man by Feuerbach, and incarnated by Marx in communism (in which man makes a complete return to himself and recognizes himself "as the highest divinity," that which "tolerates absolutely no rival"), is not only the prerogative of philosophers. This aspiration spread throughout all of humanity with a staggering rapidity through the diffusion of the "*Lumières*," which is to say, through the universal expansion of education and through the proliferation of the class of intellectuals. And this is understandable.

Nothing is more difficult than to penetrate the reality of beings and things in all their depth. The smallest grain of sand points the intelligence toward the totality of the universe and toward God. The real resists the mind. To seize the intimate nature of the real is a long-term work in which experience plays an immense role in need of constant reinvigoration. This is no less true with ideas and mental representations. They are daughters of thought. They are docile servants. They submit to the intentions, wishes, and projects of thought without rebellion. The intellectual dominates over his interior world. Nothing is more exhilarating than this game of ideas in which the player inevitably triumphs. For this to happen, the idea needs to have a weakened or cut-off relationship

---

21 Aseity: "The divine attribute of uncaused existence." Bernard Wuellner, *Dictionary of Scholastic Philosophy* (Fitzwilliam, New Hampshire: Loreto Publications, 2012), 10. [Translator's note]

with the real. Also needed is the abolition from thought and language of any mention of the harsh confrontation with experience that normally controls our images. Such deception occurs with an unheard frequency with the intellectual. The truth requires severe and harsh contact with beings and things. It also requires a lived relation with total reality and its Principle. These requirements presuppose the exercise of the mind. To the extent that, enclosed in his ivory tower[22], the thinker bears down on his ideas and their expression, this contact almost always weakens. The thinker's signs of the real are, actually, the signs and words that translate the real. Almost always, they constitute reality for him and come to replace the world that reveals itself through observation and objective intelligence. His long practice of manipulating these ideational or verbal signs with the greatest ease gives him the impression, and soon the conviction, that, in holding these formulas, he possesses reality itself. Even more, he persuades himself that the solution to the problems that he discovers by playing with all these ideas is the same solution that reality demands, but that some sort of evil genius, a spreader of secular aberrations, drowns out his voice. The spoken and written words of such thinkers removed any obstacles to spreading their lies!

How then can we be surprised that the new conception of man and the world that we have called *idealism* has had such a lively and prompt success, especially among educators? Among these people, it retains its position under various names, from existentialism to Marxism to structuralism. These solid positions are unconquerable, given the conditions of recruitment for professors. Idealism attracts all those who balk at the effort it takes to embrace the real and who claim, despite their resignation—or because

---

22  De Corte's expression, which he encloses in quotation marks, is "pensoir," which may be translated as "thinker," although that does not seem to fit here, especially with the verb "enclosed" ("enfermé").

of their resignation—to offer a solution for every human problem, even at the cost of suppressing all these problems and their human character.

Idealism fits like a glove for all those who sacrifice the lessons of experience and tradition to their own lessons. It follows the slope of the easy option by organizing the haze of sensations and multitude of images that attack us. It does so according to the superficial schemes that these sensations and images suggest and on which the intelligence elaborates within its walls based on its claimed creative power or so-called law of conquest. Or idealism follows this easy slope by feeling the presence of the humblest realities of everyday life as a profound experience that involves the collaboration of sensibility, imagination, and mind. Idealism then lifts this presence up to the level of the thought that conceives it. Where is true creativity found? In the artifice of discourse and writing? Or in the act of hard-working intelligence? This intelligence, containing the intelligible germ of the sensory faculties, offers its fruit. What is a greater malaise than this: Discovering the natural order of the universe or enclosing beings and things in the framework of mathematical formulas?

With all of its powerlessness, idealism favors the substitution of utopian intelligence for real intelligence. A conception of the world and of man that turns its back on the severe demands of humility that are imposed on the intelligence in the matter of the truth and that does not recognize the location of the human spirit in the inferior level in the hierarchy of spirits, all the while permitting those who profess this to spread their virtuosity, has every chance of obtaining an audience and the public's favors. When one thinks of the generations that were educated, or miseducated, for almost two centuries, at all levels of teaching, in an atmosphere that was oversaturated with idealist haze and smoke, one marvels at the few reserves of good sense that still exist in humanity.

## PRAXIS AND PRAGMATISM

It is natural for the intelligence that withdraws into itself and that affirms its demiurgic power to destroy the world that common sense considers to be real and to replace it with an artificial world that is built in the heads of philosophers, the learned, lawyers, and men of state, in legislatures, administrations, *thinking tanks*, laboratories, etc, and even in the cells of convents or episcopal palaces. No one can live without the world around him. If the world that man did not make were to disappear, he would be constrained to come up with another one himself. Therefore, this type of intelligence cannot but give birth to a civilization that has a technological style, which is ours. In such a civilization, wisdom is eliminated in the metaphysical as well as the moral senses. This benefits the methods used to direct operations that make all human activities rationally capable of constructing a new humanity, and a new world to which man will be perfectly adapted. The techniques of utopian intelligence permit man to adjust, ever more adequately, his psychological, economic, and social activities, if not even his personal conscience, to the exterior technified world, a little like one machine to another. In this conception of the world and of man, the *wise* (who know the nature and the end of the world and of man, which brings them back to God; in their lives they come to be, in an honorable way, the moral ideal that only someone who possesses a sure judgment in this matter can) are replaced by *experts, technicians*, by individual or social mechanisms, by competent *scientists* who can provide a practical solution to the tangle of complex problems that they face, by the *engineers of the soul*, as Stalin put it, who come before the world and man in exactly the same way as a simple engineer when he is designing an artificial form from some material through his industrious genius. Everything is determined according to decisions that are inspired by *"specialists."*

Since such an obvious fact is disregarded, it is important to state and restate that, of the three types of activities of human intelligence, which is to say, *contemplation*, *act*, and *making* (θεωρεῖν, πράττειν, and ποιεῖν), only the third remains. The contemplative life gave way to the active life. But we can distinguish, with the West's philosophical tradition and with language itself, between the *domain of action*, which is the tradition of the moral life, and the *domain of making*, which is the constructive activity of the mind. The most diverse trades make up this latter domain. This includes the fine arts and every other modification done to the exterior world by the human genius. It must be noted that, if we make such a distinction, the spheres that until now have been reserved to theoretical and practical activities have been invaded by the sole *poetic* activity of the mind. Nothing has escaped the universal transformation that began in the eighteenth century, not even man.

We have entered the era of Anglo-Saxon *pragmatism* and Russian or Chinese revolutionary *praxis*. This era was inaugurated by Cartesianism ("by wisdom ... [one achieves] a perfect understanding of all things that man can know as much for the conduct of his life as for the conservation of his health and the invention of all the arts"[23]), established by the triumphant bourgeoisie, and crowned by communism. The intelligence finds itself menaced right down to its living works and its customs right down to their roots.

Indeed, if the intelligence is no longer measured by *that which is* and by that which does not depend on it, in other words, by unchanging principles, then *the truth no longer exists*. Ostracizing speculative wisdom is rigorously equivalent to banishing all objective certitude. Now, if there is no longer any truth, there is no longer any morality

---

23 René Descartes, *Les principes de la philosophie*, "Lettre de l'auteur à celui qui a traduit le livre, laquelle peut ici servir de préface," (Paris, Bibliothèque de La Pléiade, 1953) 557.

because moral action presupposes that we know the nature of man, which needs direction, and the nature of the end of man to which he must be directed. *Nihil volitum nisi praecognitum.*[24] Without the prerequisite speculative knowledge, which is at least implicit, it is impossible to distinguish among the true good, the apparent good, and evil. All conduct becomes relative. What was good yesterday becomes bad today, and the reverse. Thrown into a world in which nothing is, in which everything becomes, man no longer has a point of reference to orient himself. Every direction is valid. Without stars or a compass, he is reduced to navigating by chance. No longer obeying any reality, not even his own, no longer receiving objects with any indication of what they are, *the only thing remaining is his subjectivity*, which he projects outside of himself and which he uses to exteriorize representations into the matter that he transforms.

The world is the result of the objectification of man's subjectivity. It is the work of an intelligence that is no longer linked to anything. The independence of this intelligence is total. It submits itself to no law or principle, only does as it pleases, and has no other course of action except the pure and simple arbitrariness of the subject. "Will it be god, table, or wash basin?" as the fabulist notes.[25] In this case it is not intelligence that adjudicates. It only provides the range of representations used to mark matter. An arbitrary decision emanates solely from the will, which is magnetized and guided by its impulse, thrust, and blind and irresistible power, except if it runs up against an obstacle that is stronger than itself. *Sit pro ratione voluntas.*[26]

In every poetical or technical form of activity that

---

24 "Nothing can be desired that is not first known."
25 Jean de la Fontaine, "Le Statuaire et la statue de Jupiter," in *Fables*, L. IX, fable 6 (Paris, Classiques Hachette, 1929), 347.
26 "Hoc volo, sic iubeo, sit pro ratione voluntas," This do I will, thus do I order (command); let my will be the (only) reason. Juvenal, *Satires*, L. VI, v. 223.

proscribes and supplants contemplation and moral action, the intelligence that is taken to be a faculty of the real finds itself eliminated to the benefit of the irrational will of power. The intelligence cedes the real to force, the sole force that can be wrapped around the most diverse things, the most seductive and most abusive fumes, to the point of no longer appearing to be what it is. Rejecting *homo sapiens* at the level of *homo faber*, it is nothing less than a brute force, a power of conquest and domination. The intelligence makes itself the servant of power in the most elementary sense, in a world that is ruled by connections of force.

Concerning the rest, how can it escape the fascination of power since it learns from itself and defines itself as a power that breaks any links that bind it? One takes refuge, as Sartre does, in the subterfuge of the betrayal that disgusts the observer and diverts his attention without resisting the vigilance of an assertive individual for a single instant. Sartre claims, while concealing himself: "I became a traitor and have remained one. I may totally put myself into whatever I start, unreservedly give myself to work, to anger and friendship. Yet in an instant, I will go back on myself, I know. I want it and I betray myself already, full of passion, by the joyful feeling of my future betrayal."[27] Only a simple-minded person is deceived. This fool's successive desertions attempt to make his *ego* free from everything, free from the jurisdiction of the universe. The intellectual who claims to be rebellious is henceforth the pawn whose ferrule wants to be the scepter of justice. The "Accused, stand up" of the comical tribunal of Stockholm is the barely-disguised reversal of the "student So-and-so, I've caught you. You will write out for me ten pages of the *Critique of Dialectical Reason!*" Such a will to power is clearly powerless and can only

---

27  Jean-Paul Sartre, *Les Mots* (Paris: Gallimard folio, 1974), 193.

maintain itself by pulling the wagon of the *real* political powers that move the planet. The pawn needs, moreover, to receive the authority that he boasts. Whoever proceeds with the psychological investments of the modern intellectual is therefore certain of maneuvering as he pleases. Sartre does not play; he is played. This is why all of the intellectuals who are devoured by power took him as model and master. He is condemned to pretend to be god, which is to say, to be an idol, an appearance, an illusion just like his adolescent idealism prevented his ever being able to become an adult, constraining this growth of himself and his imitators.

## THE WORLD OF APPEARANCES

In such a world, the intelligence is deprived of its own object of being and of all these realities that are superior to us and on which we depend. In addition, just as it nevertheless needs some object, the intelligence replaces it with *imagination*. The will to power attempts to confer a statute of reality and a rational form on the imagination. Beggars can't be choosers. The law is universal and operates at the level of thought just as it does at other levels.

It's easy to see: Since intellectual activity cannot operate without an object, it requires a product as a replacement. In order to exit its solitude and pass over the enclosure of its subjectivity, it is necessary for it to convert its internal representations into presences that are exterior to itself. To do so, it needs to appeal to the imagination that concocts a work that will play the role of the *real* object. In order to *do* anything at all, it needs to appeal to the imagination. One needs to elaborate on an *image* within oneself—a plain model, plan, or scheme of the thing that needs to be made. The work first appears in an imaginary way in the mind before it passes to the existence that the technique confers on it in reality. In this way, therefore, the refusal to submit to reality restricts the intelligence to abandon its rights, priority, and claims at the very moment in which it proclaims them and wants to verify them *with the imaginative faculty*. The intelligence becomes the servant of the imagination. It submits to its yoke at the instant when it proclaims itself master of the universe. The reality that is dismantled by intellectual analysis is put back together and reacticulated according to other configurations in an imaginary representation whose will to power is seized upon in order to construct a world that it will dominate. Even more, every intellectual activity strictly speaking (intuition, judgment, reasoning, interrogation, research, calculating, measuring, heuristics, invention, etc.) is placed at the service of the production of models that are proposed by the imagination for the will to power which will attempt to transfer it into reality.

We live thusly, or rather, we pretend to live and to exist in a world of appearances that is perpetually made and unmade, because the unique characteristic of that which is made is to be unmade, the unique characteristic of artifice is to become worn out and to cede place to other artifices that are following the same destiny. Only that which is does not change into another thing. Also, the attempt to substitute for the world of natures and essences a world created by man is subjected to perpetual restarts. As soon as it is implemented, imagination crashes upon harsh contact with permanent realities that man vainly flatters himself into modifying. The imagination then begins anew at its work. The cry of the fablist,

> I need the new, as there is nothing new in the world,

becomes the slogan of contemporary man. The worship of novelty, change, progress, and revolution that has raged for two centuries has no other origin but this enslavement of our intellectual activity. This enslavement is operated by the imagination and will to power.

Weaned off of its proper object, the intelligence is never

satisfied with the empty calories that are offered to it. It demands others and becomes exhausted in this immersion in the heart of an imaginary world like a shipwrecked man who is tortured by thirst on the "sea that is forever beginning again."[28] The imagination is exhausted in turn in this perpetual renewal of substitution. At the end of the adventure, as Baudelaire sings with bitterness,

> The Imagination that prepares its orgy
> Only finds a reef in the clarity of the morning.[29]

It turns out, however, that this dawn does not check out for us. "The diffusion of light" ends in the twilight of civilization in which not only man's will to power spreads everywhere, but in which his intelligence declines. Lest we forget that "a scholarly idiot is more of an idiot than an ignorant one,"[30] man has never been more powerful and more insane. The progressive blindness that the intelligence is struck with testifies to this. It is clear that we no longer situate ourselves in a real world, but in a world of appearances, where the only truth that man understands is that which he has made and that he has projected outside of himself like an ectoplasm from the mouth of a medium in a trance. Human work no longer adds to nature in order to bring it to its point of perfection. Human work reworks nature and thoroughly recreates it. The great suitability and friendship of man with nature, about which Montaigne writes, is disappearing. More precisely, nature is no longer. The creations of technology have replaced it. But these creations are the images of our subjectivity. We secrete them, so to speak, from ourselves. We eject them outside of ourselves and perpetually recognize ourselves in them so well that we never leave our subjectivity. Man

---

28  Paul Valéry (1871–1945), French essayist, poet, and philosopher.
29  Charles Baudelaire, "Le Voyage," in *Les Fleurs du mal, Oeuvres complètes*, I (Paris: Bibliothèque de La Pléiade, 1975), 130.
30  Molière, *Les femmes savantes*, Act 4, Scene 3.

finds himself in this world as before a mirror where he finds his image, only his image.

Marx was perfectly correct to state that with work, technology, and poetic activity, man sees himself in a world that he created and no longer in a world of beings and things independent of his thought and conscience. The modern world, dominated by the primacy of the human mind's activity of fabrication, is a *fictional* world, in the full meaning of the word. Descartes has already asserted, *Mundus est fabula*.[31] Nevertheless, man is so utterly incapable of exiting his subjectivity in order to take a certain distance from himself and his productions *that he does not see this*. Thanks to the techniques that grant him an ephemeral consistency, this world of the imagination is for him more real than the real world. Narcissus only sees Narcissus, but he does not see that his image has no other reality than that which he lends it. The world is the *alter ego* of man. It is the representation of man, his likeness, effigie, simulacrum, reflection, reproduction, his double, copy, facsimile. The world is the hallucination that man has of himself. It is an immense mirror, always magnified, that sends him a *disproportionate* image that he has of himself, a brilliant image that is in the process of exploding.

It also needs to be said, without the smallest concern for the protests that such a proposal can arouse, that the world that modern science achieves, and particularly with the sciences of physics and math (which constitute the ideal of all the others), is an imaginary world. The best physicists do not doubt this. As soon as they reflect on their knowledge, they realize that their thought is not about a real object, but that their knowledge was constructed by their mind. This knowledge is so mixed in with the data of experience that they have incorporated into their logical organization that it is impossible any longer to distinguish

---

31  "The world is a fable" or "The world is a story."

fact from fiction. One of them writes, "there is no objective experience. Experimental data are not data, but are acquired by our activity, and they bear our influence. They are abstractions that we make. The experimenter creates the experience, like the chemist creates the pure body." Heisenberg notes, "The natural laws that, in quantum theory, we mathematically formulate, no longer concern elementary particles as such, but the knowledge that we have of them."[32] Contemporary physics theory does not concern itself with the world of physical phenomena such as they are, but such as they appear in the mathematical constructions that take the place of these phenomena. For the physicist, nature does not exist, and is replaced by an image of nature. All knowledge in physics is metaphorical. It concerns an object that does not exist independently of the subject that observes it.

It has been noted countless times: The modern conception of nature, whose origins date back to Galileo,[33] challenges the testimony of our senses and their aptitude to perceive reality. The universe of physicists is that which affects the instruments that the scientist made and thanks to which he can measure this universe. The qualitative aspects of the universe, duly attested by our senses, escape science. As Eddington notes, "we know statements, not qualities, and the first resembles the second like a telephone number resembles a telephone user." If there is no objective experience and if the experimental data are not truly data, but are instead the products of our activity of fabricating instruments that measure this data and are an inseparable part of it, it is clear that the victories of modern physics are only earned on the condition of renouncing the knowledge of the real. In quantifying these "data," and in reducing them to mathematical symbols, it is clear that

---

[32] Werner Heisenberg, *La nature dans la physique contemporaine* (Paris: Gallimard, Idées, 1962), 18.
[33] See Alexandre Koyré, *Etudes galilennes* (Paris: Hermann, 1966).

the scientist bends them to the conditions of his understanding. This is after he has already bent them to the conditions of experimentation so well that he discovers in nature only the schemas of his mind.

This is what Max Planck formulates in these terms: "An experience is nothing other than a question addressed to nature. Measurement finds the response. But before carrying out the experience, it has to be thought out. In other words, the question that one wants to address to nature needs to be formulated. Before drawing a conclusion from the measurement, it needs interpretation, which is to say, the response from nature needs to be understood. These two tasks belong to the theoretician who is obliged to rely ever-increasingly on abstract mathematical language. This is why measurements have to be ordered according to a certain perspective before everything else, because each way to arrange them represents a particular way to interrogate nature. But the sound response cannot be obtained except with the help of a sound theory. It cannot be assumed that in physics we can formulate a judgment on the sense of a question without having recourse to a theory."[34]

In this way, therefore, the theory of physics comes prior to the experience and its mathematization. Now this theory can only be a work of the imagination that constructs a rational model of the world because it is anterior to all experimental and mathematical knowledge of this world. The physicist needs to construct in the imagination a model of the universe, either surreptitious or conscious, before beginning the smallest step in science. Otherwise stated, his science is in narrow and constant dependence on the imagination.

We can therefore see why nature is only known nowadays as an unknown of which we make an image, and

---

34  Max Planck, *L'image du monde dans la physique moderne* (Genève: Editions Gonthier, 1963), 111.

why the universe of modern physics is not only, according to Schrödinger's words, "practically inaccessible," but still "not even thinkable."[35] *Mundus est fabula.* The modern physicist begins to understand the range of Descartes' mysterious formula. It is also understandable why the "truths" of contemporary physics, even when they are mathematically demonstrable and technically verifiable, can no longer be expressed in a normal way through thought and, even less, through language. The attempt to express this all in a normal way, according to Schrödinger's sarcastic remark, leads to wording that is "perhaps less absurd than a triangular *circle*, but much more than a winged *lion.*" It is because we find ourselves here in a world that we are incapable of understanding, which is to say, of translating into coherent thoughts and linguistic terms, but that we are constrained *to imagine*, because of its very principle, and to *make*, because of the demand of reality that works our mind. No longer able to know nature, man can at least know what he imagines or makes it to be. The dazzling technical progress that we have witnessed for two centuries is the compensation for this latent speculative disappointment: We have multiplied the means to transform nature in an unheard of manner, for lack of being able to really know it.

THE INTELLIGENCE AND MATERALISM

The consequence follows: The distinction between the speculative and practical sciences tends to vanish more and more. Theory returns to application, and application to theory. These two aspects of research, rigorously distinct only recently, tend to become mixed up in a perfect circle. Pure science is inseparable from the technique that perfects its means of investigation, and technique is inseparable in turn from the pure science that defines it and

---

35   Erwin Schrödinger, *Science and Humanism* (1952), 26.

enables its ever more precise calculations. It is clear that contemporary sciences and technologies have renounced the contemplation of the world and henceforth aim at its transformation. The notion of the truth has ceded place to efficient action. Everything takes place as if Marx's second thesis on Feuerbach is verified in the metamorphosis of the world that modern science operates on: "The issue of knowing whether human thought can achieve an objective truth is not a theoretical question, but a practical one. It is in *praxis* that man has to demonstrate the truth, which is to say, reality, power, and the precision of his thinking."[36]

For the sciences and for contemporary techniques, deprived of all metaphysics and uprooted from the speculative conception of the universe that submits them to reality, *the truth becomes change, innovation, reform, even reversal, and, whatever the case, permanent history and revolution.* It is impossible for it to be otherwise. Sisyphus, the cleverest and least scrupulous of the mortals according to the fable, is definitively attached to his boulder. In order to rejoin the real from which it has divorced itself, human intelligence has no solution other than to *make*. Only the item that intelligence *makes*, manufactures, matches, structures, or constructs, can be real in its eyes. Being the only reality that exists and refusing everything that surpasses it, such as the universe or transcendent principle, it needs a world in which nothing enters other than what it itself produces. It needs a world where it finds itself in the presence only of itself, where man encounters nothing more than himself. A sensible person has no doubt that this is an *imaginary* world. *The intelligence submits itself with docility to the myth* and, as the achievement of myth is ceaselessly postponed into the future because the characteristic of myth is that it can never be the present reality, the intelligence is condemned to *make* and to *produce* without pause. *The*

---

36  Karl Marx, *Thèses sur Feuerbach*, "*deuxième thèse*," in Henri Lefebvre, *Marx* (P. U. F., 1969), 99.

*intelligence is the servant of the world that it claims to dominate and transform.*

This is where we are: the intelligence has been shipwrecked before our eyes at the very moment at which it believes it is triumphantly entering port. As the Portuguese proverb goes, the ship that no longer obeys the rudder—and the rudder here is contemplative wisdom—obeys the reefs. The intelligence is henceforth the prey of images and matter that force it to renewed failure, a failure that is baptized for the evolutionary, dialectical, or historical cause. The intelligence is offered in sacrifice to the myth of matter, because man cannot create anything except from matter. For having wanted to *make an angel*, it *makes a monster*. Idealism, the ailment of modern intelligence, is subjected to its last avatar, materialism. Idealism becomes, or rather *is*, materialism. There is no longer a shadow of difference between the two. For having challenged the principle of identity—the being is what it is and not what it appears to us to be—the intelligence is torn by the contradiction of two positions between which its actions oscillate. Each of the two positions is untenable.

### REAL AND IMAGINED COMMUNITY

Independently of their rivals of lesser rank and lesser virtuosity in camouflage, two philosophies (I would like to say two anthropological theologies, if I could say it without throwing around words) are in operation with growing success at concealing this decline in the mind while hastening its fall: *Marxism* and *Teilhardism*[37]. Both of them are the analogue, in the spiritual order, of that which are, in the physiological order, these products of contemporary pharmacopeia that combine in a single

---

37  "Teilhardism" refers to the thought of the French Jesuit paleontologist Teilhard de Chardin (1881–1955). His writings on the theological meaning of evolution have been considered heterodox. [Translator's note]

action tranquilising and stimulating effects. They are in effect perfect examples of the mystification that mystify the mystifier himself at the same time as they mystify his victims. Marxism and Teilhardism communicate to the imposter the unshakable good conscience that he has regarding the excellence of his cause and the inflexible conviction that he liberates his prey at the very moment at which he subjugates it.

How can one notice that these philosophies of becoming are at the same time the philosophies of the squared circle and, as Maurras notes, of the horned and crooked chimera? If everything is becoming, man is taken away in this universal flow. When will man therefore be? Tomorrow! These philosophies are in this way the philosophies of promise and, as they have to claim to be sure of the future, they are the philosophies of deceit and trickery. They have to *make* this "new man," this "new world." Now, every activity that takes place in the path of *making* is constrained to calculate the consequences brought by each step in the fabrication. It is therefore necessary to *eliminate* the *unexpected* from history. Nothing unforeseen can happen. There are therefore no events in the life of man any more than there are in his made-up world. Everything is foreseen in advance and human reason is capable of divination. Reason already knows that communism will succeed socialism just as this latter succeeded capitalism. It already knows that the "Christosphere" comes at the end of the "noosphere," just as this latter came at the end of the "biosphere." Man's reason dominates time. These philosophies are therefore hyper-rationalist. But their rationalism is unrealistic, we suspect, because it is impossible not to take into account the unexpected in human affairs, where "the unlikely regularly takes place." Reason is therefore forced to return once more to imagination and myth. These philosophies are on call to outline the specious and seductive image of what man will be, but only if he obeys the path of the future that carries him along. They are on call to propose to him his dazzling and unerring status at the end of his journey to divinity, but only if he increases the impulse through industrious effort. Who cannot see that this "achievement" of man is irrational?

*Eritis sicut dei*, you will be like the gods, is the motto of these Satanic philosophies. The will to power that animates their adepts knows it. Most men who renounced their good sense and their intelligence in order to wallow in artificial paradises of the imagination will succumb to this mirage. Consciously or unconsciously, these philosophers who contemplate themselves "in the world that they have created" and that is but the projection of their subjectivism, cannot escape the temptation to exercise an absolute power over humanity. The universe in its total history is their *ego* itself. This universe is mirrored in their ego's creation and, through that, it even universalizes in space and time. How does their *ego* not get drunk from such an edifying vision? The audience of the new class of intellectuals who are avid to exercise their earthly principality is acquired beforehand. Incapable of working on a system that justifies and conceals their will to power, they rush at whoever presents them with a ready-made victory which is adapted to their claims as weaklings who take themselves for giants.

The differences between believers and non-believers are found in the melting pot of totalitarianism. With Marxism, we have atheist totalitarianism, just as with Teilhardism we are faced with the most virulent form of clerical totalitarianism. These two totalitarian systems consist of the same elements. The latter is fatally included to connect with the first in the negation of transcendence in the exaltation of man with a capital M that it professes. Even if Teilhardism (and, later, Christianity) eventually triumphs by concealing the divine cloud and inaugurating the Kingdom of God on earth, it would be the victory of illusion and of the combined will to power. Night would definitively extend itself over humanity, and humanity would be governed by the Grand Inquisitor whose supreme hypocrisy would be to make himself venerated as the Savior of men!

It would take another book to denounce this creeping hate of the intelligence, this massive diffusion of smoke and mirrors, this itch for proselytism, propaganda, and domination that characterizes Marxism and Teilhardism, particularly with the cheap imitators of these systems, with the technocrats of new Islam and their Christian emulators.

The proliferation of partisans and militants of these doctrines, the extraordinary fashion for these mythologies, the credit that they maintain and grow in public opinion despite the severest denials that inflict facts on them, are not mysterious in any way. It is enough to reflect for a single instant on this major event that has directed human history for almost two centuries and whose consequences are coming to their end today: *The dissolution of natural communities.* The nature of the rational animal can only blossom and come to its maturity in one or another natural environment that correspond to this animal and to which his practical intelligence adds institutional extensions that support and activate vitality. For it to be the intelligence, man's intelligence needs an appropriate ambiance in which its impulse towards the beings and things to which it naturally aspires to know are reinforced and reinvigorated.

In effect, knowledge of the exterior world is not handed over to man solely through the instincts, as happens with animals. To discover this knowledge, the mind needs to be educated to orient itself towards the real. This education is received, first and necessarily, in the family, which is the original social environment from which all the others are derived and which we are at present losing. We are even losing the memory of this term. The family does not only inculcate us with moral discipline, as we tend to believe, but also with intellectual discipline.

It cannot be stated enough that it is impossible to abandon oneself to the games of the dreamy imagination, the deceptions of illusion, or utopia when one is with family. In the family, an individual's lying, sophism, error, vanity, bragging, boastfulness, etc. cannot escape the views of others and are denounced almost immediately. No one can create an illusion in the family nor create a personnage. Conduct in relation to beings and things that do not conform to their nature rapidly bring about disastrous consequences. It is not the same with societies that have grown too vast and that have lost all connections with the family. In such a society, it is difficult, if not impossible, to control distractions of the mind. The consequences of evasion in utopia occur without anyone pointing out the nuisance. The family environment is where the intelligence *as* the faculty of the real is formed. It is in the heart of the family where we learn to know the world just as it is and where we adopt the attitudes that conform to our own reality and the reality of another, and to those beings and things that surround us. The environments that are connected to the family and that develop us are watered from this natural source of realism that is natural to the intelligence.

"Oh family, abridgement of the world," sang Lamartine.[38]

It is therefore understandable why all the rootless are utopians. Their intelligence is no longer in any place. It no longer operates with the assistance of natural environments that are natural to the human being. It escapes into the mists of the imagination. It constructs a chimerical universe which their will to power aims to seize in order to dominate the world and humanity. In this respect, the priest whose superior vocation has uprooted him, and who does not become rooted again in all humility in the

---

38 Alphonse de Lamartine, Jocelyn, "9e époque: les laboureurs," in Oeuvres poétiques (Paris: Bibliothèque de La Pléiade, 1963), 748.

supernatural, becomes the greatest agent of dissolution and destruction in man and the world. He is the consummate revolutionary and the arrant leader of crowds. He is unsurpassable.

In a society such as ours, which is a society in name only, and whose true label should be *dissociety*, the French Revolution did not only ravage natural communities. *It constructed in their place collectivities that are rigorously and strictly imaginary, whose fictional existence grants every freedom to unleash its own impulses to dominate.*

## DEMOCRACY AS TECHNOCRACY

At this point, our intelligence of reality is obsessed by the prestigious aspects of the imagination that have convinced us that the greatest social and political innovation in modern times, democracy, for which millions of human beings have shed their blood, has a real existence. In fact, it is a chimera whose existence does not extend beyond the confines of our skulls or beyond the paper on which constitutions or discourses are written and that spread this word, democracy, to the four corners of the universe. The government "by the people" only exists if the people govern. It is too clear that this capacity only operates in very narrow limits and on relatively limited territories where the citizen can have the experience of the problems that are encountered and the solutions that are adopted.

Democracy is a system that is suitable for the municipality or even the region. Above a limited geographical area, it is a mere word. According to Valéry's sarcastic formula, it is the system in which the citizen is summoned to respond to questions regarding which he has no competence, and kept from responding to those that are within his capacity. The second principle is combined with the first. Bertrand de Jouvenel[39] justly writes, "In a great state, participation

---

39  Bertrand de Jouvenel (1903–1987), French philosopher and political economist.

in the government is a misleading illusion, aside from a small minority. We no more govern in participating in an election than we operate on ourselves in selecting a surgeon. And in fact, when I choose a surgeon, I am the sole elector and my surgeon is the one that I have chosen among many others. It is not the same with my "representative." My vote is a drop of water in a giant bucket, with the choice limited to the candidates.

As soon as "the people" is granted responsibilities that surpass its power of experience and understanding, politics change meaning. "The people" do not govern more effectively, nor do its delegates. The delegates pretend to govern. They are given, and give, the illusion of governing. "Democratic" structures remain, but are no longer anything more than a veneer covering a different system whose denomination, increasingly authoritative, is *technocracy*. This is necessary. We perceive its ubiquitous presence more and more every day. Despite the spoken and written inundation that is daily poured over our heads, whoever retains an objective judgment cannot help but see that society is evolving towards a division into two groups, "those who know" and command, and "those who do not know" and obey.

This technocracy itself is made up of two types of technicians whose functions complement each other: the technician in the conditioning of minds, and the technician in the conditioning of things. They both appeared as the social reserves that had been accumulated by the *Ancien Régime* in the natural communities that were depleted and left uncultivated by democracy. The ensuing broken society spread everywhere, for all to see, and needed to be mentally and materially "restructured." The democratic system that was established on the foundation of this broken society, as it was incapable of creating a new society, needed recourse to the powers of illusion and tried, through appropriate techniques, to introduce the imaginary into the real.

## THE KNEADING OF NEW MYTHS

The role of the technician in conditioning minds is to substitute the reign of so-called sovereign opinion for the exercise of the intelligence. The intelligence plays no role, except an accidental one, in the democratic systems and their vast scope of action from which the modern states were born, due to its lack of experience in setting these systems in motion. In fact, opinion is by nature malleable. The connections that it makes with reality make it easily-persuaded, fluid, and shapeable to the extreme. The strongest will to power imposes its form on opinion. In the most rigorous sense of the term, a person has an opinion, while opinion, in its more general sense, is generated. Opinion in this latter, more generalized sense is the product of a poetic and counterfeit activity in which the opinion of the producer has a major function. With the material means that technicians have at their disposal today, such as the printing press, radio, TV, etc., it is not an exaggeration to state that opinion *is mass-produced* with a consummate art of manipulation, trickery, and special effects, in the offices of information that are found in abundance on the planet. Our century is the era of *information distortion*. It is totally plausible that future historians will find it impossible to understand the historical truth of the events that have taken place under our noses for a half a century.

It is not only the knowledge of facts that has been profoundly altered. It is the conception that our contemporaries make of man and the world. The relationship of thought to the real is broken over and over by the professionals of thought: scientists, philosophers, theologians, and the countless major and minor acolytes who sail in their wake. The kneading and remaking of opinion concerning events accompany parallel operations in every domain of the mind. The generation of opinion requires breaking all the connections that unite the intelligence to being. Reduced to his subjectivism, cut off from his roots, and robbed of all his moorings, man is then nothing more than a marionette at the entire discretion of his manipulators. His mutation into a puppet is all the more easy that the only thing he has left is the *formless* impulse of his intelligence and will towards their own object, which has disappeared. It is what the technicians of opinion arrogantly call "the requirements of modern thought" or "the demands of the contemporary conscience" or "the aspirations of man," and so on. Whoever reduces himself to his own subjectivity becomes the weakest of men. The technicians of opinion seize hold of this amorphous entity and put their impressions on it from the outside, through every overt or clandestine technique of persuasion. They make the most fascinating imagery of the future man and world that they can. They crown this work with the promise, *haec omnia tibi dabo* (Matt. 4:9). The social success of their venture is secure. At this point man is a *political animal*. Every privation of his natural communities incites him to build artificial communities and castles in the air as quickly as possible.

The technician in the conditioning of minds triumphs in the kneading together of political and social matter, as experience proves. It is child's play to keep contemporary man in suspense by presenting on the screen of his imagination a future society whose advent is ceaselessly carried forward and where he will find the superman, half-god, or god. The myth of a society in which man has every right and no duty, every liberty and no responsibility, where the *ego* coincides with the human genus (according to the promise of Marx), where he discovers himself to be simultaneously "personalist" and "communitarian" (according to the imitation made by Mounier), has every chance of triumphing in a system in which there is no longer a society, where the state, no longer limited by underlying communities, possesses an unlimited power, where this State sees itself appointed by the public opinion which is conditioned by the alarming mission of creating a new man and a new world. "*Make* me god in a world over which I will reign as god": here is the vow, the plea, the request that is imperiously formulated to the State by the citizen who is mechanized by the technicians of propaganda. There is no greater devastating madness of the mind or more murderous insanity of human reason. It is everywhere. Broadcast everywhere, the idea expands to the dimensions of the universe.

### COLLECTIVE THOUGHT AND THE WILL TO POWER

It is at this point that the technicians in the conditioning of things, or simply "technocrats," intervene. Managing such an enterprise and making the dream become reality requires an organization, which means organizers. So that the conditioned man's image of himself and the world can be translated into reality, the event needs to be handled carefully and prepared through the arrangement of all that is needed to produce this world. Organizers must come up with a plan, and calculate the phases, focus effort, command operations, direct behavior, have unerring knowledge and methods, and wield absolute power. The representation that man has of himself and of the world, no longer proceeding from the real or from experience, is a pure construction of the mind. It will therefore be necessary to incorporate this representation into external matter exactly with the technique that is based on rigorous *mathematical models*. These models can then be applied to the matter at hand that they are informing. The technocrats, strictly speaking, are those who possess this science of efficiency. They are brought to supreme power not only by the perpetual vacancy of power, which is characteristic of democratic systems, but by the opinion that intellectuals have molded. In countries where the democratic facade has not declined too much, they mimic the surviving demagogues and career politicians. Elsewhere, they occupy the avenues of power. Their secret is simple.

They treat man and the world like things, like matter to be exploited, like a collection of mechanically-operating bureaucratic cogs. They look at society as the result of an organization chart and planning. They suppress every attempt to return to contemplative and moral activities of the mind. They establish the unrivaled supremacy of productive activity. They transform humanity into an immense factory for which they constitute the worldwide administrative council.

Technocracy, whether it is that of the mind or that of the mind converted into a thing, obviously includes the integral socialization of human life. Thought becomes collective because all thoughts are identical, having passed through the same mold and constituted by the same indescribable "noosphere" that Teilhard imagined for our conditioning. All the activities of the collectivized mind become collective at the same moment. Contemplative activity, or whatever remains of it, is reduced to a narcissistic vision of reason that is common to all men in a mirror that is nothing other than itself. Practical activity replaces the good with the useful, and happiness with complete subjugation to social security from cradle to grave, and above all, with poetic and productive activity, which celebrates its triumph. Workers are considered to be a single and gigantic laborer who, by working more and more, will finish by liberating himself of all work and leading an idyllic existence in an earthly paradise that is rebuilt for eternity.

This so-called inescapable socialization has only one flaw: It does not exist because it cannot exist except within the imagination as a form of mythology. Collective thinking, which commands the holistic socialization of human life, does not exist for the good and simple reason that it only exists in individual thoughts and is irreducibly united to an individual brain and individual body. Behind this supposed collective thinking, behind this supposed collective labor, there is, once again and unanimously, the will to power of those who gather together in what we can call "a collegial direction" whose delivery is in the hands of a single tyrant —οὐκ ἀγαθὸν πολυκοιρανίη εἷς κοίρανος ἔστω![40]—is foreseeable!

There are leaders who think and act. There is, according to Goethe's unforgiving formula, "the brain that is enough for a thousand arms." The other group is the bleating flock heading toward the Promised Land. When the bishop of Metz impatiently affirms that "socialization is a grace" and the bishop of Bruges follows him down this path, setting off a chain reaction that will be hidden for a long time to come given the slowness and prudence of today's bishops, let us be assured that they put in their candidacy for the title of "princes of this world," the coryphaeus[41] of a mindless humanity. They hold hands with all sorts of technocrats in order to propose to them the invaluable aid of a *new-look* clericalism that penetrates right to the roots of souls, in the very name of Christ who is put in the clothing of an instrument of domination to move with the most intimate impulses.

## CREDENTIALED IDIOTS

A society constituted of two impermeable compartments is in the act of being born under our noses from the decomposition of the society of the *ancien régime* that was devastated by the French Revolution. The last reserves of that society, which a short time ago were already thin, are today almost depleted. The classless society, the dream of democracy, and the living logic of democracy and communism constitute the smoke screen that masks *the ascension of*

---

40 "No good thing is a multitude of lords; let there be one lord." Homer, *Iliad*, 2:204, A.T. Murray, translator, https://www.theoi.com/Text/HomerIliad2.html. Aristotle cites this verse in the *Metaphysics* in omitting the imperative εστω.
41 Leader of the choir in Greek drama.

*the most despotic caste that history has ever known*, a caste without heart, soul, or spiritual life. This caste is composed of individuals whose intelligence, limited to its technical dimension, is the slave of an immoderate will to power.

This revolution that is currently underway is increasingly noticeable. The congressman is no longer made for the people, but the people for the congressman; the union leader no longer for the workers, but the workers for the union leader; the professor no longer for his courses, but courses for the professor; teaching no longer for students, but students for teaching; programs no longer for life, but life for programs; the priest no longer for the faithful, but the faithful for the priest; society no longer for the person, but the person for society. The dreadful expression, *subjected to social security*, betrays this reversal. When intelligence inverts its natural movement towards reality in order to submit itself to the reality of mental representations, we have to anticipate contradiction in every domain and an upside-down world.

The demarcation line between the managing caste and the condition of the managed, between the effective and recognized holders of power and those who are submitted to it, between the parallel hierarchy that exercises real power and those who imagine themselves still voluntarily obeying a now decorative power, is generally constituted by the presumption of formal and technical intelligence conferred via the *diploma*. Between the parchment and the intelligence that is cut off from the real, but desirous of replacing the real with its own constructions, there are today clear affinities, if not identity between the two. We see that the technocratic *intelligentsia* finds its recruits among diploma holders. In order to enter into this *intelligentsia*, one needs to provide evidence, not of the faculty to penetrate the real, but the aptitude to handle images, ideas, words, and mental or material mechanisms. The donkey's skin is conferred moreover only for a conversion of the qualitative into the quantitative.[42] Everything that is not convertible into numbers, imponderables such as character, vocation, gift, open-mindedness, curiosity, taste, honor, duty, moral and esthetic sense, etc., are relegated to the background. The false pregnancy of encyclopedic knowledge and its twin sister, specialization, eliminated the conception of the world that was characteristic of the decent man. The elite is touted and judged according to its technical capacities. The artificial world that modern man builds can tolerate no other criteria.

Universities therefore become advanced professional schools. If philosophy is still tolerated, it is to the extent that it contributes to the distortion of minds and where it attempts to justify through its sophistry that man is the measure of all things. The saint, genius, hero, wise man, or, more simply, the free spirit and the creator in any domain, have hardly anything more than a minimal influence. All of society oscillates between the side of the diploma-holders and the mandarins.

Academic titles are henceforth demanded everywhere, and with all the more rigor that minds formed (or deformed) only by courses, discourses, lessons, academic levels, and re-education, etc., are separated from reality by a screen of mental representations, spoken or printed (the thickness of which unceasingly grows), and they are particularly well-suited for the creation of a new man and a new world. The modern intellectual spends the majority of his time far from reality, in reading newspapers, journals, books, and participating in gatherings, conversations, colloquia, "dialogues," etc. The presence of the real world and real man don't make the least sense for him. He is comfortable only with an artificial world and artificial men, where he finds his own image. It can be said in this regard that intelligence

---

42   The expression "donkey's skin," or "la peau d'âne," refers to a well-known folktale of an incestuous relationship between a king and his daughter after the death of the queen.

is the faculty that the intellectual least uses. Bernanos roars, "The intellectual is so often an idiot that today we have to take him as such, until he has proven to us the contrary."[43]

## THE NANNY STATE AND THE WAR ON FREE WILL

It is increasingly forgotten that a certain amount of spontaneity, originality, and natural, naive, and gushing anarchy are necessary for every human society, to see it degenerate a little into a stereotypical animal society. Without these creative forces, society freezes, often under the cover of a non-conformity whose artificial and premeditated character accentuates the social automatisms that it claims to break. "One only grafts onto the wild one," in the excellent words of Ramuz.[44] Human intelligence grafts itself onto the disorderly impulsions of social life with which the rational animal, equipped only with instincts that are blind about matter, cannot be content. Society is a given of nature, imperfect but necessary in its origins. Intelligence brings it to perfection and channels its sap. Nothing is more fragile than this operation of which we know (in observing how difficult it is to make a true man out of this young barbarian that is the infant) that it must pursue all its life and from one generation to the next. That is the work of tradition. True tradition retains the unformed and powerful impulse of nature, its force, that it disciplines. As Maurras states, tradition is *critical*.[45] It

---

[43] Georges Bernanos, "La France contre les robots," in *Essais et écrits de combats*, II (Paris: Bibliothèque de La Pléiade, 1955), 1042.

[44] "Art, we know what it is: It is a graft onto the already-grafted.
   Now, as all grafters know,
   One only grafts onto the wild one.
   One only grafts onto the little wild one,
   That is how one grafts."
Charles-Ferdinand Ramuz, "Anti-poétique," in *Salutation paysanne et autres morceaux*, 1921, Oeuvres complètes, Volume VIII, Nouvelles et morceaux, Tome 4, 1915–1921 (Genève: Editions Slatkine, 2007), 307.

[45] Charles Maurras, *Mes idées politiques* (Paris: Fayard, 1968), 134.

constantly eliminates the dead branches and conserves only the living ones that promise beautiful fruit. It does not have its place in the artificial world of technology.

An analogous remark can be made about all types of communities: There are not any who do not have to be reinvigorated sooner or later with the help of outside elements. We know enough about the role of consanguineous marriages in dynasties and aristocracies. Universities, administrations, constitutional bodies, businesses, etc., harden through the effect of rigid rules of admission. An appeal to outstanding personalities is necessary for restoring force and inspiration. The world of technologies and artifice which we now have excludes this recourse. This world is the work of specialists who hold the plans to it. Each individual must specialize in his way in order to gain admittance. As the technologies that created it and that constantly renew its existence multiply and become more and more complex, more and more study and diplomas are necessary to penetrate into the holy of holies and the chambers of the machines of contemporary society. A human life in its entirety no longer suffices for accessing the dignity of the superior technocrat. Society is therefore composed of technicians who are spread out on its summit and who weigh with all their weight on the base that is made up of the community of mortals. This society progresses rapidly towards "the perfect and definitive anthill" where each person has his place and function labeled according to the rules that no one can transgress without condemning himself to death.

The state that organizes and directs this type of society in formation does not only assume the right to confer the license that permits each individual to take his own place there and carry out his functions. It controls not only employment, but also directs every transformation of professional life that reduces social life today. Just a while ago, it assured *the common good* of a natural and relatively stable society that independently produced its own representatives according to the necessities of time and place. At the moment, the state examines, inspects, verifies, calculates, anticipates, provokes, and determines every change that takes place in the fluid world subject to its power. The functional world which we inhabit is in fact a bureaucratized world under the aegis and impulse of the state. The citizens become the direct or indirect bureaucrats of the state. The managers are the employees of the tax authorities for this personnel. They are the employees of social security, etc. A Russian economist figured out that in 1980 the entire population of his country would not be enough to accomplish the tasks given to the state bureaucracy. We have arrived at this comical situation where the word of Péguy is no longer true: "There are those who are in front of the counter window and those behind it." All those who were in front of the window have now moved behind it. In our less bureaucratized country, Parkinson's celebrated law, "One plus one equals three," is in full swing, and those who find themselves in front of the window make desperate efforts to get on the other side.

The corruption of the world that surrounds them fills them with anxiety. They rush to the sector that is sheltered by the bureaucratic state. They have to abandon themselves to the supreme power of the state in order that the mechanisms that they activate and which they do not renounce can be disciplined. Nothing can make them happy in this so-called new world that is their work. Greedy for stability in the heart of a perpetual change that takes them away, they turn to the state, the power of stability. In this way, the great modern god rises. This is the welfare state that assures the happiness of men. But its immense and protective shadow sterilizes the intelligence by mechanizing it. Since the root of liberty is entirely in the intelligence, the welfare state kills all liberty.

De Tocqueville's prophecy is fulfilled. The welfare state "willingly works for the happiness [of citizens], but it wants to be the unique agent and sole arbiter. It provides for citizens' security, foresees and satisfies their needs, facilitates their pleasures, drives their principal affairs, directs their industry, and regulates and divides their inheritance. *Why would it not entirely do away with the trouble to think and the pain of living?* Every day, therefore, it *makes the use of free thought less useful and more rare.* It encloses the action of the will into an increasingly small space. Over time it steals from each citizen *right up to the use of himself,*[46] which is to say the use of intelligence.

### REVOLUTION AND CORRUPTION EXTEND TO THE CHURCH

The situation of the intelligence is all the more dramatic because the Catholic Church, which always presented itself to universal public opinion, to the faithful of other religions, to its own faithful, as the guardian of the truths of nature and grace, the dispenser of natural and supernatural wisdom, and the conserver of the faith and its customs, now sees a notable part of its clergy, proselytes, if not its best members, casually and even impudently flout this tradition that was its own. These members now collaborate in the radical transformation of man and the world under the sign of the triumphant technocratic revolution.

The many issues of the contemporary Catholic Church form an immense subject. One can outline one or two key elements in this subject. These issues include its relationship with the intelligence; the emergence of a parallel hierarchy contemptuous of its values of truth, which are then removed from the true hierarchy; the extraordinary isolation of this hierarchy from the real world and real man; the curtain of illusions, of chimera, of mirages, even of visions, that blind it, even sometimes with its most eminent

---

46  Alexis de Tocqueville, *De la democratie en Amerique*, vol II, (Paris: Bibliothèque de La Pléiade, 1992), 837.

representatives; its incapacity, which grows by the day, to discriminate between truth and error; its masterly and often extravagant exercises that the best-intentioned clergymen execute in a silly way, from ignorance, compromise of principles, even betrayal; the worship that is publicly dedicated to the golden calf of novelty; and the frenzy of the *aggiornamento* at all costs that causes agitation and testifies to a minuscule intellectual and spiritual discernment.

The first is, without any possible doubt, the orientation imprinted by the recent Council of the Universal Church which relegated to the background the values of contemplation to the benefit of the values of action. These in turn, in the post-conciliar mentality, were sidelined in favor of the values of fiction and the will to power. These two falls were fatal. Right from the first meetings when the majority of the fathers rejected the scholastic-styled schema on the definition of the Church, under the pretext that it was inaccessible to the modern mind, truth had to yield to efficiency, the intelligence to the will, and the eternal to the temporal. The nature of scholastic philosophy and theology is to exalt the specific difference of man and to make the intelligence, enlightened by grace, into the perfect instrument at our disposal for understanding the nature of God and of all that is. All other instruments are subordinated to this.

For the Church, it follows that the knowledge that conforms to natural and supernatural reality is the framework wherein all other human activities develop. These activities cannot extend beyond this framework without harm. The Church has always disapproved of *fideism*. She considers it beneath man's dignity, for man's principal function is reason. Also, whatever part of the will is involved in the act of faith, this intervention of the will is not a jump into the unknown. The act of faith is based on givens that, without being evident or demonstrable, are the signs of the truth for a reason. Miracles and the resurrection of Christ are the signs of his divinity. Contemplation remains the first activity of the mind that is handed to itself or illuminated by grace, and action is placed in dependence to it.

In becoming engaged in the "pastoral" path, in *aggiornamento*, and in adaptation to the "modern world," following the Council, many clergymen were moved to sacrifice the values of the truth for the values of efficiency. To reach contemporary man, it is necessary to drop the parts of dogma to which his mentality can no longer give its consent. It is necessary to weaken the needs of others, and to reorient them in such a way that they can be accepted. It is necessary to reform the moral conscience in a way that it can adapt to the imperatives of modern life, etc. The essential thing is no longer to present the true God to contemporary man for him to submit his intelligence to Revelation as he submits it to the data of experience and to the principles that regulate all the reality and all the knowledge that it contains. It is to prepare and accommodate the Gospel, and God himself who is revealed therein, to the subjectivity of the man of today, to his aspirations, desires, and intentions. Put another way, in order to achieve his goal and to restore to our contemporaries the religion that they abandoned or denied, the clergyman worries less about the truth that he declares than about the success of his action. At the limit of this perversion of the intelligence, we find ourselves with a religion without God, a religion where Christ is brought back to man, a religion of man. But as a religion of man is inevitably a religion that erects man as lord of the universe, and as the most efficacious action is that which subtracts man from his nature and then operates a radical remaking, the values of action are replaced by the values of the demiurgic transformation of man and the world, by the values of the creation of a new world and of the self-creation of man by man. Put still another way, the only Christianity that is valid today is revolutionary Christianity, in which the power of man over the world, over himself, and over others is clearly evident.

That is the abyss into which the clergyman who subordinates contemplation to action and action to the will of power topples into. This abyss of iniquity no longer has the smallest place for the intelligence.

The second key element that we would equally like to underline in contemporary Catholicism is parallel to the first: It is *the subversion of the liturgy*. This subject too is quite vast. Let us rest content with bringing out what is, in our opinion, the essential point, which is *the abandonment*, even *the proscription, of Latin*. We easily discover a single motive at the center of the dialectical argumentation used to justify this: It is necessary to make Christianity known to all men, no matter their civilization, and to renounce for the greater cause the outdated values of the Greco-Roman civilization into which the Christian faith was able to set down its roots at a given moment in history. The repudiation of Latin, and of Gregorian chant which is its diadem, is a part of the current—let us say, the torrent—that takes Christianity far from its *natural* bases.

Ultimately, for the believer, it is not by chance or arbitrary decree that Christ was born in a given place, at a given time, *within the orbit of the civilization of the intelligence and realism of the mind*. The disposition of Providence is obvious: Greco-Roman civilization is the sole civilization that, having confidence in the human intelligence, in its capacity to be measured by the real and to understand it, had a universal reach. This universalism, founded on the definition of man as a rational animal, was able to serve as the basis of the Church's ecumenicity. Greco-Roman civilization is *the* civilization par excellence, where all men can be united by virtue of their nature. Christian civilization, which in a way sublimated this civilization, is its most perfect expression.

It is true, so prodigiously true, that we are currently witnessing *its extension and planet-wide corruption*. The myth of man's triumphant excess and demiurgic activity could not have arisen without the theoretical intelligence of the Greeks or practical intelligence of the Romans. Today's excess distorts, falsifies, and squanders the immense resources of Greek and Roman intelligence. The myth of man's deification through collective work could never have spread throughout the world without the Gospel. Man's deification is a perversion and cancerous proliferation of the Good News. Maritain said it before us: "Revolutionary ideas are not Christian ideas, but are corruptions of Christian ideas. From this point of view, it is correct to say that the Revolution did not know how to invent anything, and that it had to borrow everything from its old enemy, Christianity. Its myth of *Humanity* and of the *Future City* is the idea of the Church and of celestial Jerusalem, fallen from the divine plan to the earthly one. The *Revolution* itself is conceived as a Last Judgment, the *Regeneration* of the human species, allotted as an end to our hopes. It is the counterpart of baptismal regeneration. Regarding *necessary progress*, it is quite simply an unfortunate *ersatz* of Providence. The reason for this general process of the slouching and degradation of Christian ideas in the course of modern times is very clear. It is that Christianity only preserves its essence and life in the Church. The secularization of Christianity, which had begun with the Reformation, thus led to a simultaneous corruption of religion as a direct consequence. *Now a corrupted divine ferment can only be an agent of subversion of incalculable power.*"[47]

Let us continue with the citation, as it confirms our diagnosis of the moral ailment that intelligence is suffering from and that has transformed it into a demiurgic faculty of nature:

> The order of grace is **OTHER** than the order of nature, but being **SUPERNATURAL**, it adds to nature, perfecting it without destroying it. *If now we deem as*

---

[47] Jacques Maritain, *Theonas* (Paris: Nouvelle Librairie Nationale, 1925) 154. The italics are De Corte's.

NATURAL *that which is from grace, and we claim at the same time to conserve its ghost, and impose it on things, then we begin to substitute, with force,* ANOTHER *order for the order of nature. We thereby ruin the natural order in the name of a divine principle and a divine virtue. This is everything that the revolution is.*[48]

This text is from 1925. It is eminently current. In many cases, pastoral work and liturgy were abandoned to the bilious zeal of innovators, the darkness of an intelligence gorged on illusions, and the will of clerical power. This work and liturgy have incited the faithful to work with all their strength in collaborating with those who dream of changing man and the world. There are countless examples of this.

What brainwashing or deluges of demagoguery are we made to see in this "religion of St. Avold"![49] Like democracy and communism, the former preparing the way for the takeover of the latter, the Church becomes, in the scheme of the falsifiers, a gigantic soul-stamping machine whose levers are in the clergy's hands. "The people of God" are subjected to the avatars that all peoples have crossed and still cross in the hands of their democrat or communist leaders. This people is a smooth and docile lump of dough that is imprinted with a single mold. It is transformed into a giant robot, a mechanical Leviathan that the clergymen direct at their discretion. "The general will" that this mechanism is apparently equipped with is nothing other than the will to power of the engineers of the new human intelligence. This intelligence has nothing more than the name that is declared at its moment of exultation! It is enough to attend a so-called "community" Mass, hear a certain homily, or read a certain episcopal or parish circular letter, to realize that the parallel hierarchy that was brought into the Church wages a war against the

---

48  *Ibid.* The words here in capitals were originally put in italics by Maritain. The last phrase is put in italics by De Corte.
49  Jean Madiran, *L'hérésie du XXe siècle.*

intelligence in "demythologizing" and humanizing the Gospel on the one hand, and "mythologizing" humanity and divinising it on the other. The community myth, preached wrongly yet everywhere, is the surest way to suppress in man his specific and radically individualized difference, and to transform humanity into a flock of sheep.

What conclusion can be drawn from this analysis? As Maurras foresaw, intelligence has entered "its Iron Age." Today it propagates its own defeat. It degrades itself to the point of being nothing more than the shadow of itself, its dream, nightmare, and lie. How can one "request an act of good sense from that which is henceforth deprived of sense," of this intelligence that is degraded into imagination, that now only achieves its own constructions and encloses itself in the ever-rising walls of the jail it built around itself?

But Maurras shows us the way. From the depths of his tomb, we hear his inextinguishable hope:

> It is characteristic of the intellectual to lead the reaction to hopelessness. Faced with this threatening horizon, the national intelligence [I would add today: the universal intelligence] has to become connected to those who try to do something beautiful before sinking. In the name of reason and nature, conforming to the old laws of the universe, for the salvation of order, for the long-term and the progress of a civilization under threat, every hope floats on the ship of a Counterrevolution.[50]

---

[50] The square brackets and the words therein were added by De Corte. Charles Maurras, "L'Avenir de l'Intelligence", in *Romantisme et Révolution* (Paris: Nouvelle Librairie Nationale, 1924), 87.

## 2

# The Romanticism of Science

**SCIENCE'S RUPTURE**

While the *intelligentsia* and its will to power are a recent phenomenon, the influence exercised by "science" on spiritual and intellectual behavior, on the moral, political, and social conduct of men, is perhaps greater. The empire of "science," its universal expansion, the tyranny that it makes to weigh on the human spirit and on customs, the totalitarian reduction of its norms, methods, and way of understanding and conceiving the world, its mode of argumentation, and even the language that it inflicts on all the other types of knowledge and on all types of human activities, began two centuries ago. We have gone from the "learned ladies" of comedy, where the event begins,[1] to a "learned" humanity that is explored by sociology today and that celebrates the extirpation of illiteracy with statistics every year. The major evolution that prevails around the world today is on its next-to-last stage. This is the prelude to the definitive mutation of man into superman and of the round machine [i.e. the earth] into earthly paradise. The motto, *Rerum novarum nascitur ordo*, assigned by Diderot to the conception of nature of which he is the protagonist, signifies that humanity stepped over the "pre-scientific" phase of its history to accede to its apotheosis under the aegis of science. "Science" makes us into "mutants."

---

[1] This is a reference to Molière's comedy, *Les femmes savantes*.

We are so used to this phenomenon that we have to make an effort to see how ancient, medieval, and even the *honnête homme* of classical culture were able to live outside of this universe of science that is ours. Their "physics" asserted for more than two millennia that the world was composed of four elements, earth, water, fire, and air, along with the "quintessence." This fifth element, ether, constituted the noble matter of the stars, which were submitted to perfect regularity. We laugh at this childish knowledge. We unquestionably condemn the naive ignorance and credulity that it displays. Aristotle's mental age is that of a six year old child, Léon Brunscvicg[2] impatiently utters. The adult man of today, educated by science, has completely banned from his field of vision this archaic conception that corresponds to nothing in the real universe that is penetrated and mastered by modern science. There is a total rupture between the physics of the ancients and that of the moderns.

### THE WORLD OF ELEMENTS

Can we be certain that the ancient conception of the world that we so deride in the name of science does not match reality? Undoubtedly, this conception has nothing scientific about it, at least in the sense that we give this word. However, it corresponds to the world that is directly perceived by our senses and immediately recapitulated by our classifying intelligence. It is radically realist, from top to bottom. The reality that it expresses is perceived without the least distortion. It is the world such as reality presents and represents itself to us at the moment that it appears in our faculties of knowledge.

I never understood this type of knowledge better than when on an early morning walk with an old and spritely farm relative on a vast, deserted beach. She interrupted the enchanting silence that we beheld in front of an immense

---

2  Léon Brunscvicg (1869–1944), French idealist philosopher.

nature that enveloped us, saying, "Can't we just feel the elements invade us down to our lowest depths: the earth, water, sun, and wind? We are simply one with them." I had just discovered, with a delighted stupor, that the physics of the four elements of the Greek and medieval philosophers was not a theory, but a reality, the reality that the human being originally feels when existing in relationship with nature.

The elements are the objects of instantaneous sensory experience that we have of nature that surrounds us and with which we communicate without any intermediary. We seize it immediately and present both its organization and our mutual relationship with it to the intelligence, which is hungry for being. These elements so fittingly constitute the most appropriate place for our being to be that, in order to express the idea of "being where one best flourishes," popular language has an expression whose depth of meaning we can still just barely perceive: "To be in one's element." And this reciprocally-harmonious connection of coexistence between the human being and the universal being rings out in the mind without restraint as if this rapport were the object, standard, and ideal of all perfect knowledge that offers uncorrupted reality to us. This is so because the same mode of expression, in this most profound conservatory of lived experiences which is language, signifies that one easily and methodically discusses the things that one knows particularly well.

If it is true that language is a system of articulated signs by which man communicates his thoughts to man, the elements must have provoked the appearance of the first signs that man used in order to make known for himself and others the being of nature. The world of the elements was, according to all plausibility, the very first reality, the original being that the human being was able to grasp in a lived experience and with primordial reason, and that he expressed to himself and to other men.

The nature of the sensible, which is to say, of the material constituents of the universe, even more powerfully incites the reflection that the exclusive absence or predominance of one of them to the detriment of the others makes all human life impossible. How can we not perceive and understand that we live in a world that is comprised of earth and fire, water and air, by their mixing and union? The very first intuition of the *being* of the things of the sensible world was that of the elements. It is on this being that the initial certitude of being and the unquestionable experience of the *principle of identity*, the law of the real and of the mind, were established. There is being, and being cannot not be.

## MAN'S NATURAL METAPHYSICS

The world of the elements was the first world of being, and so it remains in spite of the mockery of modern philosophers and scientists who forget it. The man of agricultural civilization, which was ours until these last two centuries, always felt himself in faithful and persevering relationship with the elements. At every moment, they engulf his senses and impose their presence on his meditation. It is enough to walk in the countryside to discover the ubiquity and perpetual manifestation of the elements.

As ironically as one may discuss this elementary knowledge of the world that today's primary school student has mostly surpassed, isn't its disappearance problematic? In an urban civilization, where modern man finds himself caught in a trap, won't the elements, neglected, forgotten, and ostracized by science, take revenge? How can one live without land or green space? How can one escape the almost constant mineralization in this artificial light in which we are immersed? How can we adapt to polluted air or to water that itself has been washed of its contamination with so many chemicals? Has the great city of today been made unlivable by this creation of science and modern technology that are victorious over all resistance of nature? Doesn't the weekly exodus of crowds from the city, and their massive annual flight, however vain their movements are, demonstrate that they are obeying a profound impulse that springs from the depths of man? Though this impulse is also corrupted, it pushes them to rediscover their natural place in life where the human being recognizes himself once again in his element.

The man of traditional civilization is content with little in limiting himself to this holistic knowledge of nature that comes from his familiar interaction with the elements. In comparison with the knowledge of the material world that we have accumulated, it is not an exaggeration to claim that he knows nothing and that his ignorance is total. He sticks to the basics, which are, first, *being*, the proper object of human intelligence and, second, *intelligible being*. This latter is perceived confusedly and so to speak piecemeal among the things of the sensible universe. From that, the traditional man was able to build this philosophy of common and good sense, which is immune from wild raving and mirages. Bergson correctly called this philosophy "the natural metaphysics of human intelligence" and the root of all truth-seeking thought. This physics, as meagerly scientific as it is for us and as childish as we judge it to be, forms the solid basis of *metaphysics*. This is the science of ultimate causes, if not the science of natural theology. Its irrefutable affirmations, inaccessible to the corrosion of sophistry, implicitly contains in a rough yet healthy state (which communicates the indispensable health of the normal exercise of our highest faculty) the conditions of certitude that permit it to reach the summit of supreme knowledge.

The heart of nature is irrigated by the elementary energies that outline its arrangement. These energies are consequences, connections, recurrences, and rhythms. At this heart of nature, man's intelligence perceives the presence of an order that does not depend on itself. This intelligence then asks whether this order depends on a higher cause. This spontaneous use of the *principle of causality* can undoubtedly be called unrefined, brutal, and defective. Even so, it does map out the path upwards by clearing and marking it out, with a view ultimately to reaching definite certainty. Contingent being points back to necessary being.

Concerning the rest, it was in this way that ancient Greece developed the first and only conception known by humanity of the real that is founded on experience and reason. What is called "presocratic philosophy," as Aristotle shows us, is nothing other than the application of the principle of causality brought to bear by man's intelligence on the reality of the sensible world. This intelligence still has an elementary and rudimentary awareness of reality that is true in the order of *being*. Also, the emergence of this first philosophy, a prefiguration of later refinements on it, culminated in the affirmation of the existence of a supreme and ordering intelligence. This was declared by Anaxagoras, who, Aristotle explains, appeared to be the sort of man who remained sober at a banquet while all the other guests were drunk.

### THE METAPHYSICS OF DIRECT EXPERIENCE

It is from this start that human knowledge followed its course until more recently. The modern understanding of science, taken as the study of phenomena that are envisaged in their quantitative correlations, remained practically unknown to the ancients. With the exception of astronomy, where a few rare specialists submitted to geometric treatment, all knowledge was encompassed in the field of philosophy.

The intelligence's approach was vertical. It went from communal experience to superior principles that command and illuminate it. It mattered little to the man of an agricultural civilization, who was constitutively submitted to nature's great rhythms and suspended in an order of immutable being, to know the laws that governed the phenomena of a sector that was determined by the real and to be able to act on these phenomena thanks to this knowledge. Man does not command the seasons, nor this intertwining of various causes that we call chance or fortune! You cannot make a plant grow by pulling on its leaves!

Obedience to destiny or to the will of God, stated otherwise in philosophical language as the respect for the nature of things and the attachment of their being to transcendental causes, diverted this type of mentality from horizontal and detailed analysis of natural phenomena. What is the good of persisting in the research of minutiae when the Essential and the Necessary Unique can be attained? When it is understood that it is impossible and vain to want to modify the changes that nature impresses on the elements, and that these drives are unable to extract from their origin anything but one or several transcendent universals, does one not possess the best of knowledge. Aristotle wrote, "We reckon that we possess the science of something in an absolute manner, and not like the Sophists, in a purely accidental manner, when we believe that we know the cause by which something is and that we know that this cause is the cause of the thing, and in addition that it is not possible that the thing be anything other than what it is." This is Aristotle's methodical and rigorous definition of the spontaneous approach to common intelligence.

Contrary to a widely-held opinion today, this type of experience is founded on absolutely general and radically primary facts that are accessible to immediate observation. The simple and universal presence of this experience is applied without possible opposition from the less-informed. If we base things on the principle of causality, this type of argumentation goes back to the reason of being of things.

This generates more consistent and unquestionable certitudes than experimental sciences, which are always liable to appeal to changing theories in order to coordinate and systematize the data. This is why humans brought up in an agricultural civilization gave hardly any credit to the official sciences of nature. Their sense of the real, preference for solid being that does not deceive, and passion for eternal truths that illuminate the general course of things was fulfilled more through philosophical inquiry and its indisputable conclusions than through scientific research.

This type of knowledge excluded all subjectivism. Humanity was content with this knowledge for millennia. The farmer knows that he cannot command the facts and events that he faces. These are independent of his intelligence and will. His direct experience this is as objective as possible, and the consequences that he derives from it in applying the principle of causality are not at the mercy of his fantasies regarding any implicit philosophy. They are prescribed with the very authority that emanates from superior truths and are not a function of the appetites of his ego. Submitting himself to the injunctions of the ego is a death sentence. He would not survive for a single instant without constant and strict submission to the real, to the nature of things. Undoubtedly, this experience and argumentation must be purged of all imagery where these injunctions are expressed. They also have to be purged of all extensions by which an undisciplined intelligence constrains it to have recourse. But this experience and argumentation maintain unmatched rigor and truth with regards to their roots in and impulse towards the absolute explanatory principles.

All agricultural civilizations consist of an identical metaphysics and natural theology under the variegated appearance that distinguishes them because they respond in the same manner to objective demands of reality and the same obedience to its architecture. It is not an exaggeration to say that the highest certainties in the matter of metaphysics and natural theology proceed, regarding the psychological or sociological conditions that concretely command them, from the agricultural mentality. The counter-proof equally proves it: to the extent that certainties are let go and unmade, agricultural civilization regresses.

## THE HARMONY OF THE MICROCOSM AND THE MACROCOSM

This helps us understand why the man of traditional civilization does not worry much about measurement, which is the very basis of all modern physical sciences and constitutes the pole of attraction of the natural sciences, which have not yet, in many respects, been completely mathematicized. Such a type of man, far from measuring things, is continually measured by them. We had to wait for Protagoras to proclaim that "man is the measure of all things, the measure of their being for those that are, and the measure of their non-being for those that are not."[3] *Sophistry* is an urban phenomenon that presupposes the gathering of great gullible crowds and, as we are assured by Plato (who witnessed their birth), the manipulation of the "*large* democratic *animal*"[4] and his capacity for illusion. It requires the existence of a favorable terrain where the will to power of some individuals can work for the submission of the aptitude to powerlessness and the mystification of others. It demands that some be sufficiently liberated from the constraints imposed by the nature of things and that they derive from their very rootlessness their propensity for excess, while the others, debilitated by their break from the natural environment of life, unfailingly become their prey. Man frees himself from the physical and metaphysical conditions of his natural environment only to transform them into an ever more merciless empire at the heart of social life.

---

3   Plato, *Theaetetus*, 152 a, 1–3.
4   Plato, *Republic*, VI, 493 a–d.

When society is developed beyond its limits and allows excess to spread without immediate resistance, the only means that the sophist disposes for deploying his will to dominate are violence and speech. They give him every license to affect others and get them to submit. Most frequently, it is a combination of the two, and a learned dose of violence and words of violence. This is why Gorgias proclaims that the λόγος is discourse, "the Great Prince" (μέγας δυνάστης),[5] that restricts the lives of men to the injunctions of his persuasive force and makes their lives into what he wants. The human being who shirks the laws of being conforms to the seductions of language that the sophist has mastered. Such seductions envelop and capture him. It is not man who becomes the measure of all things, but the specialist of the word and handler of liberalized crowds who does.

For a long time, sophistry's prestige was held in check thanks to the powerful reserves that had accumulated in souls by the natural metaphysics of the human mind. For centuries, man, who was measured by the laws of being and by God, resisted the temptation to measure others and things and thereby to dominate them.

It is not that he disregarded measurement, but that he turned this regulating measurement towards himself and his own activities. Far from using measurement as an instrument of fascination, deception, or tyranny, man introduced measurement into the heart of his own conduct in imitation of the measurement that made the universe a harmonious whole, directed by a superior principle. The measurement of the microcosm was borrowed from that of the macrocosm, and became the essential factor of the moral order. A measurement coming from the superior faculty was needed to bring concord among the numerous

---

[5] "Discourse is the great prince who, with a very small and barely visible body, accomplishes truly divine works." Gorgias, *Encomium of Helen*, Fragment 11.

forces that divided the human being and to impose direction on the movements that took hold of him. This measurement was man's reason. This reason was capable of contacting and knowing the nature of the rational animal and regulating it according to its norms of human conduct.

This sense of measurement, applied to man and not to the exterior world, appeared for the first time in Greece. The man who was educated in this privileged place of the globe by the spontaneous certainties of *common sense* and the metaphysics prolonging them, deeply felt it more urgent to discipline himself than to rule over the world. The *Greek miracle* not only consisted in the discovery that the universe is ruled by intelligible laws over which the ordering Spirit keeps watch. The miracle also consists in the natural revelation that man is ruled by the law of his intelligence. His intelligence is a reflection of divine reason in him. In this way, according to Pindar's admirable formula, "the law is the queen of the universe."[6]

In a civilization that is governed by the principle of reality, the ultimate human act is the harmonization of man in a manner in which man can contribute to universal harmony. How can he achieve this without submitting the various parts of his being to measurement, in such a way that none of those parts encroach on the others and that an order is established among them which is analogous to the order that rules the elements of nature? Through the experience and reasoning that man has of himself, he knows that he can only truly be himself in integrating the universal order into himself. He knows that this incorporation can only be accomplished if he measures his acts according to the standard of his being. Excess is, on the contrary, anarchy introduced into his being, even causing the ruin of the human being.

---

6 · V. Pindare, *Isthmiques et Fragments*, fragment 49 (Paris: Les Belles Lettres, 1961), 218.

## A NEW KNOWLEDGE

Because of its foundation, all of western civilization is simultaneously oriented towards the explanation of reality through metaphysical knowledge and the fulfillment of human reality through the practical science of measurement.

The individual exceptions to this double and unique direction are obvious and as numerous as one may wish to note. These exceptions only confirm the rule: Without this orientation, the most significant works, those that are most representative of this civilization, are unintelligible. In the current meaning of the term, science merely plays an unassuming role, as much from the point of view of speculation as from that of action. This type of knowledge, rarely practiced by the man of traditional civilization, was spread by Leonardo da Vinci, Galileo, and above all, with Descartes and Newton.

The chronology for this is revealing. From the moment that the Christian religion began to lose its vigor and influence, modern science grew in status. Christianity's weakening led to the disgrace of the natural metaphysics of the human mind and the morality related to measurement. It is symptomatic that the promoters of the Renaissance get their philosophical justification for the new conception of man and the world from neither Aristotelianism nor Platonism, but from neoplatonist doctrines. Metaphysics established on the principle of causality were set aside in favor of a reflexive, idealist philosophy. Knowledge of the world disconnected itself from the theocentric perspective. Contemplation lost its place to the action of man, the primacy of the object to that of the human subject.

The exaltation of man during the Renaissance was a point of commonality. Man was not only at the center of the world, but he also cast off his limits. Pico della Mirandola proclaimed that God allows man to decide on his nature, according to his preferred form, in accord with the free will that is his nature. Man is in that way a being who creates and actualizes himself, unconstrained by any necessity. How could he not launch himself on the conquest of the world, and how could the world not appear to him as a sort of plastic, malleable matter to be manipulated at his desire once he was familiar with this? This was achieved by abandoning the old relationship of nature to its first cause, which had now become useless. It is obvious that the humanism that erects man as *causa sui*[7] is the origin of the new scientific conception of the world as we know it today, along with the associated technologies. Christianity's internal crises only explain modern science's appearance. These crises not only weakened belief, but also undermined the natural philosophical and moral certainties presupposed by the faith and that the faith raises to the supernatural light. And as man cannot live without certitudes, he will attempt to find these in himself and in a new type of knowledge.

## SCIENCE AND THE NEW COSMOS

There is no other alternative to theocentrism than anthropocentrism, and this anthropocentrism inevitably clothes itself in the divine causality that it repudiated. It is henceforth no longer a matter of contemplating nature in its relationship to the transcendent cause that orders it. Nor is it any longer a matter of accomplishing by human acts the being that was allotted man with moderation in the general economy of the *cosmos*. It is a matter of following *the only path* that is still available when one has left the paths of speculation and of action. This path is to be someone who deploys his *poetic* energy in a universe that is considered solely under its material aspect. With respect to this universe, such a human behaves as the demiurge or sculptor of the clay that he forms into something.

---

7  Self-caused.

*Making* comes to monopolize all the contemplative and active energies of man to his profit. Θεωρία and πράξις get mixed up with ποίησις[8] to the degree that all thought is henceforth a sort of work of art, and every action is the construction of a new world and new man. This is modern science. *Homo faber* supplants *homo sapiens*.

Descartes' prodigious, intuitive genius sensed this. The *Discours sur la Méthode* testifies to this in a passage whose magical virtualities have not yet been exhausted by our era:

> Instead of this speculative philosophy that is taught in the schools, we can find a practice by which, knowing force and the actions of fire, water, air, the stars, the heavens, and all the other bodies that surround us, as distinctly as we know the various trades of our artisans, we can in the same way take advantage of all the uses that are proper to it, and in this way we make ourselves nature's masters and owners. This is desirable not only for the invention of an infinite number of devices, which would enable us to enjoy the fruits of the earth and all the commodities to be found therein without any bother, but principally for the conservation of health.[9]

This is where the romanticism of science spreads, visibly but unnoticed. It is in this romanticism that our era flounders. The noxious air of this romanticism throws into panic weak and false spirits. All of man's activities are from this point on diverted from speculative knowledge and the precise observation of the rules that permit man to carry out his task as man and to fulfill his human measure in orienting himself towards contemplation. A new type of knowledge appears, which is modern science. We persist in dividing it, according to the norms that it challenges and that can no longer be its own in any way, into "theoretical" and "practical" sciences, when it

---

8 *Theoria*, *praxis* and *poiesis* are the words in Greek.
9 René Descartes, *Discours de la Méthode* (Paris: Librairie philosophique J. Vrin, 1967), 61.

is, in fact, *poetic knowledge of nature*. This is to say, it is knowledge that makes man master of the forms that he imprints on the world in the exact same way that the artist is the master of the figures and images in which it frames the material of its work. The *intelligible* and the *viable* cede their places to the *practical*.

This error is enormous and has completely invalidated the interpretation of the avatars of the human mind since the Renaissance and the shock of Cartesianism. The error is to believe that the new science of nature defined itself in divorcing metaphysics (and morality) and in joining up with mathematics. Undoubtedly, mathematics was the only science that remained intact after the shipwreck of the ancient conception of the universe, and which could, in this role, set itself up as the pole of attraction for all empirical knowledge of nature that was now abandoned to uncertainty and the precarity that resulted from their decommissioning. But the victory of mathematics over the metaphysical and theological explanation of nature is due to another factor. Mathematics triumphed from the principle of causality only insofar as man no longer perceived the exterior world as an object of contemplation, but as the material destined to receive the imprint of his conquering intentions. This was due to Christianity's fall from grace, which had distracted him from his natural end and emancipated him from its norms.

A world that is no longer formally understood as being subordinated to a supreme cause that confers its existence and intelligibility is no longer a world, a *cosmos*, a set, an arrangement, or a system of parts that fit together. Once deprived of the superior illumination that outlined an order for it, the world became for man a *chaos*, a flux of elusive sensory phenomena, a jumble of disparate energies that, abandoned as they are to their apparently incoherent and confused course, now arouse man's will to power. When Zeus no longer has his lightning, Prometheus takes over.

Man cannot live without a world surrounding him. Because there no longer is a world, man creates one. For the harmonious world of nature and the supernatural that disappears over the horizon, he substitutes a world that, to the extent possible, will be his work. From that time on, this world will be transparent to his reason through and through, on the same level as reason. It will be submitted to reason's injunctions and intentions. In this universe in which the God of nature and grace, of metaphysics and Revelation, fades in the twilight's last glimmer, where the lanterns of common sense and the beacons of the faith go out little by little, man swells up, imagining that he will shed some clarity on the becoming of things, and takes himself to be a *demiurge*. After having disenchanted the world and deprived it of its meaning, he proclaims himself as its enchanter and gives it a meaning, which comes from his creative will.

This new world, the world that is reborn under man's power, must have a meaning. It must follow rules, obey an order, and submit itself to laws in order to become once again a *cosmos*, but a human *cosmos*. Where will this methodological disposition that will make it habitable come from, if not from man himself, who establishes himself as "king of creation," with the title of creator? His will to power over everything that is not himself is directed towards the *end*, which is henceforth his end. This will seeks the *means* to achieve it. Man begins to make a world that is worthy of his superhumanity, if not his very divinity.

### CONSTRUCTING THE NEW WORLD

Every problem therefore comes down to the sole problem of art, technology, method, directions, means, and instruments that will assure man's regency over a world that is deprived of transcendence and moderation and that has become malleable and disposable. This world is devoted to constraint, to "hominization." We are in the age of transitory activity, of ποιεῖν, of *making*, which subordinates all other activities, whether speculative or moral. Henceforth, the sole question that man asks is, "*What do we* MAKE *in order to* HAVE *a world?*" while I find myself faced with a flux of phenomena whose changes, variations, and vicissitudes assail me without respite. Everything is called into question according to this reversal of the axis of the real, including political and social existence as much as the conception of nature and man. What could undoubtedly exist for a long time in people's mentalities are the resources of country and religious life and reservoirs of wisdom, judgment, and good sense. These gather in the most secretive of souls as a result of lived communion with the universe, according to the principle of being and obedience to their requirements, and with the conception of knowledge as reception and submission to the real. Such notions will no longer be playing a directing and regulating role. Instead, it is a matter of *constructing, inventing,* and *believing.* Again, of what *means* does man dispose in this respect? These are the means that his will to make tirelessly uses in manipulating the new world in order to be its master.

REASON AS A TOOL

We do not have so many of these means, though man's *reason* is obviously one. It will no longer be used to abstract the intelligible from what the senses receive and thus to take the path that leads towards metaphysical knowledge. Reason no longer has any object *that is given to it prior* to its exercise. There no longer is *being,* in the strong sense of this word, to feed intelligence. There will only be that which the senses perceive. Even this does not matter! Reason will generate its object from itself. It will come up with plans, build models, create ideas, construct logical systems, trace out frameworks, even design utopias, and draw from itself rational archetypes to which the new world will have to conform itself in order to be a human world. Reason will somehow build the universal place in which all human knowledge will take its place, *with its own objects*. Nothing henceforth will be real that does not adequately respond to this general structure of the world. Reason's acting and dominating force will establish the norms of this world. It will promulgate these norms itself in order to assure its own perfect possession and comprehension. Its design for the construction of a world that is livable for it is totalitarian. In this design, reason can exclude nothing from its jurisdiction. Reason is the milieu in which everything that merits existence will be classified. Reason itself is this milieu, and does not tolerate anything else around. Even more, reason is itself the *instrument* by which this milieu is drawn up, made, and extended. The *rationalism* that germinates from the decomposition of metaphysics, the morality of moderation, and ethics, is a *poetic* knowledge, a demiurgic activity. Every particular science that will go around its orbit will be compelled to change into a manufacturing activity and a working knowledge of its object. In assigning itself the goal of building and possessing a homogeneous world, reason *instrumentalizes* all the sciences and *instrumentalizes itself*. The world thereby becomes a construction site where everything totally changes and is transformed according to the pillars of reason. The universe declined due to contempt for and forgetfulness of *being*. In order to grasp *becoming* after this decline, reason has no other tool than the network of logical relations that it tirelessly weaves. Reality is whatever it catches in its net. As an ichthyologist said to Sir Arthur Eddington who was asking him about the object of his science, "Whatever my net cannot trap is not fish." The *models* constructed by reason are not only images, two-sided ideals of reality, and sublimated Platonic forms. They are above all the tricks that reason weaves, the machinations that it contrives, and the traps that it sets to capture the uncatchable becoming of things and make it intelligible.

## REASON AND QUANTIFICATION

Even so, this poetic and creative reason, which will be the sole conception of the intelligence to possess monetary value in the modern world, cannot believe itself capable of drawing a world out of nothingness. However "divine" it proclaims itself to be—and its infatuation will sometimes reach delirium—it requires a "matter" on which to imprint its forms. This matter must be suitable to receive these forms.

The world that is deprived of its being and "substantial forms" is reduced to sensory phenomena. Are these phenomena suitable for this imprinting? Doubtful. That which can be sensed is, by its nature, not accessible to the intelligence. In order for reason to comprehend and come to dominate whatever is sensed, and to bring it to conformity, it must be rationalized and have introduced into it something that is the act of reason, the product of reason's generative power, the network of reason's artificial ideas that can delight in the phenomenon of the energy of the creative reason of forms.

Yet every sensory phenomenon has an aspect, *quantity*, that is offered for the use of architectonic and conquering reason. Regarding quantity, Aristotelian scholastics forcefully underscore that it is *the first accident* of all material bodies.[10] All the evidence shows that this quantitative aspect of sensory reality is real, but its reality can only be grasped by the artifice of reason. All quantitative determinations of the fleeting nature of things (number, size, volume, weight, density, speed, frequency, proportion, etc.) are measurable, but to capture them, reason needs to establish measurements. The real only provides the measurable. Measurement does not naturally occur in nature. It is the work of the mind, the result of *an arbitrarily-established*

---

10   St. Thomas Aquinas in IV Sent., d.12, q.1, a.1, qla.3, c. Also in VII Phys., lect.5. In V Metaph., lect.15.

*convention that the mind establishes.* This instrument, which can also be a device or machine that the mind invented, allows it to dominate not only the quantitative aspects of the real, but also its qualities, when it compares these latter to each other by some number measurement or according to their degree of intensity. This is the case with heat, for example.

Thanks to the establishment of such standards and to the measurement devices and machines that are built for the same purpose, calculating reason is introduced into the very heart of phenomena as metrically determined. It discovers there the constant relationships that will in turn become the means that will serve to expand its empire. All mathematical entities that it generates are the beings of reason, the creations of the mind, that are based on a certain aspect of the real, the *entia rationis cum fundamento in re*[11] from which it weaves the nets it uses to capture the measurable properties of things and thence to erect a world that comes to duplicate daily experience and, ultimately, to supplant it.

## A MANUFACTURED PHYSICS

From Galileo, Descartes, and Newton down to contemporary physics, the new conception of physics did not cease to advance along the path that regards and uses mathematics as an instrument whose objective is to scrutinize the measurable properties of matter. Its motive is theoretical only in appearance. This knowledge does not come anywhere near to grasping the nature of matter, but only the objects that relate to quantity. It does not

---

[11] The *ens rationis* is "a being of reason; a purely logical being," according to Wuellner, 41. This means that this entity has no being outside of the reason that thinks it. The entry on "Reism" at the Stanford Encyclopedia of Philosophy covers Brentano's discussion of the *entia rationis* at https://plato.stanford.edu/entries/reism/. [Translator's note]

know anything more about the nature of the quantitative aspects that it gathers together, though it does discover the laws at the *quantitative level*. Not only does it have nothing theoretical—or speculative—in the proper sense of the word, but the object that is undoubtedly real that it connects to and defines is found connected to the technological procedures and to the devices that capture it, in such a way that it cannot be split apart. It becomes *a technical object* as a result, a type of work of art in which the constructive activity of the mind necessarily increases in proportion to the scientist's will in attaining the object that he pursues *as the object is in itself.*

In other words, *the more the new physics wants to be theoretical* and, in pursuit of this, aspires to penetrate the secrets of matter and its intimate constitution, *the more it becomes a poetic knowledge that transforms its object.* Filippi writes,

> the classical theory of the microscope teaches us that the corpuscle is all the more better localized in the space that illuminates it with a radiation of a shorter wavelength, which is to say, with a higher frequency. But to send a high frequency photon $\nu$ to a corpuscle is to inflict on it the shock of a high energy photon $W = h\nu$ (the Compton effect). Its speed is thereby altered. The consequence is clear. Diminishing uncertainty on the position means increasing uncertainty on the quantity of movement."[12]

This is the great obstacle of contemporary physics which Heisenberg, in a celebrated demonstration, proved to be absolutely insuperable. In addition, Louis de Broglie perhaps correctly writes that "the results of the measurements that constitute the scientist's knowledge will not describe *the physical universe such as it is*, but *such as it*

---

12 Ulysse Filippi, *Connaissance du monde physique* (Paris: Editions A. Michel, 1947), 286.

*is known by the scientist following experiments that comprise unknown and uncontrollable disturbances.*"[13] There is therefore no knowledge of the intrinsic properties of the electron nor of any particles that make up matter, but only of the matter that is transformed when it is seized and measured by the device.

It is not only the device that disturbs observed reality and makes it into something else, but the mathematical instrument that is used to understand it. In approaching reality, the mathematical device is made so dense, narrow, and complex that, at its limit, it seizes only itself. The electron vanishes in a way that makes of it a "package of probabilities," a bundle of equations, a symbol.

Let us quote three declarations from Heisenberg: "The natural laws that, in quantum theory, we formulate mathematically, no longer concern the elementary particles strictly speaking, *but the knowledge that we have of them.* The conception of objective reality of the elementary particles is therefore strangely dissolved, not in the fog of a new conception of obscure or poorly-understood reality, but in the transparent clarity of a mathematics that no longer represents the behavior of the elementary particle. Instead, this mathematics represents *the knowledge that we possess only of the mathematics itself.* When speaking of nature according to the exact sciences of our day, understand *the image of our relationship with nature*" rather than the image of nature itself.[14]

This relationship of the physicist with reality strongly resembles the relationship of the artist to his work, except that the product of physics is not arbitrary, nor the product of the dereistic imagination. It is pregnant with a certain measurable entity whose existence is independent of the

---

13  Louis de Broglie, *Physique et microphysique* (Paris: Éditions A. Michel, 1947), 149,
14  Werner Heisenberg, *op. Cit.*, 18, 33. The italics are Marcel De Corte's, except the last eight words.

mind that measures it and is dependent, on the contrary, on the constructions of this same mind, regarding the knowledge that this latter has of it. It is clear that heat or weight *exist* in the universe outside of all devices of measurement or all mathematical equations, which is to say, outside of all thought that measures them. But the knowledge that the scientist can have of this comes from a series of operations that he executes, exactly as the knowledge that the artist has of the reality captured in his work correlates the work he has done on a certain matter to what he has *made* or *produced*. It is a poetic knowledge or, to use a more pedantic term, a *poematical* knowledge that *makes* the object, not relative to being, but relative to knowledge. Eddington confirms this interpretation: "The magnitude of physics discovered thus is above all the result of our operations and calculations. It is, so to speak, a *manufactured article*—manufactured by our operations."[15]

## THE SCIENTIST AS CREATOR OF THE NEW PHYSICS

In physics, which serve as a model, to some degree, for all the other positive sciences, it is therefore impossible to separate that which is nature-based from that which is the modern scientist's contrived part of reality—just like we cannot dissociate in knowledge the part of the real object represented (figuratively or not) by the artist from the part that is invented by the artist. What is captured by physics is simultaneously the product of measured reality and of the instrument used, the latter being the work of the mind. No physics—in the modern sense of the word—no positive science, as long as it leans towards the current status of the reign of the sciences, can be classified within the division of knowledge, neither among speculative knowledge (which has no other object than to know and explain reality as it

---

15  Sir Arthur Eddington, *The Mathematical Theory of Relativity* (Cambridge, 1930).

presents itself to the mind), nor among the practical sciences (in the sense of knowing what determines human conduct as such). Physics and its emulators are *poetic sciences* that result from an intelligent and voluntary activity that works on the world that surrounds us in a way such as to transform it. Except in the broadest sense, pure physics or exclusively theoretical physics research do not exist. Theoretical physics *includes in itself* a construction of mind that creates in some way the datum and what constitutes the world where it takes a form that is accessible to thought. Theory and practice are indivisible.

Every fundamental concept of physics is therefore defined in an *operational* manner: "If you want to know the basics of the scientific method, do not listen to what the scientist will tell you, observe *what he does*," notes Einstein justly. As Bridgman underscores in his *Logic of Modern Physics*, there is not a single concept of physics that is not tied to a series of operations that are carried out on a material substrate. The notion of length is typical in this regard. It is impossible to define it without a concrete, man-made standard. In the same way, the notion of temperature cannot be defined without a thermometer. The object and the instrument constitute a unity. And the instrument, whether it be material like a dial, or intellectual, like a system of equations, is a work of the mind. Binet, the inventor of intelligence tests, already noted this a long time ago: "Intelligence is simply that which suits my calculations."

The modern scientist manufactures not only measurements and mathematical snares that are capable of imprisoning sensory phenomena that obediently provide their quantifiable aspects. The global approach of his thought is commanded by the construction of an intellectual *model*—still centered on mathematization—of the concrete object that it attempts to know. But given the absence of fixed boundaries between the subject and the object in the very act of physical-mathematical thought, the scientist will ceaselessly oscillate between the construction of a real model and that of a nominal model, which are equally impossible.

The scientist who uses experimentation will try to design a model that reflects the true structure of the real as perfectly as possible and that can be retranslated into a language that is adapted to the sensory universe in which we live. But however scrupulous his intention is, he will never be able to reduce the artificial part of his method. It is common today to use words that are pregnant with realism. This will undoubtedly help his model get closer to the image that we have of the world. But who will be able to guarantee that the intelligible model conforms to reality when the latter is only perceived by the senses? The *adaequatio rei et intellectus* that defines reality will never be anything but hypothetical because it is a matter of making the two radically different domains of the real conform to each other. The "truth" of the model thereby elaborated is taken from the experimental results that are drawn from the formulated hypotheses. It is nonetheless a precarious "truth" because nothing proves that another model would not have "saved" the observable aspects of reality equally well.

The mathematically-inclined scientist proposes integral mathematics as a means to systematically order the data of experience. He will build a model that cannot be transcribed into everyday language to express the perceptions that we have of the world and that exclude all concrete representations of reality. In other words, the atom will always be a system of equations. It is clear that such a tendency is the practical equivalent of the abandonment of the notion of objectivity. This is replaced by *coherence*[16]

---

[16] "The image of the world that physics proposes only has to satisfy the condition of *coherence*. Other than this demand, the theoretician can operate *with total liberty*, without any curb on his

and the rigor of systematization. Mathematical physics is a language that was created by man[17], that reveals to us the existence of a scientific world whose relationship with our familiar world is as distended as possible. Eddington writes, "modern physics was forced to recognize the abyss between the exterior world, such as it appears in our perception of familiar history, and the exterior world that presents its messages at the gate of our mind. For this reason, the history of science is no longer the weaving together of a history that is familiar to us. Instead, it follows its own path... There is nothing in the descriptions of the physical world that we accept that owes its acceptance to the fact that we possess a sense of color. All that we affirm can be verified by a color-blind person."[18]

An event therefore falls under *physics* when it is described in the terms of physics, in the logical-mathematical language natural to physics and in the symbolic forms utilized by physics. Yet these symbols are clearly *artificial* signs, invented to designate an assembly of factors whose unity depends on reason alone, the reason that made and established it. For example, the T symbol represents the whole collection of heat that is existentially captured in a given object, the devices of measurement that capture it, the "theories" that are made concrete in these instruments, and all the non-inherent elements that intervene in the processes of measurement. This symbol is combined with other symbols that represent other factors in groups of equations. In the constructions of signs (and signs of other signs), the

---

imagination. This is to say that his research contains an appreciable amount of *arbitrariness* and *uncertainty*." Max Planck, *op. cit.*, 56.

[17] "The scientist's clear-sightedness comes uniquely from the fact that this world of physics is nothing other than an image of the real world *created by the human mind* that, for this reason, evidently has a *perfect* knowledge and dominates it in its details." *Ibid.*, 109. De Corte's italics.

[18] Sir Arthur Eddington, *Nouveaux sentiers de la science* (Paris: Hermann, 1936).

symbol takes the place of the defined object, *exactly as a work of art takes the place of the object that it represents*. At the limit of this, the sign has completely absorbed the signified. The mathematical model that implements the complex of signs is sufficient in itself in the arrangement and coherence of all its parts.

In the case of the real model, the problem of correspondence to reality can never be resolved. In the case of the nominal model, no solution is offered because the problem is no longer addressed. It cannot be otherwise. As soon as a model is constructed, whether it is real or in name only, we place ourselves in the perspective of poetic knowledge where the subject cannot get to know the object except with *constructions* that are made on the base of experiences that are limited to the measurable aspects of the sensory phenomena. This is exactly like the artist, whose work constructs a fake and materialist idea of an object. The comparison of the model with reality is impossible because the reality is never directly perceived as such.

As Einstein wrote, "the concepts of physics are the free *creations* of the human mind and are not, as one might believe, determined only by the exterior world. In the effort that we make to understand the world, we resemble in some way the man who attempts to understand the mechanism of a closed watch. He sees the dial and the needles move, and he hears the tick-tock, but he has no way of opening the case. If he is ingenious, he can *form some sort of image* of the mechanism, to which he will assign responsibility for everything that he observes, but he will never be sure that his image is the only one capable of explaining his observations. He will never be able to compare his image with the real mechanism, and he cannot even envision the possibility or the significance of such a comparison."[19]

---

[19] Albert Einstein and Leopold Infeld, *L'évolution des idées en physique* (Paris: Flammarion, 1948), 35.

This is why the new science of physics cannot be a *speculative* knowledge of the universe, despite the aspirations of its scientists. By an inescapable slope inscribed in its very epistemological structure, in the operations and manipulations of the experiment that are inexorably connected to it, physics is led towards what today we call "practice." That is, as we have established at some length, a *poetic* knowledge, a transformer of matter. It is combined with a more-or-less covert and vehement desire to be master of the world, to which the intention of speculative knowledge of the world is subordinated.

It is clear that scientists seek to know the universe of the measurable in a disinterested manner, and that they remain mostly indifferent to the practical results of their investigations. But the scientist's state of mind is one thing; quite another thing is the method that he adopts and that constrains him, under threat of failure, on paths that his mind rejects. It can even be said that the passion for the truth that animates the scientist is precisely that which inclines the science that he is building to transform the world. Given his point of departure (which is to know the sensory phenomenon by deliberately renouncing metaphysical illumination), the intellectual curiosity that moves him forces him to discover a new mode of knowledge, which until then had lain fallow without exiting the brush of artisanal empiricism. Its true name is *technology*. The method is only scientific if it rigorously *applies* its rules. *In applying its rules*, the new science can only begin the great movement of the *creation* of a new world (distinct from the familiar universe and, if it is restrained by metaphysical and moral reason, hostile to this universe) that characterizes the modern age. The *Discours de la méthode* is not the charter of modern science in the speculative sense of the term, but it is the charter of this amalgamation that is inseparable from the scientific intention and technology that we call "science."

In his biography of Einstein, Philip Frank notes that the crowning glory of the famous scientist is to have deduced the famous law E=mc2 of the theory of relativity, but that he only made it *after* he had reported the practical applications of the theory, among which is the central place of the atomic bomb. Louis de Broglie equally underscores that "the speculations of pure science, in appearance the most detached of all utilitarian worry, hardly waited before developing in practical applications." In fact, every theory of physics has been articulated, in an intrinsic and organic way, in material or mental existence, in a work that brings about utilitarian achievements. A theory that revealed itself to be incapable of explaining scientific facts, awaken the creativity of the mind, and arouse inventions in weaving a network of hypotheses and mathematical relations that serve to capture measurable reality of phenomena, would be sterile and soon abandoned by the scientist. Every theory must be *verified*, which is to say, submitted to a series of tests that show him to be capable of "making the truth," of *producing* something that can be controlled. It is necessary to hold firmly to this evidence, misunderstood to an unimaginable point, that physics never tells us the reality of *that which is*, but of *that which it becomes* when the scientist manipulates it.

**SPECULATIVE SCIENCE**

The truth of physics is therefore never the truth of speculation. It is practical truth or, more precisely, *poetic* truth. The scientist does not resemble the philosopher. He is the superior and perfected replica of the *artisan* or *artist* in the most universal sense of the word. The truth that he discovers does not consist in knowing in a manner that conforms to that which is, but consists in *producing a model*—a *work*—that corresponds to the rules that govern the measurements that he operates in sensory phenomena. If we define art as *the precise rational determination of things to make,* modern science in its physical-mathematical archetype is an art in the strictest sense of the term. It is, as Aristotle said of τέχνη, an ἕξις τις μετὰ λόγου ἀληθοῦς ποιητική, "a poetic disposition of the mind that accompanies true discourse."[20]

In his precise scholastic vocabulary, John of St. Thomas said: *"Proprie enim intellectus practicus est mensurativus operis faciendi et regulativus. Et sic ejus veritas non est penes esse, sed penes id quod deberet esse juxta regulam et mensuram talis rei regulandae."*[21] The scientist only finds the truth if he knows how to produce a work, a model that answers to its end, which is to measure the quantitative aspect of phenomena, just as the artisan only achieves this if he knows how to produce a work, such as a habitable house or a knife that can cut. The truth is not here except for practical or *poetic* truth—we tirelessly repeat this for fear of not being understood because the prejudice is so tenacious. Whatever he claims, his knowledge gives him power over nature, not only because this power is the sole proof of the truth of his knowledge (which is immediately colored with a practical and poetic character) that he can *truly* put forward, but because this power is incorporated into the very structure of his knowledge. This knowledge concerns the physical science that builds a world with man as the master, just as the artist is the master of his work.

This is what the founder of experimental medicine generally expressed in terms as clear as possible: "In the experimental sciences, man observes, *but he also acts on matter,* in analyzing its properties. He *provokes the appearance of phenomena for his benefit.* This appearance undoubtedly takes place according to natural laws, but in

---

20   Aristotle, *Nicomachean Ethics,* VI, 5, 1140 a 20–21.
21   "The practical intellect is the measurement of the work to be done and regulated. And thus it does not possess the truth of being, but of that which concerns the norms and measurement of such things that are to be directed," John of St. Thomas, *Cursus theologicus.*

conditions that nature did not yet often achieve. With the aid of *these active experimental sciences,* man becomes an *inventor of phenomena,* a genuine *foreman of creation.* And concerning this relationship, one does not know how to *assign the limits of power that he can acquire over nature* through future progress in experimental science."[22]

Jacques Maritain admirably recognized "the striking kinship" that unites "theoretical physics and its most brilliant discoveries" to "artistic creation"[23], but perhaps he did not sufficiently emphasize the cause. The dissolution of the links that unite man to the universe and to God obliged man to create a new world. Man alone was to be the measure of this world. This was to be *the real world,* to which his brand new knowledge, shorn of the limits imposed on it by traditional metaphysics and morality, would have to adjust. And yet, the scientist still considered this world, and still considers it if he is not careful, from the perspective of the old philosophy of nature that was ostracized for its incapacity to seize the essences that abound in the physical universe and for its abdication before ontology and theology. In other words, in taking over the place of the obsolete philosophy of nature, the new science, which is inept and unfit at discovering the secrets of matter, took on once again the aspiration to be the genuine explanation of the real and to reveal the intimate structure of things.

Ever since Galileo, this pretension has not ceased to animate modern physics and, in particular, the majority of those who measure the truth by its successes. Thus despite the warnings of the knowledgeable, such as Poincaré, about

---

[22] Claude Bernard, *Introduction à l'étude de la médecine expérimentale* (Paris: J. De Gigord Edit., 1930) 34. The italics for *"these active experimental sciences"* are from Bernard; the others are from De Corte.

[23] Jacques Maritain, *Distinguer pour unir ou Les degrés du savoir* (Paris: Desclée De Brouwer, 7th édition, 1963), 319.

the incapacity of physico-mathematical theories to reveal to us "the real nature of things,"[24] such as Eddington on scientific research that "does not lead to knowledge of the intrinsic nature of things," or yet such as Claude Bernard about "this blind faith in theories, which is actually a scientific superstition,"[25] nevertheless Reverend Father. Rideau, in a beautiful zeal for openness of the faith in the world of matter, does not hesitate to declare that contemporary theory in physics, which has gone well beyond superficial and empirical relationships, "reaches little by little the very essence of things, well above superficial and empirical connections."[26] Countless other examples can be cited, particularly from a clergy that is eager to become allied to communism in the work of conquering the masses, which is to say quantity. This clergy shakes with admiration before the "science that is available to everyone," but that it generally knows only second- or third-hand.

Modern physics *is therefore set up as a speculative science*. It takes the place of the speculative philosophy of nature. It renounces being specified only by its object, which is quantity, because quantity reflects back the corporeal substance, whose first accident it is, and corporeal substance returns back by its contingency to an absolute metaphysics whose jurisdiction must then be recognized by the new science. In searching its object, modern physics

---

24  "Mathematical theories do not have the object of revealing to us the genuine nature of things. This would be an unreasonable pretension." Henri Poincaré, *La Science et l'Hypothèse* (Paris: Flammarion, 1968), 215.
25  "We must not believe in our observations or theories that are only subject to experimentation. If we believe too strongly, the mind finds itself tied to and narrowed by the consequences of its own reasoning. There is no longer freedom of action, which leaves us with the lack of initiative that comes to possess whoever knows how to free himself of this blind faith in theories, which is, in fact, a scientific superstition." Claude Bernard, *op. Cit.*, 66.
26  Emile Rideau, *Philosophie de la physique moderne* (Paris: Editions du Cerf, 1938), 18.

realizes that the scientific fact is a synthesis of symbols, laws, and theories that result from the constructive activity of the mind. It only finds in the fact, which is baptized as reality, what it puts there. In mathematizing measured reality, it builds something in its place. Duhem writes, "When Regnault conducted an experiment, he had the facts before his eyes and observed phenomena. But what he transmitted to us of this experiment was not the account of observed facts. He transmitted abstract symbols that he was permitted by accepted theories to substitute for the concrete documents that he had gathered.

What Regnault did is what every research physicist necessarily did. We can therefore outline this principle, and develop it in the conclusion of this book:

> An experiment in physics is the precise observation of a group of phenomena accompanied by the INTERPRETATION of these phenomena. This interpretation substitutes for the concrete data truly gathered by the observation of the abstract and symbolic representations that correspond to them according to the theories that are admitted by the observer.[27]

Louis de Broglie adds,

> This is why experimental discovery, at least as developed in our day, has as its condition *the creative activity* of our thought and form that possesses the character of an *invention*.[28]

## THE ROMANTICISM OF SCIENCE

We are here at the very heart of our subject: *the romantic-idealist temptation* to which the new knowledge is submitted and to which it infallibly succumbs as soon

---

27 Pierre Duhem, *La Théorie physique* (Paris: M. Rivière et Cie, Éditeurs, 1914), 221. The italics are De Corte's.
28 Louis de Broglie, *Continu et Discontinu en Physique quantique* (Paris: Ed. Albin Michel, 1941), 79. The italics are De Corte's.

as it claims to replace philosophy, to become a speculative knowledge of the real just like philosophy, and to reach the very being of things. If idealism is defined as the doctrine that reduces all existence to thought and presents being not as an independent reality equipped with its one existence and essence, but as exclusively relative to the mind, and if it is claimed that physics succeeds at grasping the intimate nature of things, one is immediately pushed into this enormous and shocking conclusion that the physical being is the very being of thought and that this produces the scientific world—"the real world" that soon displaces the familiar and everyday world in a demiurgic or godlike way. If physics is a speculative science that concerns the essence of things, this is because it makes this essence and places it in existence as the daughter of its works. According to Kant's formula, "reason only sees what it itself produces according to its own plans."[29]

The universe of science, which it proclaims to be the real universe, is therefore that which man constructs through nonstop labor. The results of this labor add to the other results in an endless line of progress of his creative intelligence. To the "natural" universe of animality succeeds the "real" universe of rationality. Thought produces the object of thought and man becomes, in the strongest, most rigorous, and most precise sense of the term, "the measure of all things": for those that are, the measure of what they are; for those that are not, the measure of what they are not. Protagoras is right. Thanks to science, sophistry is no longer falsification of the truth. Sophistry is the truth. There is no being except by man's free decision. There is a universe only because man has become Prometheus through science. The great philosophical lesson of Einstein's theory, according to Léon Brunschvicg, "the thing that will remain in human thought, is the general

---

[29] Immanuel Kant, *op. cit.*, "Préface de la seconde édition (1787), 17.

conception of measurement."³⁰ "Einstein knew how to orient the definition of measurement towards the reality to measure, and to define this reality according to the measuring device itself."³¹ Henceforth, man knows that "time is born at the moment it is measured, which conforms to the axiom laid down by Einstein regarding simultaneity,"³² and that "space is not anterior to measurement. *It is born from the measurement* that is made part-by-part according to the procedures of Gauss and Riemann.³³ There are no longer "things in themselves," "natures," or "substantial forms" that are independent of the human mind, as the Aristotelians, stuck in their infantilism, believe. There are instead phenomena onto which reason introduces its own measurement and laws, thereby producing the universe of science. The everyday universe is not even the promise of this, but simply the passive expectation, the indeterminacy that receives the determination of the mind, the amorphous matter that Promethean thought, industrious and artistic, brings to form.

One of the fathers of modernism and Christian progressivism, Édouard Le Roy (1870–1954), adds,

> It is not objective facts that interest science, it's *their artificial aspects*. The 'datum' of scientific thought is not the immediate reality, *but the positive representation that we have formed of it*. Substitute for this latter *a new representation that is the work of our reason alone*. This is the problem to solve. The subtle purification that results in our ideas from the crystallization of science is achieved by rejecting overly-elusive psychology, the concrete object that our logic fails to penetrate, and the body's lower needs. Science's program, its ambition, is to integrate the world to the mind, work

---

30  Léon Brunschvicg, *L'expérience humaine et la causalité physique* (Paris: P. U. F., 1949), 536.
31  Ibid., 537.
32  Ibid., 395.
33  Ibid., 414.

out the universe in broad outline into a hierarchy of logical points, *establish an image of nature through the single activity of the ego,* and to get to the point where the work of building knowledge only depends on oneself. Science's supreme goal is the total reduction of the universe to the mind. Scientific truth does not consist in a scrupulous labeling of a given matter. It is the coherence, stability, and harmonious progress of a certain approach of the mind. *It is the increasing success of our conquest of the world.* In short, scientific truth resembles a moral good: It is not received from outside. One practices and *does it*.[34]

It is understood that by reflecting on science and becoming convinced that it is capable of embracing the ultimate reality of things, the scientist only discovers the world of the symbols that he created. He thereby persuades himself that he is indeed an artifex. He shuts himself up in a constructive idealism in which the being that is sighted in the phenomena is nothing other than the being that is produced by thought. The new physics, if it proclaims itself as the holder of the speculative keys that pry open the secrets of the universe, cannot avoid pushing the poetic character right to the most extreme consequence that affects all coherent idealism. If there is nothing higher than thought, as the idealist proudly affirms[35], the being that the physicist has his sights on is the being that he himself has constructed. Presence is the progeny of representation and the scientific universe is the ontological expression of its own generative idea.

---

34  Édouard Le Roy, "Science et Philosophie," in *Revue de Métaphysique et de Morale* (1899), 518, 539ff, 561. Italics by De Corte, except the words "reduction . . . mind."
35  Cf. Léon Brunschvicg's terse formulas: "Knowledge constitutes a world that is for us the world. Beyond that, there is nothing." *La modalité du jugement* (Paris: Librairie F. Alcan, 1897), 2. "Every man contradicts himself or, rather, commits suicide, when he makes his thought into another reality than this reality itself." *Ibid.,* 188.

## The Romanticism of Science

### THE BREAK WITH NATURE AND WITH ITS PRINCIPLE

Such is the world of science when the scientist refuses, implicitly or explicitly, the competence of metaphysics and, ignoring the intoxication that his discoveries communicate to him, he slips step-by-step into excess. One can say or do what one wants, but this is the world that is increasingly being imposed on scientists and on humanity. Scientists are, increasingly, the counselors of humanity to the extent—to the enormous extent—to which metaphysics and the morality of measurement lost their credibility. The inevitable tendency of a science that rejects this metaphysics and morality as outdated is to construct a Promethean philosophy in morality. In other words, it gets all things to orbit around the demands of human subjectivity, which is taken as absolute, even if this means conferring on this subjectivity the extensions of the universal socialization and divinization as Teilhard so modestly proposes.

The new science will transform nature, on the one hand, and disturb human minds right to the point of vertigo, on the other. This is due to the following reasons: First, for not having soberly and truthfully confessed the poetic knowledge of the measurable aspect of phenomena, *inasmuch as they can be measured*. Second, for not having limited itself to being what it is: it is the science of the first accident of corporal substances. The other accidents are grafted onto this first accident without, however, attaining the immutable nature of things except in an indirect or oblique manner (as the accident is concretely inseparable from the substance itself). Third, for not having recognized that information and transformation of things (as permitted by the measurements, devices, and machines that it invents) are subjected to the metaphysical order of the universe and to the measurement that must morally characterize all human activity. Fourth, for having exceeded the limits of its epistemological structure.

We will hardly touch on the prodigious transformations that the new science forced on what was recently called nature, the human environment, the milieu where man *dwells* and where he *remains* what he is. I have stated elsewhere that:

> it is a commonplace to affirm today that man's relationship with nature has completely changed. Modern man no longer follows nature as his Greek ancestor did. He no longer experiences himself, as his forebears did, as a natural element in a natural world that was created and redeemed by God. He no longer even dominates nature in obeying it as prescribed by his teacher Bacon. Modern man has arrived at the precise point where his exploitation of nature transforms it into its opposite, into an artificial milieu that progressively drives real nature out of the human sphere. It is not an exaggeration to claim that between man and nature there is an absence of relations that is as radical as possible. The familiar, intimate, and physical relationship of man with nature, that Europe's agricultural civilization knew for millennia, is constantly shrinking. Already at the beginning of this century, the Swiss novelist Ramuz said, 'farmers are dying out.'[36]

The new science strongly contributed to this death since physics and its related disciplines do not consist only in constructing an architecture of beings that come from reason, in place of sensory reality, but in constructing a world that is uniquely the creation of man. It replaces exiled nature, or nature that has been reduced to the state of slavery, with the technocrat. The farmer creates nothing. He experiences things according to nature and is rooted in his reality, in continuity with it. Through his activity, he brings nature to the perfection of its form. He humanizes it. His life surroundings therefore retain the

---

36 Marcel De Corte, *L'homme contre lui-même* (Paris: Editions de Paris, 2005), 18.

characteristics of nature, which are stability, rhythm, and harmony. These nevertheless dominate his violence and anger, without which it would be unlivable, and receive at the same time a human face.

This "great concord and friendship" between the farmer and nature, as Montaigne noted, this multi-millenarian nuptial pact was broken to the benefit—or curse—of prosthetic devices that science tirelessly produces. The modern city, the spectacular creation of science and technology, produces a type of man previously unknown in history. He considers the cutting of his ties with nature and with its mysterious principle to be freedom, and he is only limited by the external, by a network proliferating with laws and regulations that turn him mechanical, and by social constraints (or, rather, socializing) whose degrading burden is his to bear. It is therefore understandable that in this urban landscape, deprived of presence and comprised of frozen representations, where man only encounters the infatuating idea that he has of his empire over things, the transcendent God of the neolithic farmer (derided by Teilhard de Chardin, who wants to exorcise its persistent influence at the heart of Christianity) does very poorly. This God, considered incongruous, must yield to the "God of going forward." This latter is the projection of the demands of a human type that is born from science. Science provided this human type with the power to modify its milieu indefinitely and thereby to create itself indefinitely because the metamorphosis of its environment leads to his own metamorphosis, and vice versa, in a dialectic without any conceivable end.

In this sense, Marxism, which finds its breeding grounds in the contemporary *Megalopolis* and in mass society, demonstrated an undeniable flair in basing its ideology on the materialism that is called "scientific," in dooming the farming class to extermination or reducing its numbers to the condition of agricultural workers. Driven to the conquest of the world, fanatically atheist, and opinionated in its intention to eradicate the smallest roots that could remind man of his human condition and dependence regarding the Absolute, Marxism was launched in permanent revolution because the offspring of what it hates pushes back ceaselessly. For this reason, Marxism had to link its fate to the science that "renews the face of the earth" when it is left to itself. It is bound to parasite off of science, develop it into an extreme artificialism, and spread its influence over the new social structures that it creates. The totalitarianism of Marxist *praxis* (which is a ποίησις with a different name) responds, with its will to substitute man's creations for God's Creation, to the totalitarianism of science. In order to be detached from metaphysics and morality, science no longer knows the limits of the expansion of its epistemological structure that condemns it to the transformation of the universe and man.

#### SCIENCE'S FALSE PROMISE

The problem of the mastery that science has over things is often reduced to the problem of the ambiguity of this mastery. This is connected simultaneously to the promise of a marvelous future and to the somber perspective of an alarmingly destructive power. Louis de Broglie writes, "Every increase in our power to act over nature necessarily increases our power to harm," and man, knowing how to "demonstrate the power of his intelligence in the work of science," must now "demonstrate the wisdom of his will if he wants to survive his own success."[37] Such a proposal, which is often topped off with a simple appeal to the "beautiful risk" that humanity must henceforth take, or a pathetic plea to the famous "extra touch of soul" as vainly proposed by Bergson, seems academic to us.

---

37 Louis de Broglie, *Physique et microphysique* (Paris: Editions Albin Michel, 1947), 364.

## The Romanticism of Science

The problem is not the good or bad use that we can make of science, or if it is, it is this only very superficially. The problem is found precisely in modern man's incapacity to perceive this ambivalence and to be able to resolve it, as he has broken his traditional ties and immersed himself in the urban society of the masses. The human being has always operated on nature because he surpasses it just as much as he is a part of it. All of civilization consists precisely in a constantly renewed and precarious effort to give nature a human face in domesticating and making it habitable, a dwelling where man can become what he is and transmit his work to his descendents. The man of traditional rural societies or of cities that prolong the countryside's rhythms and sharpen their movements instinctively knows, prior to all reasoning, discourse and moral exhortation, that his development of nature has limits that he cannot breach without causing harm. Because poplars do not climb indefinitely towards the sky even if he succeeds in stretching their branches, he thinks that measurement is the queen of all things. Nature is not the work of his hands or mind. He therefore foresees that sooner or later it will oppose his intentions, which will come back on him if he crosses the boundary. Knowing his own dependence on the gods or on God, just like nature itself, his concern to order nature only goes up to a certain point, beyond which he would bring on himself the horror of sacrilege.

All that is lived rather than thought in him. The brake that he applies to the rest and the *no* that he silently offers when he is gripped by the temptation for excess result from a tendency oriented in another sense and from a *yes* that is clearly and strongly articulated and that bursts forth from the depths of his being. It affirms the existence of a *superior law* for all knowledge, techniques, and arbitrary will. Even Homer's gods are subject to Μοῖρα, and their caprices return to the norm that confers on each being an unalienable lot, whatever that lot happens to be, in the universe.

As has been noted a thousand times, the Greeks, who invented the mathematical tool of modern science, could have discovered *poetic* knowledge and spread it throughout the world. They didn't do it because their preoccupations were elsewhere and their souls turned towards contemplation. They did not place measurement in measurable things, but *in themselves*.

Therefore, the problem of man's mastery over nature, including its limits, was already resolved. The problem was not unheard of in human history. Never before seen was the conviction, spread by millions of voices and proclaimed by the elite, even the religious elite, that man, through science, and solely through science, has crossed a decisive step in his history and is henceforth virtually the master of himself as of the universe. What is new is precisely this resolution to establish all knowledge, whatever it may be, and all activity, even if it was at first glance stubborn at following this intention. This resolution rests on the apparently unshakeable bases, first, of a validity that was speciously proclaimed as universal and, second, of science as defined and elevated by the modern mind to being the supreme degree of knowledge. Nothing can better push the intelligence, and therefore the rational animal, to death.

## MAN'S DEIFICATION OF HIMSELF

This increasingly dogmatic pretension, less and less submitted to the test of critique, is today so common everywhere that it constitutes the indubitable first and major step in every intellectual or spiritual approach and of every action of whatever domain. The mental performance of "the man of the past" was secretly or consciously regulated by the metaphysical evidence of the *principle of identity*, the supreme law of the real, and of common sense as pure thought. All conduct of "modern man" is governed by the unconditional primacy of science (with

## The Romanticism of Science

mathematical physics being modern as much in its method as in its triumphs) and justified by the decision of the scientist that it concerns. This conduct is suspended by the first evidence of success won by the operational concepts that are implemented and by the constructions that scientific thought establishes. It is gauged according to a model that made its proofs in the neighboring sectors and that the scientist will suffice to adjust in the case in question so that he finds a happy outcome. Just as a work of art is judged to be successful when it conforms to the rules that make it do good in its order, so a conduct will be successful and declared perfect when it corresponds to the scientific method that impresses its impulse on it and makes it good for its type. Science is queen. We have entered an era of *scientism*.

Marcellin Berthelot has already noted that "the experimental sciences create their object" and that "the artificial beings that they create exist in the same way, with the same stability as natural beings." This leads to the caveat that "the play of forces, which is necessary in bringing them about, is not found in nature." Knowing exactly "the sense and play of eternal and immutable forces that rule in nature over the transformations in matter, we become the masters of the natural mechanism and make it function at our discretion." "This method, this *poetic knowledge*, that tackles the problems of the material and industrial world every day, is the only one that can resolve and that will eventually work out all of the other fundamental problems." "The power that it gives man over the world and over himself is the most solid guarantee." Also, "today, science claims both the material and the moral direction of societies." "It has transformed humanity in improving the material condition of individuals, however humble and miserable these conditions are; in developing their intelligence; in destroying the transitory economic organisms that oppress individuals, and that, many claimed, kept them in chains;

and finally, and above all, in impressing on all consciences the moral conviction of universal solidarity and the imperative task of justice. Science dominates everything and gives ultimate power to its own agencies. Henceforth, no man or institution will have a long-lasting authority if these do not conform to the teachings of science." The study of science excludes the world "of the influence of every individual will, in other words, the supernatural element and metaphysics." It is henceforth possible to conceive humanity as in a state of perpetual growth, with "the sum total of goodness rising as the sum total of truth rises and ignorance declines in humanity." The notions of science and progress are indissolubly linked. "The scientific mind never stops. It always pushes forward and sparks ceaseless activity that is more intense than intelligence and industry. It has already begun to transform the distribution of wealth and image of human societies, and will transform them ever more quickly." Emancipating and managing science infallibly directs itself in this way towards the creation of an ideal type of man that slowly becomes more concrete in existence. "Whoever tasted this fruit will not know how go without it." "All thoughtful minds are thereby won, without any return to old ways, as time erases the trace of old prejudices, and a collection of convictions that will never be reversed grows in the highest regions of humanity."

Around the same time, during the celebration of the centenary of the Revolution, a member of the Comédie française, dressed as the goddess Reason, addressed a crowd that had gathered in the theater in these lyrical terms: "Man who, through me, becomes God!"

All Renan would do was to orchestrate this theme of the self-divinization of man by science or that of Reason whose only paradigm is human. This Reason is, through science, coterminous with the totality of the real. Being found in all things, it experiences itself, *causa sui*,[38] and

---

38   Self-caused.

deifies itself. The moment has come when, according to the formula of *L'Avenir de la Science*, "knowledge will equal the world, and where, the subject and the object being identified, God will be complete." It is no longer the divinity who condescends to humanity; it is humanity that makes itself sublime in divinity, which is science's Omega point.

The texts are clear in this regard: "To know is to imitate God." "Science is therefore my religion." "Intellectual matters are all equally holy." "My religion will always be the progress of reason, which is to say, science,"[39] Renan wrote again in 1859.

## REASON AND THE IMAGINATION

The origins of scientism and the religion of science are clear. Once again, Renan saw things clearly: "The great progress of modern reflection was to substitute the category of *becoming* for the category of *being*, the conception of the relative for the conception of the absolute, movement for rest."[40] The great crisis of Christianity, which begins at the Renaissance and which has not yet come to its end, is the discredit of the scholastic theologians, the decline of metaphysics, and the disappearance of the sense of measure. This crisis led to the dwindling in man of the specific act of his intelligence, namely abstraction of the intelligible essences that are immanent to the realities of the sensory universe where it is physically and intellectually rooted through birth and nature.

One always comes back to this simple explanation. It is as simple as a law of physics. If the human intelligence is incapable of seizing that which is (that is to say, the profound determinations that persist below every superficial modification and that make it so that the thing can be nothing

---

39  Ernest Renan, *L'Avenir de la Science* (Paris: Calmann-Lévy Éd., 1923, Préface), vii.
40  *Ibid.*, 182. Renan's italics.

other than what it is), there is no longer anything before or outside of it. There is no longer anything fundamentally inaccessible and impenetrable to it, than the sensory phenomenon of which it *will construct* a representation that will attempt to capture and adjust it as adequately as possible, if not substitute for its flowing reality.

It is impossible for an exclusively intellectual device to connect to sensory experience. Therefore, the notion that reason *is made* from this *experience weighs reason down with whatever has the strongest impact on the senses without forcing it to leave the imagination, which is its immanence*. Reason will be able to imagine that science is solely the deployment of its creative energy and that it attains the real in attaining the rational of which it is the generator. The fact remains that this rationalism can only be fully accomplished *in secretly resorting to the powers of the imagination*. In its act of insubordination to being, reason is forced to derive everything from itself. As its creative faculty is limited to the form to be imprinted into a given pre-existent matter (like an artist, as we have already seen), it needs to call on the resources of the imaginative faculty in its effort to draw near to the concrete object. A concrete representation that is constructed by the activity of the mind is in effect nothing but an image. It is the definition that every good philosophical dictionary provides. In this regard, Kant very keenly saw that the categories of understanding cannot be directly applied to the objects of experience. Building a bridge between reason and sensation requires an intermediary activity that he calls "transcendental schematism," which is the imagination that is produced by "schemes," or mental representations, that are intermediary between the mind and the sensory intuition. It is in this framework that we arrange our perceptions.[41]

---

41   Immanuel Kant, *op. cit.* 151.

## THE IMAGINATION AND THE SCIENCES

"To think is therefore to make schemata," wrote Goblot, for "we do not have another means of understanding things except to reconstruct them according to theoretical views." If so, *to think is to imagine*. The acts of reason and the imagination get confused.

Actually, it is like this in mathematical-physics. To find the measurable aspect of sensory phenomena, it is necessary to imagine measurements, devices, machines, symbols, signs, models, and theories that are mental representations. These *beings of reason* only exist in the intelligence that forms them, but they are extended in concrete representations of physical reality. In other words, they are extended in images as soon as one wants to surpass pure mathematical formalism and regain contact with the experience that set in motion the scientific process of explanation. The measurable is precisely the place of election of the imagination. It is impossible to measure without imagining. Duhem rightly wrote, "a size is not simply defined by an abstract number, but by a number linked to the concrete knowledge of a standard."[42] This concrete knowledge is the fruit of a creation of the mind which therefore adequately responds to the definition of the image. The physicist who admits the existence of an independent physical reality of the observer cannot avoid using his imagination to get closer.

The immense difficulty into which contemporary microphysics sinks is, as Louis de Broglie notes, that "its theories lead to a complete abandonment of concrete representations of physical reality at a very small scale. In this way, they tend to abandon the very notion of objectivity. "The atom is no more than a system of equations," according to one qualified theoretician. That point of view, pushed to the extreme, will join up with the idealism or positivism

---

42  Pierre Duhem, *op. cit.*, 174.

of certain philosophers in their most accentuated forms.[43] This conception conceals a good number of contradictions (for example, "concrete images are rejected and conceptions drawn from these images are constantly used, such as the position of a corpuscule, the quantity of movement, etc., conceptions that our mind cannot do without"[44]). Even more, the ultra-mathematical formalism of contemporary microphysics leads to the construction of creations of the mind that are the symbols of the phenomena that are absorbed in one way or another. Even so, however abstract a symbol is in appearance, it remains the product of the imagination. The symbol $P$ for pressure, in Mariotte's Law for example, implies an act of imagination that assembles together the theories, instruments, and devices of measurement. It is the same with all symbols used in equations. If one admits with Heisenberg that the mathematical formulas of microphysics no longer represent the corpuscules, but the knowledge that we have of them, and that idealism is therefore the philosophy that is immanent in it, one will find the imagination at work in all the signs that figure in the equations. Of the rest, *idealism is the ultimate philosophy of the imagination* because it assigns the intelligence, as an object, not the presence of being, but the representation that forges the mind. Short of lapsing into radical a-cosmism, the representation of the concrete universe will itself be concrete and, as such, the work of the rational imagination.

In any case, at stronger or weaker doses, the imagination is everywhere present in physics and in the sciences that trace their appearance to it. This is not to say that the imagined or imaginary entities employed do not correspond to anything. The measurable is a reality without being *the* essential reality of things. But they oscillate and

---

43  Louis de Broglie, *Certitudes et incertitudes de la science* (Paris: Editions Albin Michel, 1966), 36.
44  *Ibid.*, 36.

cannot but endlessly swing between a movement that brings them closer to sensory experience and one that draws them, in the opposite direction, towards reason. We recognize here, under another point of view, the rolling motion that moves contemporary physics we spoke of earlier. It is clear that it is usually a matter of more or less. The physicist is constrained to verify the results of his inquiry in contact with experience. He cannot simply settle in "this world of shadows" that his equations weave. He must return to the everyday world in the measurable formality that is natural to his knowledge and that cannot do without the imagination.

As long as the scientist does not cross the boundaries of the measurable that determine the object of his knowledge, the method that he uses to deal with the obstacle adapts itself to reality. This is the obstacle that sets in front of him the rejection or omission of the philosophy of being and the deliberate choice for becoming that characterizes the perceptible universe. There is no other means of seizing the ever-changing and imperceptible sensory phenomena aside from submitting them to measurement. The warmth of bodies endlessly changes and even more so does the assessment by the senses.

In order to obtain its measurement, it is necessary to imagine a device that measures according to the height of a line of mercury in a glass tube. In order to understand what the physicist calls "nature" (which in no way is its essence or its "being in itself," but is its mental representation), it is necessary to *imagine* a model that is called "real" (in which the atoms collide and the heat is defined by the number as determined by this agitation), or *imagine* another model by Fourier called "nominal." This model defines heat more geometrically by the surface of the body and by mathematical coefficients. Despite its more abstract character, this theory remains a tributary of concrete mental representation because it must make a concrete aspect of the body intervene, which is the precision of its polish. In any case, the scientific imagination is found in the last analysis submitted to the measurable aspect of reality taken *as measurable*. It is tamed. It no longer escapes the adventure that is outside of the real.

## SCIENCE'S WORLD OF BECOMING AND IMAGINATION

But what gives science its power also gives it its weakness (just as happens with the rest of the philosophy of nature and of everything that is human). As soon as science liberates itself from its own object, by which we mean the measurable *as measurable*, the constructions of the imagination, which are integral parts of its epistemological structure and type of poetic knowledge that it incarnates, detach themselves from the reality of which they are the representation. These constructions—no longer regulated by the independent determinations of their mental architecture—invade the entire mind and the universe. Here we can repeat Pascal's words. An expert on matter, he wrote on "the imagination, that mistress of error and falsehood, and all the more deceitful that she doesn't always deceive."[45] The emancipated imagination pulls reason and being along in its wake. Being is the object of intelligence. A new metaphysics that dares not speak its name is sketched out by scientism. A new morality emerges for the use of those who no longer have one or do not have one but who have to pretend to have one. These then replace the metaphysics that comes from common sense and the morality that is grafted onto the measure specific to man's condition, which the tradition of humanity elaborated, and that the West brought to its point of perfection.

It is necessary to repeat here what has already been laid out at length because nothing is more misunderstood:

---

45  Blaise Pascal, *Pensées*, édition Jacques Chevalier (Paris: Bibliothèque de La Pléiade, 1954), 116.

## The Romanticism of Science

The void left by the eviction of metaphysics and morality gave the new science a greater incentive to proclaim itself as the exhaustive knowledge of nature. This major change in human history unleashed the will to power that works inside every man. The distance that separated the mastery of measurable phenomena by physics, and that of the very nature of things whose quantitative aspect is concretely inseparable, was all the more quickly surpassed when science ousted the philosophy of nature and took its place without worrying about its own limits. The sense of limits is basically philosophical and pertains to wisdom: "*sapientis est ordinare.*"[46]

The result has been a disequilibrium in the order of knowledge. The attempts at the classification of the sciences from Descartes to Comte, and the brutal reduction carried out by scientism for the benefit of a single type of knowledge, give only a vague idea of this. The disorganization of the hierarchy of knowledge is, moreover, nothing but the reflection of the disorganization of the hierarchy of our faculties. This latter disorganization is the consequence of the upheaval to the hierarchy of being due to the intrusion of modern science with its totalitarian pretension. This pretension is latent or outwardly verified according to the temperament of the scientist. A physics that, through its measurements and imagery, had captured the becoming of things, while knowing what it was doing and while taking its appropriate place in the assembly of human knowledge, would have had to admit the existence of immutable essences. The laws of these essences that it discovered in the succession of phenomena are moreover the sign of these essences. But a physics whose expansion is metaphysical can only conceive the universe and all that it contains under the unique and exclusive aspect of a *becoming* of which it becomes the master by its operations.

---

46  St. Thomas Aquinas, *C. Gent.*, I,c.1.

Without stating it, and in concealing the reason for doing so, it is therefore constrained to value the imagination to the detriment of the other faculties. The imagination swells to the exact dimension of universal knowledge that the new science wants to be. It encompasses the universe in the fantasy web of representations and perspectives that it tirelessly spins.

When it is understood that *becoming can only be grasped by the imagination*, because the simple sensory perception cannot get hold of it in its present moment and because the intelligence surpasses it in favoring its own object, which is being, so is also immediately understood the most important consequence of modern science for the human mind in becoming unhinged. This consequence is that *if everything is becoming, everything is imagination, everything is fictitious, and everything is the work of man.* The characteristic of this man is to create an image of himself and make himself into a perpetual progress and a continuous surpassing of himself. Man is an animal that manufactures chimera that come about, and that make him come about, in an endless dialectic or, if there is an end, one that can only ever be his continually-renewed apotheosis. *Mundus est fabula*: The world is a fable that is narrated by the scientist.

### THE MAGIC OF THE SCIENTIST

Such is the new scientism that saw the light through the development of its prototype from the Renaissance to the nineteenth century. Science gives man the means to surpass man and to have access to the superhuman in achieving or becoming the image that he makes of the world and of himself in always perfecting it. This evolution permits no stopping. Evolution is the supreme law of the universe and of humanity that it leads towards better things, since man is the only animal that is able to represent, which is to say, to imagine, his own future and that of the world. This scheme is ascendent and progressive. It is the only possible one. The undeniable progress of means which is inseparable from its end and of knowledge which is independent of being and generative of its own object cannot be regression except in appearance and according to an outdated and static perspective. The world is the future of the world. Man is the future of man. Contrary to the old scientism, for which the perspective of the future was still only an ideal, for the new scientism, it is *evidence*, something that is viewed as an image but that is already found to be achieved *by the very fact* in the strongest sense of the word.

> *All of hideous and deformed ancient history*
> *Flees like smoke on the horizon.*
> *The time has come.*[47]

The time of scientific romanticism has come.

If romanticism is defined as a disequilibrium, as a disorganization of the human mind, the primacy of becoming and the pre-eminence of the imagination (penetrated or not by "scientific" rationality) on the intelligence (devalued due to the sin of its submission to being) are superabundantly romantic. According to Goethe's profound word, romanticism is an ailment, a reversal of the organic hierarchy of the characteristic faculties of the human makeup, and a revolution that inverts their mutual relationships. In this regard, and without the least paradox, modern science is thoroughly romantic when it is left to itself and is not purified of its original demons by good sense and the scientist's implicit metaphysics.

Nevertheless, it is not by chance that the scientist is today seen as a sort of wizard by the majority of men and that he exercises in their eyes a function not long ago attributed by Hugo to the poet. It is not by chance that

---

47 Victor Hugo, "Plein ciel," in *La Légende des siècles*, Oeuvres, I (Paris, Bibliothèque de la Pléiade, 1950), 725.

expressions such as "miracles," "marvels," and "wonders" of science are common nowadays. Even if the current inflation of language is taken into account, these formulas testify to the spiritual state that the impact of the scientific imagination has provoked in the imagination of our contemporaries. The scientist is endowed with an occult power. He has the power to grasp that which is hidden to other men. Having knowledge, he has the power and, possessing the latter, he is capable of foreseeing the future because he can make it. He holds first place in modern society from which he ousted the priest and, if he does not occupy it, it is due to an injustice that is unduly perpetuated and that must be eliminated. He is capable of giving satisfaction to all of man's aspirations, provided he is given the time and means.

We are still in the "morning of the magicians." An unheard of *mutation* is operating on the scientific brains that will gradually take over all of humanity. We are witness to a progressive acceleration throughout the world of mental faculties that also corresponds to the progressive acceleration of physical faculties. The phenomenon is so clear that doctor Sydney Pressey of the University of Ohio has just set out a plan for the instruction of precocious infants. According to him, his plan can provide three hundred thousand highly intelligent individuals each year. In addition, when the principles of science are massively propagated in every country, when there will be fifty or a hundred times more researchers, the multiplication of new ideas, their mutual fertilization, and their multiple alignments will produce the same effect as an augmentation in the number of geniuses. In the heart of Catholicism, which is open to scientific reflection, Teilhard de Chardin himself also affirmed that he believed "in a deviation that is capable of leading us towards some Ultra-human form."

Scientists and writers ceaselessly refer to Teilhard. These people influence public opinion through the means of publicity at their disposal. They deliberately aim to transform science into *anthroposophy* and *theosophy*, often enhanced with sexology and collectivism. With the necessary warning, it is enough to browse through the writings of Haldane, Sir Julian Huxley, Henri Laborit, Jacques Dartan, Jacques Bergier, Louis Pauwels, and *tutti quanti*, and to leaf through the journal *Planète*, without mentioning the scintillating articles by churchmen. The favor and innocent blindness or stupidity of their superiors lifted them up to positions from which they spread the Christian faith according to the surest methods of ideological propaganda. They therefore spread the worst nonsense because it was useful to them and the audience willingly accepted it.

FALSE INTELLECTUALS AND FAILING LEADERS

The laity is matching this with philosophical and religious knowledge that would class them, despite all of their science, among the feebleminded in less unfortunate times than ours. In our time, an advertising hardsell and a caricature of the Good News cheerfully transforms the last into the first. This is surely the case with Mr. Leprince-Ringuet. His title is leader of French Catholic intellectuals, without counting the honors with which he is covered—*honors* in the plural! If it's in the plural, as Péguy said, it is worth stopping here for a moment.

Four decades ago, the *Dictionnaire apologétique de la foi catholique* was content to show, for the use of its readers, the "compossibility" of science and faith, their situation in different planes of the real, and the vanity in every attempt to place them in opposition to each other. It listed a crowd of scientists who did not hesitate to subordinate their science to a superior knowledge that is called Christian Revelation.

The new apologetic, parallel to the medicine that Molière mocks, changed all of that. It spares no effort in getting science—majestic science—to support religion.

## INTELLIGENCE IN DANGER OF DEATH

As the high seat of a Divinity could only be located in the brain of a scientist on his way to the hyper-humanity that is so dear to Teilhard, we see our twentieth-century Tertullians rush to the search of a renowned Catholic who would deign to authorize the Christian religion to occupy a place in a corner of the scientist's mind that is so weighed down by intellectual brilliance:

> Hard pomegranates half-splitting open
> Giving way to the overabundance of your seeds,
> I seem to see sovereign brows Bursting with
>     their discoveries![48]

True scientists are hardly inclined toward histrionics. They flee the stage. Also, our contemporary "defenders" of the faith—it's necessary to say "offenders"—fall back to the same adulterous glories that the world generously dispenses to those who bend to its injunctions. Mr. Leprince-Ringuet[49] stands out in this masquerade. It is not enough to be an honest physicist—I imagine this at least. He has to be a Father of the mutating Church. It is necessary for him to pour out the blessings of science—of his science!—on the new religion that conforms to the "spirit" of Vatican II. He is seen everywhere. His thought, obviously adult, condescends to instruct even the young, the French Catholic youth of the *Club Inter*. One does not know a man who is more "open to the problems of his era." The "great smiling brain," as one of our Fathers said without the slightest frivolity, is a shack that is swept aside by all the winds of the century. And he never catches a cold.

If I am so severe towards Mr. Leprince-Ringuet, it is because he represents the type of scientist—the perfect type due to its purity—whose conceit has become so much

---

48   Paul Valéry, "Les Grenades," in Œuvres, vol. 1 (Paris: Bibliothèque de la Pléiade, 1957), 146.
49   Louis Leprince-Ringuet (1901–2000), French physicist and historian of science. He was the president of the Catholic Union of French Scientists and member of the Pontifical Academy of Sciences.

## The Romanticism of Science

a part of his being that it has lost all self-awareness. Such a type can be a show-off, swaggerer, or dupe. It's only human. But to no longer be aware of this, to be so mired in his own sufficiency as to become incapable of measuring the amount of ostentation that one needs to project in order to dazzle the world, is surely the characteristic of the mediocre. Not long ago, intelligence's brake still worked on the conceited intellectual. The very worry of carefully handling its effects inspired moderation in self-love. Mr. Leprince-Ringuet no longer has these precautionary manners. He is the model of these scientists without modesty whom I have seen for half a century invade every kind of faculty, academy, institute, and company. They are all the more ignorant in the vast areas where they settle and carve out for themselves a narrow sector of knowledge that corresponds less to their competence than to their art in being deceptive.

Ever since companies have become peoples, it is no longer enough to be learned and hold a doctorate. It is also necessary to be a flatterer. From the eighteenth century onwards, associations of intellectuals have claimed to be regents to the world, and ambition has become unleashed, to the detriment of intelligence. True scientists have despised this free for all. Mediocre individuals saw this as an unparalleled occasion to transform their insignificance into genius at low cost, through the simple application of advantageous strategies that diligent attendance of groups and factions develop to the most sublime degree. There are hardly any affinities between knowledge and character. Their separation generates the "pontiff" who has pride of place with all the more ostentation in the world as he has less personality. Perpetually on scene like an actor who claims to mimic every character he is not, his being is devoured by *appearance*.

It cannot be imagined to what point this itch for appearance has raged among "intellectuals" since the art of governing the people has been ousted to the profit of the association of Science and Technology. These have become the sole instruments of politics when natural communities and their leaders, who were traditionally admitted, no longer play any role in social life. Add to this the primacy of poetic knowledge proper to a knowledge that, extending beyond its limits, almost always sways the learned heads in the passion to know and direct everything. In the clear and precise vocabulary of the *Schoolmen*, one may say that science that has become *univocal* has evolved into an immense swamp with slack water in which all the frogs who want to be as large as a cow croak. Mr. Leprince-Ringuet is the unsurpassable example of this.

He claims that "there is the scientific pole that is universal and without barriers," and "the human pole," with all its particularisms and divisions, notably religious ones. He evidently claims that the religious pole is inferior to the first pole, and that the attraction to the religious pole fades as science progresses. Most religious problems will be eliminated "in one hundred years" when "we know more about certain mechanisms of the human being." The eminent physicist, perched at the summit of his scientific pyramid like God the Father at Sinai, does provide an exception, however: "Evangelical love will remain."

But beware! This is not the Gospel, the whole Gospel! It is "the spirit of the Gospel," "the spirit of love and fraternity," which knows neither God nor boundaries, and joins in the universality of science. The Catholic scientist of today can no longer admit "the doctrinal formulas" of the faith. He gets rid of the prologue of the Gospel of John as superstitious, not to mention the miracles that he disdainfully and silently glosses over, nor the Resurrection of Our Lord, that his pride ignores. Only the love of humanity remains of "the Gospels in general." The dogmatic truths have "something unreal" and constitute "problems for which we, Christian scientists, do not always have perfectly defined positions." "All that is in evolution," and Mr. Leprince-Ringuet finds that "it is astonishing to be in this world in evolution." "The Catholic Church currently takes careful notice of this and is very happy." "Science gives you the liberty to think" what you want to think until the moment when its progress will decide otherwise.

Mr. Leprince-Ringuet's thought, if we can use this word, is the quintessential sparkling of fires that combine audacity with silliness. It falls under the diagnosis that Étienne Gilson formulated in *Christianisme et Philosophie*:

> One of the gravest ills from which Catholicism suffers today, particularly in France, is that Catholics are no longer sufficiently proud of their faith.... Instead of saying in all simplicity what we owe to our Church and faith, instead of showing what the Church and faith bring us and what we would not have without them, we believe it is good politics or good tactics, in the interest of the Church herself, to act as if, ultimately, we are not distinguishable from others. What is the greatest praise that many of us can hope for? The greatest that the world can give is: "he's a Catholic, but he is really a good egg. You'd never guess he Catholic."[50]

Perhaps that is not saying enough. Until recently, the Catholic who begged for the world's approval hid his Catholic identity as much as possible. Now he displays it, but in emptying his Catholicism of all its substance and in only leaving the exterior surface, turned with precision towards the world. He ceaselessly rekindles the fake splendor of this exterior surface.

The world is humanitarian? Nothing is more humanitarian than Christianity! The world adores Eros? But sexuality is a part of the human order, and therefore the Christian order. We apply it everywhere! The world

---

50   Étienne Gilson, *Christianisme et Philosophie* (Paris: Librairie philosophique J. Vrin, 1949), 159, and *Itinéraires*, n. 118, December, 1967, 84.

becomes socialist, collectivist, and communist? No one is more so than we are! Between Kosygin[51] and Mao, our choice is made! The world only believes in science and technology? But we too, and even more! We repudiate all Christianity prior to Galileo. St. Thomas, Aristotle? Come now! We need Teilhard! To a world in evolution, we propose a Catholicism in evolution. Our faith assumes and fulfills all of the requirements of the world. How could Christianity and the world not align? *They are identical.* Science eliminated from the faith all of the philosophical and theological aberrations coming from human naivety and ignorance. It is nevertheless necessary for those responsible for the barque of Peter to realize once and for all that Mr. Leprince-Ringuet can no longer adapt to a Christianity of Fatima! A scientifically formed and informed humanity, populated by countless young and old Leprince-Ringuets thanks to the law of progress, can no longer adhere to a *Credo* that dates back to Nicaea. What the hell! Christianity no longer saves us. Science is enough. We nevertheless have to save the essence of Christianity by passing it through a sieve of scientific knowledge in order to satisfy this fondness for the "religious" that still works in us and makes us hope to be like the gods one day. What remains, Teilhard magnificently called *Metachristianity*.[52] The nuptials of science with this faith that is purged of its obscurantism open up a radiant future for us.

This is exactly the opposite of what the Church always taught, as noted by Étienne Gilson:

> Progress in the sciences and the success in avoiding or refuting the miserable errors of our era, wrote Pius IX, depend entirely on our intimate adhesion to the

---

51  Alexei Nikolayevich Kosygin (1904–1980), Premier of the Soviet Union from 1964 to 1980.
52  "Can you tell me who will finally give us this metachristianity that we are all waiting for?" In Étienne Gilson, *Les tribulations de Sophie* (Paris: Librairie philosophique J. Vrin, 1967), 75.

revealed truths that the Church teaches. It is in leaning on this truth that true and wise Catholics were able to cultivate the sciences in safety, reveal them, and make them useful and certain. This is impossible to do unless human reason supremely reveres, as is befitting, the infallible and uncreated light of the divine intellect. This can even be achieved within reason's limits through the pursuit and study of these truths that reason can attain through its own powers and faculties. This intellect shines marvelously from every part in Christian Revelation. Although indeed these natural disciplines rely upon their own principles such as reason knows them, it is nevertheless necessary that the Catholics who cultivate them have divine revelation as a guiding light.[53]

The *stella rectrix* proposed to Catholics today is no longer Revelation. It is Leprince-Ringuet's "great smiling brain." What happened in the Church is the indication that man's highest faculty has been compromised at its root. The faith falters because the intelligence falters, and reason is shaky because it is deprived of its natural nutrition and is content with the substitutes that false science, the hollow idol, tirelessly bestows on it to calm its bulimia. There is an abundance of these products. A genuine industry has been made that spreads them everywhere.

### THE FALSE PROMISES OF A TOTAL SCIENCE

I admit that I had to overcome a strong feeling of nausea to read this literature, with its sweet odor of the miasma of "science fiction." The decomposition of the mind and the rotting of the sensibility that occurs in this domain are the phenomena that make the specific difference in man and provoke in him the worst degeneration. This

---

53 Étienne Gilson, *Christianisme et Philosophie*, 140 and *Itineraires*, no. 117, November, 1967, 81.

degeneration is camouflaged as promotion. But, as [Léon] Bloy said, a garbage collector needs a strong nose.

Everything is all set when, for example, the German logician and mathematician Gotthard Günther haughtily proclaims that current mathematics will permit us "to travel somewhere beyond space," and that the further step forward, with the same courage as needed "for becoming a good creative mathematician, requires a strong neurosis." If we add the following text of Arthur C. Clarke, we have nailed it: "Since only the structure is of importance, can't the mind and the intelligence exist and work without the presence of matter? Can they exist in the relationship between pure entities such as electronic circuits and radiation waves? In the same way, the intelligence was formed in the interactions with matter and utilized matter as a vehicle for such a long time. Could it not one day tear it off as a butterfly does its cocoon? And as the butterfly flies ever higher in the summer sky, so the intelligence can soar up towards experiences that are of a totally different nature from those of its former transformations." Undoubtedly, whoever makes a monster, makes an angel.

A French biologist and supposed inventor of tranquilisers, Morand—he really needed them!—coldly writes that this mutation of humanity has had sporadic precedents: "Such special cases included Mohammed, Confucius, Jesus Christ." The mutation is henceforth collective, he adds. A universal Conscience, apparently with a capital C, is being born, undoubtedly from the bursting of particular brains. Marx's old dream of the individual identifying with the species, taken over and staged by Mounier in his personalist and communitarian "philosophy" (used by Catholics in the Parousia of Humanity, which they contemplate in their visions and their heads), is currently being achieved under our eyes.

Undoubtedly, a "superior race" is being built in history. Geneticists can add to this race with selections from the rest. Haldane writes, without wincing, that "the production of such an 'artificial' being from the cells of people of recognized value could open to human evolution fantastic perspectives." He humorlessly adds, "It is probable that the great mathematicians, poets, or painters would pass their lives from the age of fifty very usefully in educating their own artificial descendents." Moreover, mathematics will permit man to analyze information that contains a given genetic message. In this way, the physicist dreams, humanity could be rendered not only more intelligent, but also more beautiful. "By combining human genius with the calculating power of machines, formulas will certainly be found that will define genetic beauty." Beauty salons, hairdressers, estheticians, etc. will evidently have to undergo a radical reconversion. This is the moment to recall Bernard Shaw's response, as a seasoned bachelor, to a young woman who wanted to have a child with him who would have her beauty and his brilliance: "And if the inverse happened, Miss?"

Nothing is more possible than this in the domain of the mind and that of matter. Whereas primitive thought was *monovalent* and Greek thought was *bivalent* (the author adds that these formulas "would need commentary," but let's disregard this), scientific thought, modern thought, in fact, just thought, is *infinivalent*. Diafoirus writes, "We can certainly *imagine* the bond that Knowledge will make when the languages of mathematics, physics, biology, psychology, and philosophy succeed in suppressing the barriers that forbid them from communicating in a great collective synthesis. Undoubtedly, that is what future Humanity will achieve. It will succeed in harmoniously articulating the different languages with each other. It will know how to overcome the divisive stage of simple languages in order to pass to the unifying step of a language of languages. It will know how to carry out a generalization of human Knowledge towards a planetary Knowledge. It will have achieved the stage of the 'noosphere' whose early warning signs were seen so well by Teilhard de Chardin." Thanks to "the permanent university," to periods of "retraining," which are attended by everyone (the old curés d'Ars going back to the seminary to have the senility of their brains washed clean by specialists, notably by accredited sexologists), thanks to never-ending education, indoctrination, and brainwashing, it is all of Humanity that "psychically" participates in Evolution.

Another doctor Pangloss utters, "thanks to globalized information, almost all human groups have overcome a certain threshold of humanization." But thanks to the new, burning hot science of generalized semiotics, as dazzling as the supernovas that spring up in the astronomers' sky, a new threshold is passed, that of the superhominization of the individual conscience that is coextensive with the universal conscience, at least for the great contemporary scientists and thinkers. We see outlined the most fantastic reality behind their attempts, which is science. In this, all scientific knowledge is surpassed by a sort of internal push. This Science totalizes all the other sciences and includes them in a single and same language, that of machines with perforated cards that are capable not only of taking inventory, classifying, and conserving human knowledge in magical cabinets, but also of helping this knowledge progress by working on numerous and complex masses of documents and discovering therein simple relationships in uniting the most distant elements, which is to say, discovering new scientific laws.

We can henceforth *imagine* the machine directing a business, an administration, a people in exercising on the planet a sort of infallible electronic government. Because science will soon "produce in abundance, with water and chalk, food for animals and humans, fuels, plastic materials," it is clear that the most equitable distribution could be carried out through the automatic calculation of machines. A scientist comfortably seated in his armchair can then prophesy that "all the other problems—we really say, *all*—will be able to be solved." The "economic machine for the planning of the development of nutritional resources for the globe" will be the extension of our conscience that has become almost total. It will receive and translate, in all vernacular languages, man's evaluations of his creations. It will provide, via a complex and subtle application of its standards, the best logical solutions to these human-posed problems. And this solution will never be inhumane because man will have estimated all the data."

And this is why man is the future of man. Limits must be drawn on science's untold future-oriented probing. "A new romanticism, a cosmic romanticism," spun by Science from one end of the universe to the other, and beyond the galaxies, "today impacts human consciences." It is as you say. The scientists whom I am quoting are not crazy. They are clear-minded. Transcendence is no longer the attribute of God, but of man, who ceaselessly surpasses himself. If it is true that romanticism is defined by excess, the scientific imagination amputated of its object (the measurable as such, which entrusts science with reality and opens science to the perspective of productive inventions) no longer knows any limits.

## THE SCIENTIFIC IMAGINATION WITHOUT LIMITS

Let's not believe that this is a matter of isolated cases. Science's romanticism penetrates everywhere even right to the areas that have been the most resistant to its influence. Since the Renaissance, when this "point of perfection, as goodness and maturity in nature," of which La Bruyère spoke, we have not stopped being prey to the romantic fever. The only exceptions to this are the brief period of neo-classicism, intellectual and spiritual health, mental equilibrium, and the seventeenth century. The cordon sanitaire established by the Catholic Church is no longer there, and it is perhaps in the heart of a certain clergy that this fervor for the future that is promised and constructed by science rages with the greatest intensity.

When we count up what the offsprings of science, which are modernism and progressivism, have left intact in the faith, what will remain? Belief in God and in his only Son Jesus Christ? It's not so certain. It presupposes the realistic scope for intelligence, the capacity that the human mind has to grasp the being of things, and the evidence from the principle of identity. Our thought cannot reach God, at the level appropriate to nature, unless this thought is objective and can grasp the realities that exist independently of its knowledge about nature. Becoming as such is not intelligible. Depending on it amounts to depending on nothing. Becoming that is separated from nature is nothing. It only exists in the imagination.

From this point, when the image of becoming chases from a mind the reality of being, we can be sure that this mind, having at its disposal nothing more than its subjectivism and mental representations, is ripe for atheism. Undoubtedly, this atheism does not always declare itself with virulence. Nor does it weaken the faith any less. It is, in fact, impossible for the faith unless there is a permanent miracle. Yet maintaining such a faith without the prerequisite certitudes of the objective intelligence is a contradiction. What remains of this faith, once it is deprived of its foundational demonstrations, either implicit or explicit, is a belief that is without object. It is a subjective belief. The individual believes that he believes in God, but, in fact, he no longer believes in God. The romanticism of science paradoxically influenced certain clergymen who were struck by the appearance of a type of religion that is unprecedented in history. This is a religion without God, in which God is no longer anything but the pretext for the surge of subjectivism.

The concept of universal evolution is an extension, from sensory phenomena, of the scientific imagination that is emancipated from all submission to measurable reality and all relationship to the facts. The success of evolution can be explained by that as much as by the religious character in which it covers itself. It is an error to think that it purely and simply originates from a legitimate generalization of evolution restrained to the phenomena of life, whose existence and fruitfulness have been demonstrated by the biological sciences.

In fact, the inverse is true. As Cassirer[54] noted, the world of historical culture, that romanticism so proudly claims to have discovered and whose evolution is such a dominant theme, was not revealed in its universal scale until the Enlightenment and its philosophy and will, characteristic of the *Aufklärung*, to reject traditional metaphysics and morals. "In this domain, the eighteenth century also portrayed the problem as philosophical by questioning the 'conditions of possibility' in history just as it had questioned the conditions of possibility in physics... Romanticism mostly failed to recognize this decisive pioneering work, and in many cases disdainfully distanced itself from it. This attitude will not influence and trouble our judgment for too much time to come."[55]

It is enough to read Leibniz, Lessing[56], Herder[57], Diderot, and still so many others, to immediately realize that *the eighteenth century broke with the principle of identity*. For them, history does not stop generating new creatures. The domain of history is that of perpetual creation and covers the totality of that which exists. The Leibnizian monad

---

54  Ernst Alfred Cassirer (1874–1945), German philosopher trained in the Neo-Kantian Marburg School.
55  Ernst Cassirer, *La philosophie des lumières* (Paris: Fayard, 1966), 207.
56  Gotthold Ephraim Lessing (1729–1781), philosopher and dramatist whose writings and plays had a profound influence on German literature.
57  Johann Gottfried Herder (1744–1803), philosopher, theologian, philologist, and poet.

mixes its being in its dynamism and development, which are inseparable from the dynamism and development of all. It can already be said that the essence of being evaporates here in temporality. Lessing conceived religion as a divine plan of education. He sets forth "a theodicy of history, which is to say, a system of justifications that appreciate religion not in function of a stable being given at the beginning of time, but in function of its becoming and the finality of this becoming." "The historic does not oppose the rational. It is the path of its achievement, the authentic place, the sole place, of its accomplishment. According to Lessing, religion is the manifestation of the infinite in the finite, the eternal in becoming in time." Teilhard invented nothing.

All of Lamarck's[58] career developed in this overheated atmosphere, stoked by the specter of radical change in mentalities and manners, and boosted by the Revolution. Lamarck was the creator of transformism applied as much to geological phenomena as to biological phenomena, and, with this double title, the first to have the idea of universal evolution. It is important to strongly underscore, with Maurice Caullery, that, if the theory of Lamarck is very coherent, it is not founded on facts nor experiences. Lamarck's point of departure is the rejection of the Linnean notion of the absolute reality of species. For Lamarck, there are only individuals. As the stability that is characteristic of species disappeared before his eyes with species itself, as the individual is only the object of sensations, as a series of individuals who descend from one another without anything specific linking them, it follows that Lamarckian transformation is a mental construction and representation anterior to all experience and from which experience receives its mold. The proof of evolution by acquired characteristics, far from being a proof, is a consequence deduced from the *a priori* principle of evolution.

---

58  Jean-Baptiste Lamarck (1744–1829), naturalist, biologist, and one of the earliest proponents of biological evolution.

It is the same thing with the origin of species, which Darwin explains with natural selection. *First of all*, it is necessary to imagine evolution in order to *then* affirm that selection is capable of generating a new character or improving an old one. By itself, selection can only reinforce and stabilize the species. In order for it to play a differentiating role, it is necessary *beforehand* to place it in the framework of an evolution that has already been imagined.

As for mutationism, it takes nerve to affirm that a phenomenon is the cause of biological progress after one has already affirmed that it weakens the vitality of the organism. Here still, it can be quickly grasped that it is necessary to imagine an ascending universal evolution in order to grant to mutations, which are almost always lethal or abnormal, a power of transformation that would advance life.

The *dogma* of universal evolution therefore possesses an incontestable priority with regards to what is customarily called transformist theories. These are simply extensions of the theory of evolution. Haeckel writes, "Nothing more absurd can be imagined and nothing demonstrates more clearly that our theory of evolution is not understood, than the demand to establish it on experimental proofs."[59] Delage admits, "I recognize without pain that we have not seen one species engender another, nor be transformed into another, and that we have no absolutely formal observation demonstrating that this has ever taken place. I nonetheless consider evolution to be as certain as if it had been objectively demonstrated."[60] One wonders what has happened to the intelligence and its conformity to the real. It is now a faculty that has gorged itself on illusions.

---

59 Letter of Haeckel to the anatomist Virchow, cited by Louis Bounoure, *Déterminisme et finalité, double loi de la vie* (Paris: Flammarion, 1957), 49.

60 Delage, *"L'Hérédité et les grands problèmes de la Biologie générale*, cited by Louis Bounoure, op. cit., ibid. Delage boldly adds: "Those who will be shocked by these premises only need to close the book!"

## EVOLUTION AND THE IMAGINATION

It could not be otherwise. The human mind, frustrated in its normal attention to the metaphysics of being, and having surpassed the boundaries that limit physical science to the measurable as much as it is measurable, is faced with universal becoming about which its knowledge is nothing more than a pure and simple poetic knowledge. First, it has to create an image of total evolution, and then project it onto existence just as the artist does with the image of his work. At this point, the poetic knowledge that characterizes science reaches the limit. It sees nothing in reality that can be compared to the measurable aspect of things, except an indefinitely malleable becoming which is susceptible to being *informed* according to the whims of the author. The immense variety of false phylogenetic trees drawn up by the evolutionists is the proof. The trunks that have been successively cut down by critique could make a totally new forest if they still had roots.

Evolution is therefore a *myth*. In the strongest sense of the term, it is a *word*. It is the expression of the mythological mind in the most frustrated state, that in which the word, far from being the sign of the thing, is the thing itself. Still another blow: the diagnosis is fatal. It is a mental representation which, far from being derived from reality, is completely fabricated by the imagination and can only have a verbal existence. Poincaré already noted that "everything that the scientist creates as a fact is the language in which he expresses it."[61] Nevertheless, the fact is that regardless of the form of language into which measurement conforms, the measurable exists prior to language because physics cannot go without an appeal to experience. At the end of a famous study, Meyerson concluded that science demands the concept of something. But here generalized becoming is insubstantial, and the evolution that claims to seize it

---

61  Henri Poincaré, *La valeur de la science* (Paris, Flammarion, 1970), 162.

resembles the shadow of a net that attempts to seize the shadow of a fish. It is then understandable that diehard evolutionists, such as Teilhard, use so many neologisms, bristle with superlatives, and brim with redundancies. These are edemas of deficiency that compensate for the absence of reality. It is therefore understandable why Teilhard capitalizes the majority of his concepts. He instills them with a sort of personality. He transforms them into active principles. He hypostasizes them. Balzac already wisely noted in 1840 that "scientists live by nomenclature." With the evolutionists, it's exactly the phenomena of *nomen-numen* and the extraordinary catalog of the names of the Roman gods. Once again, the word is the thing.

This myth of evolution, as with all imaginary representation, is dedicated to being outwardly incarnated in a work. This is the fundamental law of poetic knowledge. The visionary would not be a visionary if he did not believe in the reality of his vision. Teilhard is always astonished that others were not seeing what he saw. A person who is hallucinating perceives a cat when there is no cat. Evolution is therefore a projection of the mind that only ever encounters itself and that, not dependent on anything else, is dedicated to absolutizing itself. It is a system of thought that is closed in on itself and is self-sufficient.

This is where the two essential characters of all generalized evolutionism of any sort come from. Evolution is the work of the mind. Evolution is a *faith*, a new religion that is destined to gather together and replace all the others.

It is inevitable. The characteristic of scientific illusion is to be scientific, which is to say, *coherent*, for want of being true and adequate for the real. In his critique of rationalism, Chesterton noted that "the fool is not the man who has lost his reason. The fool is the man who has lost everything except reason."[62] Because it cannot be *ontological*, evolutionism will be *logical*, and evolution

---

62   G. K. Chesterton, *Orthodoxy*.

will ultimately discover by the end what it had within itself from the beginning.

Evolution must therefore arrive at the Spirit, whether human or divine, because it begins with the spirit, which imagines! Also, the spirit is not introduced into matter from the outside. According to Teilhard, it is present in matter, as far back in the past as we look. It constantly activates a generative power. For Teilhard, as for the most archaic cosmogonies, a mother-god (matter) engenders a son (spirit) who then fertilizes her and triggers the evolutionary movement. "Matter is the template of the spirit," but the spirit in turn engages matter in "a process of increasing complexity." Teilhard therefore finds in matter the feminine and maternal element that his spirit fertilizes. He cannot "think" of matter without spirit because his spirit is not distinguished from it.

Matter does not exist independently of his "thought." It is indissociable from it. He does not break the umbilical cord that links them. Matter begets its spirit, and its spirit begets matter in return. He also writes with passion: "In fact, and even at the highest point of my spiritual trajectory, I would not feel at ease except when bathed in an ocean of matter." His *panpsychism*[63] is entirely the consequence of the incapacity from where he is to take a certain retreat with regard to the object—in which consists the act of judgment and thought—and of his prodigious force of imagination. For this last level, the object (matter) is not distinguished from the subject (the spirit) and the visionary himself from his vision.

The case of Teilhard's evolutionism, which is the most total and totalitarian that has ever appeared in history, thus comes to light in all its hidden recesses. Teilhard is

---

63 Cf. Louis Jugnet, *Réflexions sur le teilhardisme*, Revue des Cercles d'études d'Angers, janvier-février 1963 et *Problèmes et grands courants de la Philosophie*, Les cahiers de l'Ordre français, septième cahier, 1974, ch. XXI.

all imagination. His mind has never contacted any reality. *The other as other* does not exist for him and cannot exist. The premise of universal becoming is the premise of the barren imagination because becoming only exists in image and in an act of the mind that adds up and fuses together successive sensations. As soon as that happens, all the realities of the faith are transformed into mental entities kneaded and informed at his discretion. He admits it himself in rare moments of lucidity when he is frightened by the distortions he forces Christianity's fundamental concepts to submit to. Christ, in particular, changes from a person in flesh and blood situated at a unique historical moment into a fluid entity that Teilhard's imagination amalgamates into the becoming of the *cosmos*. Henri Rambaud correctly states that, despite the desperate efforts of certain Jesuit fathers, Teilhard is not Christian.[64] To be a Christian is to believe in a Presence. Teilhard only believes in a Representation, which is the divine Evolution. This has no other existence than the imagination.

His counterpart on the atheist side, Sir John Huxley, has exactly the same mentality. This is the representation which, with him, eliminated the presence of the real and simply stripped off the Christian elements that Teilhard synchronized in his representation. This is due to the residues of a different intellectual and spiritual upbringing than that of Teilhard. The imaginations of the two evolutionists do not work from nothing, but from mental representations, habit of thought, reflexes due to education, a language that is used from childhood, etc. All of these factors are redeployed in the two cases in order to create the vision of becoming. With Huxley, this vision is humanitarian and socializing in the Anglo-Saxon tradition. It is humanity that evolves in the universe and that

---

64  Henri Rambaud, "L'étrange foi du P. Teilhard de Chardin," *Itinéraires*, no. 91, March 1965, 114–143; "Les habiletés du R. P. de Lubac," *Itinéraires*, no. 114, June 1967.

permits man, thanks to science, to assume his destiny and that of the universe in the current age. Evolutionism leads to integral humanism.

### EVOLUTION AND MATERIALISM

Both a restricted evolutionism and a more generalized one are clearly the object of faith and are *a religion,* as they are not founded on experience or demonstration. Teilhard does not hide this. Nor does Sir Julian Huxley. Both men participate in this form of religion (so widespread nowadays, particularly in intellectual milieus and, unfortunately, also among clergymen) that is the religion without Revelation, the religion of the most extreme modernism, the religion that belongs to all those minds who substitute, for the presence of beings and things, the internal representations that they distill in the recesses of their imaginations. Christian Revelation is the revelation of presence: *Et Verbum caro factum est et habitavit in nobis.* This Presence does not let itself be manipulated by our phantasies. Therefore, it is necessary to eliminate the real one way or another, radically or surreptitiously, in a way that always produces a plastic representation of nature as the replacement. In this way, the mind will not encounter more than itself. *Myself—that is enough.*

Such a mentality is all the more widespread since contemporary man finds himself in a *society of the masses* for which poetic knowledge, immanent to modern science, tirelessly produces artificial objects that are the work of man himself and reflect back his own image. The ego never has any other object than the ego when man encloses himself or finds himself enclosed in such an atmosphere. The mind never seizes this more than when it is in its laboring activity. Man finds himself perpetually beholding man occupied with his own edification.

The only idol that man can substitute for God is the ego. All the others are coarse or subtle metamorphoses.

When God is dead, the absolute moves into the ego. The ego that is separated from the real, closed in on itself, is the sole power in the world that is capable of killing God *in the imagination* and, through a ceaseless effort, to bring these attributes into its own reality. But the ego loathes to proclaim itself God. It is not because it fears ridicule. The ego takes everything seriously because it takes itself, which is everything, seriously. It learns competition: another, stronger ego, can arise and reduce its divinity to the abyss. Deception is therefore needed to achieve the sublime level of apotheosis. As well, the ego always hides itself behind the *We*, the Social, the Collective, Humanity, etc., whose levers of command it attempts to take control of by deceiving his competitors. In this way, the idolatry of the ego camouflages itself in the religion of Humanity. For Huxley, humanity is self-sufficient and stretched out towards an Omega Point. The pantheism that Teilhard confesses is indistinguishable from this. Evolutionism is therefore a religion without God, an atheist religion. Communism is the perfect expression of this and simultaneously its vehicle. We also see all the other forms of evolutionism, with Teilhard and Huxley at the head, submitting to its attraction and considering "scientific" materialism to be an attempt (in need of improvement) of true humanism. Teilhard and Huxley are foolish once again with their imagination. They do not succeed at grasping in the "science" and dialectical evolutionism of whitewashed Marxism *what this latter really is*.

**THE RELIGION OF NARCISSUS**

Like all dupes, they dupe others in order to escape their inner lie. I've said it a thousand times and I will state it once again because the spectacle of the contemporary world is eloquent in this regard: When everyone is a fool, no one is a fool. Also, the evolutionists have the soul of an apostle. Teilhard spent his life convincing himself and, connected to this, convincing others, that his "thought" would give to Christianity a new life and an unparalleled blossoming. His sycophants celebrate in him a new Aristotle, a new St. Thomas, and even a new St. Paul, if not a new Christ. He goes so far as to proclaim loudly and clearly that if he comes to lose his Christian faith, he will retain his faith in the evolution of the world. He died in betraying the vow of obedience made to his order, which should be his only inheritance, and in taking care that all of his writings can be spread after his death. Papal warnings, the encyclical *Humani generis*, the letter of Reverend Father Janssens, the general of the Company of Jesus (the publicity of which was curtailed in the extreme), a whole series of measures aimed specifically at him, had no effect on the mission that he believed he had. This mission was to announce to men the good news of the evolution of humanity towards the Omega Point. It is the same with his disciples, whose zeal was not halted by the Holy Office's *Monitum*.[65] They developed the most remarkable propaganda in the world since Lenin and Goebbels. As soon as the sales of Teilhard's books weaken, the circles founded to diffuse the message of "the Master" get busy. Teams of lay and clerical lecturers set off to redress this fall, right in front of mesmerized or complicit bishops.

---

65  On June 30, 1962, the Holy Office (renamed The Congregration for the Doctrine of the Faith) issued a monitum (warning) on the writings of Teilhard de Chardin: "Several works of Fr. Pierre Teilhard de Chardin, some of which were posthumously published, are being edited and are gaining a good deal of success. Prescinding from a judgement about those points that concern the positive sciences, it is sufficiently clear that the above-mentioned works abound in such ambiguities and indeed even serious errors, as to offend Catholic doctrine. For this reason, the most eminent and most revered Fathers of the Holy Office exhort all Ordinaries as well as the superiors of Religious institutes, rectors of seminaries and presidents of universities, effectively to protect the minds, particularly of the youth, against the dangers presented by the works of Fr. Teilhard de Chardin and of his followers."

Some day we shall have to deepen our understanding of the sociological phenomenon of the penetration of Teilhardism inside and outside of the Church.

Let us quickly underscore the essential element. Teilhardian evolutionism has with the greatest ease infiltrated the mentality of every man who appears to mass society, whatever his social level. Such a man is unable to control categorical affirmations that are orchestrated by an adequate publicity of the mystique of evolutionism. He is established in a sort of imaginary world constructed of reading second- or third-hand works hastily thrown together, of digests, journals, radio programs or television broadcasts that include no personal experience whatsoever. *Such a man is unbelievably gullible.* His faculty of belief is without limits. The more an allegation is questionable, the higher the chance it has of being favorably received by him provided that it is dressed up in a "scientific" language. The authority of "science" guarantees its "reality." The universe of fictions in which this man wallows is thereby reinforced. He shuts himself in a citadel that cannot be taken by any argumentation.

Modern man cannot check the relationship of the words that sustain him against the realities they signify. "Evolution" is one of these words, and among the most efficacious. Its influence is directly related to its verbal character and vacuity of substance. It corresponds to the needs of change, to the continuous state of dissatisfaction that the ego has of itself. The characteristic of the idol is deception. The ego seduces, but ceaselessly deceives the ego. This latter thereby lets itself be carried away in a movement that does not stop, in an infinite aspiration towards its always-changing image. Evolution is the euphoric justification that diverts the ego from its fundamental malaise, from the anxiety that it feels when it encounters its inner emptiness. It stuffs its worries with optimism. Evolution is the greatest spiritual tranquilizer that stokes the grievances of the ego without ever being presented with the bill. Evolution absolutizes these grievances in inserting them into the line of its "inevitable" progress. All of the ego's requests must be granted. This is a universal law. And whoever opposes this is a "dirty reactionary" who will be swept aside by History.

It is easy to see the prodigious force of mystification that evolution possesses. This force supplies the weak, mediocre, and incapable with a will to indefinite power. It cannot be pointed out enough enough that as soon as one believes in evolution, one is immediately at the head of the class. It is impossible to be surpassed or left behind. The supporter of evolution is guided and led. In this way, evolution transforms failures and malcontents into leaders. Humanity is in their hands and their imagination represents it as a fluid mass on which they print their own ever-transformed image. In order to retain this place at the summit of evolution, one must constantly change. One must be elusive, evanescent, and enigmatic, speak without saying anything, and adopt the character of speech that signifies nothing and that can be easily and immediately betrayed because such speech flows like evolution itself. Gossip, wordiness, and verbiage are always the dominant characteristics of evolution fanatics. When a man, by misrepresenting his opinions, comes to occupy in the hierarchy of being a place that his aptitudes, gifts, and very being have not destined him for, it is certain that sooner or later he will champion generalized evolution. He needs to become a guide, leader, or apostle to save himself from this intolerable error. In this regard, the majority of priests who failed in their vocations and substitute the god of their imagination for the God of the Gospel are prone to Teilhardism. Evolution communicates to them a good conscience regarding the power which they exercise over souls. They use this power to mold, shape, and adapt these souls to evolution. *This is also their will to power, their itch for domination, the totalitarian expression of their ego, and the triumphant outpouring of their subjectivity.* They are all suffering from a shrill "apostolate." They all cheerfully sacrifice the truth for efficiency, that is to say, for themselves.

Evolutionism is the religion of Narcissus in ecstasy in front of his image reflected in universal becoming. It rings the death knell of the intelligence. And if Teilhardism hardly seems to occupy a major place in the Church at the end of the twentieth century, it is because it has totally invaded the Church and become one with it.

# 3

# Information that Deforms

**THE NATURE OF MODERN INFORMATION**

The *intelligentsia* and its utopias, along with the exaltation of science as the universal criterion of knowledge and the panacea of all the evils and the substance of the future society, is the phenomenon that characterize our century. Supporters of all this witness the divorce of the intelligence and its proper object, which is the extramental real. They also witness the correlating triumph of the poetic imagination. This imagination is the constructor of a universe that is strictly the work of man. But however powerful our imaginative faculty and capacity for illusion are, they cannot succeed at building something based on nothing, or on their own contents whose trickery passes into reality. They may deliberately renounce, with a sort of Olympian reassurance, the data of experience and tradition, but they cannot obtain nourishment from the abyss. They need *something* from which they can extract a part, just as much for justifying the objectivity that they wish to dress themselves in, as for continuing under this mask their work of the destruction of the real. But this *something* must be as little independent of their domination as possible. It must be malleable to the extreme. It must be able to welcome with docility the *form* that man's will to power wants to give it. The will to power, based on the imagination, can do pretty much whatever it wishes to this *something*. This something has received a name: *information*.

## Information that Deforms

What is information? Its meaning today obviously exceeds a narrow technical domain of Littré's definition of it as the simple reading of data. Increasingly, information tends to signify knowledge and the diffusion into the public of all that happens in whatever domain of human activity, from a short news item to religion, art, science, technology, politics, etc. Information concerns *all that happens* in the immensity of the universe. It unfolds with a background of *continuous change*. If there is no change, there is no information. What is acquired once and for all, what is incorporated into knowledge, the eternal truths, is not, properly speaking, information. One is not informed about the rotation of the Earth around the sun or about the multiplication table. Information essentially concerns that which appears or is produced *in the present* and, as the present ceaselessly moves, *into the new*. This unheard sense of the word "information" corresponds to Valéry's remark regarding how the new fact takes the place in contemporary civilization that until now was reserved for experience and tradition.[1] There is therefore information that one calls "event."

The word "information" is nevertheless not a simple synonym of "news" or "current affairs." The "news" or "current affairs" do not possess the "exact knowledge" that information has from the outset in the eyes of the man of today. The "informed" man is the man who knows and "informs" those who do not know and will therefore in turn be "informed." The word "information" therefore takes on an immense scale that encompasses and surpasses the sense of the word "science" or "knowledge of reality," while joining the aspect of the "truth" or the "conforming to the

---

[1] "The *new fact* tends to take all the importance that tradition and *historic fact* possessed until now." Paul Valéry. "Propos sur le progrès." in *Regards sur le monde actuel et autres essais, Oeuvres,* tome II (Paris: Bibliothèque de La Pléiade, 1960), 1025. The italics are Valéry's.

nature of things" that this normally involves. Information tends to cover the entire field of knowledge, including scientific knowledge. The essential quality of the scientist today is to be "informed." He needs to know everything taking place in the domain of his competence so that he can add a "new fact" to this ceaselessly transformed knowledge. Journals that specialize in exhaustive "information" are now available to me. Each journal identifies all the recent publications of such and such a sector of human knowledge. It is a matter for the scientist of being "up to date" on research and scientific production in his sector so that he may carry out his own research and in turn produce something "new." To accentuate this movement, congresses, colloquia, and scientific meetings multiply for scientists to exchange and discuss their respective information. The sciences have increasingly become a network of information relative to a given object whose design is modified and scope is broadened day by day. While until recently information and simple documentation were for Littré almost synonyms, information and knowledge identify with one another more and more in the language of the twentieth century at the level of new scientific knowledge and in the spheres in which scientific knowledge appears.

In this way, information in the modern sense tends to be, on the one hand, "knowledge of the new" and, on the other, through its scientific uses, the precise knowledge of transformation that operates in the course of knowledge. The two significations are currently congregating in the mentality and language of contemporary man for whom the truth no longer corresponds to what is, but to what becomes. In his eyes, everything that occurs and is broadcast through the channels of information takes on a value of reality and is even found to be the sole value of reality. It is not at all by chance that the results of scientific calculations that are obtained by cybernetic machines are called "information." The machine is not only more precise in its calculations than the human brain, but it can extract solutions that no person could have arrived at and that are consequently unheard of. But with appropriate programming and inputting of variables, the machine can also explore the future of a project and determine its best future state for any given situation. What is newer than this mathematical knowledge of "a brighter future"?

The famous scheme that is assigned by positivism to science, "to know, foresee, and be able to," no longer appears to have anything utopian. Thanks to information, man is already master of his collective destiny. He can do as he wishes at the level of a restricted society that is identified with the economy. He waits to do something individually according to his own will which is liberated from the servitudes to matter due to exhaustive information. With all the information and knowledge from all the events that spring up and constitute his becoming, man is therefore capable of being his own demiurge, his own maker, and his own *homo faber*. Such is the backdrop on which the new signification of "information" is drawn. It accords with the sentiment, which is largely spread by information itself, that contemporary man is a "mutant" who has the power to master and orient his own "mutation."

What is the cause of the apparition of this new sense of the word "information" and its universal expansion? The preceding chapters have already prepared a response to this question. In the modern sense of the word, information's first cause is the new conception that modern man makes of himself as emancipated from every relationship of dependence with regard to the universe and its Principle. Since the Renaissance, according to Pico della Mirandola's formula, man has conceived himself as his own modeler and fabricator (*plastes et fictor*), and he imagines himself to be capable of "shaping himself according to all the forms preferred by his free will."[2] This

---

2  *De hominis dignitate, op. cit.,* 8.

conception, which reached its theoretical culmination in the eighteenth century, and which reached its threshold of practical realization in the twentieth—with the attendant consequences!—socially and politically results in a communal system of life that received the name *democracy*. As the genius Augustin Cochin foresaw, it is the *sociology of the democratic phenomenon* that *completely* explains the phenomenon of information and, as we will establish later on, the deforming action (at the destructive limit of human intelligence) that this universalized information exercises.

An introductory precision is required here. The democracy that we know today does not have the least commonality with the democracies of the past, with Athenian democracy, for example, with the communal democracies of the Middle Ages, with the legitimate democracy that Pius XII described following the great political philosophies of the past, or with today's Swiss democracy. The difference that separates them includes physical space, since these earlier philosophies were geographically and demographically restricted. The democracy of today spans great physical terrain and numbers of people to make *the world safe for democracy*, according to Roosevelt's promise, and to make the global machine a universal democracy equipped with a universal government.

As we have already stated, and it needs re-stating, much political and social vocabulary has become deceitful so that the citizen does not conduct himself in the same way in the two systems that seemingly resemble each other because they are given the same descriptor. In a human-scale democracy, the citizen directly knows by experience the data of the problems that need resolution. If he does not know about them, he knows a man or men who do know and in whom he can place his confidence. It is not the same in the enormous modern democracies, whether they are bourgeois or communist, "formal" or real, claiming to be democratic or not. The questions that are posed to the citizen are so abundant and complex that he cannot know the data by the sole source of authentic knowledge, which is experience. The beings and things that depend on his decision are for him, whether he is a representative or represented, simple mental and abstract representations, not real and concrete presences. It is exactly the same for whoever is called the "democratically elected head of State." One of them said an extraordinary thing that, for once, expressed his hidden plan: "All of my life, I *had* a certain *idea of France.*"[3] The France of the flesh is no longer for him but a clay pretext into which he introduced the mental representation that he had of it. This comes from the lack of identification of dynastic interests with the national interest as established by a hereditary monarchy.

The citizen can therefore make up his mind or form an opinion about the beings and things of which he has no experience. He can *imagine* them. He can never effectively know them. The result is that the citizen in modern democratic regimes can only resolve the problems that he faces at a verbal level. He is like the Merovingian king whose Mayor of the Palace has to be called up. Having no lived affinity with his social and political environment, he is forced to use the image that he has forged in the interior of his thought, and to project it onto the soft and amorphous lump that we call "society" so that it can take form. But since his imaginative capacity is generally very limited, he is forced to call on experts who offer him ready-made models. And he will adopt one or another of these, not in virtue of the model's correspondence with the reality that it is powerless to discover, nor in the knowledge of the cause and his intelligence's judgment of its adequacy, but for impulsive and affective motivations that the informer has an interest in inciting in him in

---

3 Charles de Gaulle, *Mémoires de guerre, L'appel* (Paris: Bibliothèque de La Pléiade, 2000), 5. The italics are De Corte's.

order to be the master and to eliminate the rational or real. Bertrand de Jouvenel has pertinently written: "Our ardent desire for union with our companions is such that the less we realize this in our daily commerce, the more we *dream* of 'instituting' it on a great scale."

Nature always gets its vengeance. Due to the lack of being able to understand the data of experience, man's intelligence, immersed in immense accumulations of things, can only escape through the imagination. The nation, in the modern sense that the word has taken since the French Revolution, and nationalisms, internationalisms, and supernationalisms are the images of society that only exist in the mind of contemporary *homo democraticus*, and that tend to take shape in the constitutions and institutions (without speaking of 'structures'!) that are submitted to perpetual questioning and incessant reforms. Another example of this is the crazy foolishness that has been the rage since decolonization. This rage consists in creating completely new "republics" from a mental fiction that is then put onto paper. Nothing produces more hatred and ruin than this type of political hallucination that preys on human beings who are suddenly uprooted from their customary environment.

### THE THEATER OF DEMOCRACY

We could have suspected as much. Modern democracy is based on the isolated individual. To express his political will, the citizen enters the polling booth. He is called *to do the social with the mental, the real with the imaginary, and the ontological with the logical*. The tentative inevitably ends in failure. The inescapable failure of the modern democratic system was long hidden by the accumulated social reserves that had built up from traditional behavior (the regime depleted this accumulation to inoculate itself from a fake life) and by the accumulation of laws, rules, and bureaucratic structures that served as prosthetics for anemic or defective social behaviors. We are now at the end of our tether. The resources accumulated in the old natural communities have almost dried up, and the crutches that were accumulated to allow citizens to walk — if we can still use this word — have become an intolerable burden causing immobility. The explosions of social instinct which are deprived of expression, reduced to brute animality, and multiply everywhere under our eyes, along with the lethargy that affects almost everywhere the electoral liturgies, are signs that do not deceive. Only in a fog would modern democracy build the bridge from imagination to social reality.

The difference between the ancient democratic regime and the democratic regime of the huge contemporary states therefore comes down to that which separates the real from the unreal. The ancient type of democracy existed and functioned within reality. We could compare its advantages and inconveniences with those of other political regimes. *Modern democracy does not exist.* As long as no one understood Maurras' diagnosis in all its sparkling lucidity ("There was an *ancien régime*. There is not a new regime. There is only a state of mind that blocks this regime from being born again"[4]), no one understood the historic evolution of contemporary societies or, more precisely, of contemporary "dissocieties." We are then reduced to finding situations that are politically disastrous and in which communities find themselves forced to accept ineffective solutions that abandon them to the inevitable process of social disintegration or that hide ongoing decay under an iron corset. This is what a "conscious and organized" citizen from recent times called "a brighter future," the "noosphere," the "New Frontier," etc. Unable to look for long at death any more than at the sun, the citizen takes refuge in the myth of the future city in order to escape his destiny and, according to the poet's

---

4  Charles Maurras, *Mes idées politiques, op. cit.*, 49.

verses, in order not to perceive that *a god is missing at the altar where he is the victim.*

Democracy is essentially the deprivation of this good which is required by the human condition and that is the life of an organic society. This good is born of the demands of nature and brought to perfection by intelligence. Democracy is therefore evil. It is death. It substitutes non-being for being. It does not exist, or, more precisely, it only exists to the extent that it can destroy the existence of man. There is no paradox there. It is our current situation. We have just read on the pediment of the Sorbonne this childish declaration of angry students: "The imagination has seized power."

Bernanos roared, "Imbeciles! How can you not see that it has already [seized power] for so many years and that this power at its disposal as well as whoever you imagine has it, are ceaselessly delighted by the crafty, if we can call them as such, the exploiters of the appalling credulity of contemporary man!"

Modern democracy does not exist. What exists in the pure theatrical decor of democracies are the directing minorities that conquered *the vacant state* and occupy the vacant positions of command, either directly or through intermediaries. These minorities who hold the levers of the democratic state can only act, sincerely or not, *in doing things as though democracy existed*, whether they know or do not know the truth. They can only govern citizens by tricking them and persuading them that they, the citizens, hold all the power, even though citizens are deprived of the essential power of decision and direction that they possess verbally and that determine all the other powers. Their good or bad faith, once again, has nothing to do with this. In no other period of history has the citizen been more deprived of real power than in modern democracy. And yet, everything is *said* as though he were king, and everything takes place as if he is a mere figurehead.

*Information that Deforms*

## THE SUBJECTIVE INTELLIGENCE

The sociology of this system, with the real power of a minority and the imaginary power of the majority being combined, explains the phenomenon of information and its distorting activity. Augustin Cochin admirably demonstrated this for all "societies of thought" of the eighteenth century. These societies prefigured with precision the current situation of democracy. All of these "societies," groupings of "the Republic of Letters," academies, lodges, etc., have the same characteristics. They are *egalitarian* in form and their members are *fraternally* united and *free*, stripped of all attachments, obligations, and social function. To gain entrance to these societies, they leave behind all the qualities that they enjoy, or would enjoy, in their natural communities, which include the family, occupation, parish, village, region, etc., if they still had the sense of these communities.

They insert themselves into a type of society where "morality is exercised far from action and politics far from public affairs."[5] They "have neither direct interest nor are engaged in the affairs of which they speak."[6] Their associations have "no other object than to free themselves by their discussions, determine things by voting, and spread ideas through correspondence. They *express*, in other words, nothing more than the common opinion of 'their' members."[7] Cut off from every effective relationship with the social realities of daily life, they can only impose things in advance and without appeal, to themselves first of all, then to the public that they catechize, the point of view of subjective intelligence, the unreal that must, as we have said one hundred times before, beg for extensions of the imagination and of the word in order to give themselves

---

5   Augustin Cochin, *La Révolution et la libre-pensée* (Paris: Plon, 1924), Introduction, xxx.
6   *Ibid.*
7   *Ibid.*, 7.

an *ersatz* object. In these cities of "thought," everything is said and imagined far away from beings and things, outside of experience, tradition, and the realism of the common sense that imposes the world of objects on the intelligence. Everything is said and imagined as faith that proposes to the same intelligence the dogmas whose substance does not depend in any way on it. Cochin notes, "The training of free thought has grave consequences in the intellectual order first of all. Thanks to this the privileged forget their privileges; the scientist forgets experiments; the religious forget the faith."[8] In all of this, we are in the presence of "cognition that is as unconscious as custom and folklore."[9] "It is a drama in which *personal man*," in daily association with the beings and things that he did not make, with the situations (such as the principal ones of *birth* and its procession of necessities, or family, time, place, etc.) that he did not create, "is little by little eliminated by *socialized man*," identified with his artificial "society," with the word that nourishes him, with the image that configures him, and that "will no longer be but a number, an abstract feature."[10] For the *real* and *personal* being of man is substituted, in this city of "thought," a *social* and *fictive* being.

We are no longer in a genuine world where one collides with the resistance of things. We are in a universe of words where one encounters only the softened realities that are informed by the requirements of a discourse. This discourse *aims to influence the members of the group and to obtain the agreement of everyone*. It is covered with an *ecumenic* value and is addressed, beyond the restrained circle of listeners, to all of *humanity*. In the real world, this intellectual agitation and traffic of discourse, writings, and correspondences would be laughable, and those who give themselves over to it (the moralist who rebuilds society

---

8   *Ibid.*, Introduction, xxxiii.
9   *Ibid.*, xxxviii.
10  *Ibid.*, xliv.

without recourse to the faith or to the realities of birth or history; the politician who creates a brand new state without appeal to tradition; the man who defines the rights of man without calling on the experience of the ages and the models of humanity that the wisdom of the ages from the best people enthroned) would be doomed to defeat and scorn.

But in this special milieu in which the specimens spread everywhere, coordinating the dispersed movements of all those who let their intelligence wander far from the real, the young, "intellectuals," men of law, of the pen, of the word, skeptics, the vain and superficial, *"the deficiencies" of uprooted man "become strengths."* The information that they exchange, and that go in the inverse sense of daily life in natural communities, appears to them, in their verbal refinement and even in their emptiness, like an unparalleled acquisition that they do not delay in attributing to "the progress of the Enlightenment," about which they boast as soon as they are the authors and ringleaders. Their desire to persuade and win all the members of the group over to their views incites them, first, to identify with humanity itself (to which they address themselves) and, second, to establish their particular reason, as bloodless as it is, and the cause of this reason's weakening, to be the universal reason, deified and deifying.

As Cochin writes,

> on the other hand, sincere and true spirits, who look to what is concrete, to effect more than to opinion, find themselves disoriented. Little by little, they stray from the world that they have made. In this way, the refractory eliminate themselves. They are what philosophers call "dead weight," which is to say, men of work. They eliminate themselves to the profit of the more fitting, who are the men of words. This *mechanical selection* is as lethal as the triage between the heavy and light bodies on a vibrating plaque. It has no need for a master,

who designs, or of doctrine that excludes. *The force of things is enough.* Among themselves, the lightest will rise the highest, while the heaviest and those weighed down with reality will fall. This double social law of triage and training does not cease to act and push the reasoning and unconscious troop of brothers away from real life, towards the dawn of a certain intellectual and moral type that no one foresees, that each one would reprove, and that everyone is building.[11]

It is sometimes shocking that the majority of "intellectuals" are "of the left" and inclined to pardon communism for everything. It is often asked why the great centers of information, such as news agencies, newspapers, movie newsreels, radio and TV stations, universities, research centers, etc., are stuffed with revolutionaries, with proselytes of subversion or friendly "liberals" who smile in their role as harbingers of nihilism. The opposite would be surprising. Despite the exceptions, which are not all that numerous and which are due to chance and to the necessity of the fight, all of these centers are peopled by individuals who are disgusted by the human condition and would like to shake up the foundations because it suits them, because they are automatically called to this, because they are as far as possible from the everyday lives of men, and because these are the means of expression of a regime whose members, with varying degrees, are almost all cut off from their fundamental relationship with reality and with the principle of reality, especially today.

The environment of "information" is as distant as possible from the natural environments where the true life of men takes place, where nothing new takes place except the ceaseless renewal of life, where the masterly finalities of human existence peacefully unfold like the courses of rivers towards the ocean. The environment of "information is that of *accident* as opposed to environments of nature,

---

11   *Ibid.*, 23.

which are rooted in essence." Is it paradoxical that the intelligences that are cut off from their relationship to being are attracted to those environments and consummate their separation there, as their models from the eighteenth century did in clubs and societies of thought? The environments of information are the salons of democracy where anonymous beings that swarm about in the regime are revealed like microbes and viruses under the microscope.

In these diverse environments, large or small (at least according to the echo that they provoke), the real fact is broken down into its elements and recomposed according to a form-type with few variants. These variants boil down to a few procedures or cliches that assure most efficiently the influence of the orator or the informer over those whom he addresses and from whom he wants to obtain assent. If "the shepherd" or "the good savage" of the eighteenth century, to which the model of the mind of the new society in gestation had to conform, has been replaced today by "the proletariat," to whom belongs our future by predestination, there is no doubt that "liberty" has conserved in our days the same power of fascination that it had in the revolutionary era. A people that "fights for its liberation" will in our day always have the support of our contemporaries and the events that mark out its emancipation will be broken down according to this mythical model.

Some day, someone will count up these driving images that are preliminary to the events and to their disclosure, whose form they shape. The work of the historical critic will be indispensable for untangling the true from the false, inextricably mixed up as these two are in the contemporary accounts. The information of these accounts inundates us and weaves the narrative. It is noted that the recipe has remained the same for two hundred years. Very simply, it is a matter of emptying the fact of its substance and seizing in it the aspects that are suitable for a work of transformation to thereby make it communicable to the minds that are uprooted from reality and reduced to their subjectivity. Persuading such minds and rendering docile subjective thinkers, who are apparently sealed up in their isolation, is an easy thing. It is enough to reach out to the subjectivity of the other, to accentuate it, to give it the only support that can sustain it in its state, and to introduce an image as distant from the real as possible, which is to say, a word that reflects a determined reality as little as possible. The brute fact is coated in illusion and immediately absorbed.

A thousand examples of such work can be found with *les philosophes* whose critique sapped the foundation of the *ancien régime* with information that twisted real facts. The *philosophes* were detached from complex relationships formed with their environment and circumstances, and they were deprived of the living sources that make such things understandable. Facts are seen and known, but not understood. They are invested with a whole other signification that is entirely subjective, unreal, fictional, and wholly fabricated, in proportion to the uprootedness of the minds that make up the group in which the information spreads. Again, nothing is easier. It is precisely because the reasoning of the *freethinker* in the eighteenth century is the same in all the other freethinkers in the society that they formed, being out of tune with the real because of their "liberation," that "the thinker does not need to consult the reasoning of others, but only to follow his own." The subjectivities meet and fuse with each other, akin to the clear unanimity of highly-charged crowds. The democratic informer is in the same situation with regards to the democratic masses that he informs. In every case, the clever and the power-seeking who are conscious of their actions, work on artificial, inorganic, and homogeneous groupings that are reduced to the state of docile and perishable amalgamations. The clever and

## Information that Deforms

power-seeking dispose of a genuine machine that, if it is handled according to the rules, is capable of forcefully forming the minds and making them think or act as they decide. The democratic milieu itself carries out almost all of the work. Its members are outwardly verbally and imaginatively active, but in reality passive and malleable.

The same law that directs the society of thought and imposes on it one or more machinists to maneuver "the machine" wants modern democracy to have continually at its head informers who forcefully stamp the amorphous opinion and permit it to express itself. In this regime, information constitutes the *fourth power* that, by the very force of things and by the unavoidable evolution of the system, is in the midst of insidiously substituting itself for other powers. The legislative power by definition is dead after the birth of this other power. Proudhon noted at the end of his parliamentary experience, "One may say that the man elected or representative of the people is only the mandate of the people, the servant of the people, the justified powers of the people, its delegate, advocate, agent, interpreter, etc. In spite of this theoretical sovereignty of the masses, and of the official and legal subordination of its agent, representative, or interpreter, it will always be the case that the authority and influence of the agent will not be greater than those of the people, and the agent needs to seriously accept a term of office. Always, despite the principles, the delegate of the sovereign people will be the master of the sovereign... Bare sovereignty, if I dare call it as such, is something still more ideal than bare ownership."[12] Parliaments have only survived to the extent that the sociological law of triage, which governs this type of assembly just as it regulates societies of thought, has not yet eliminated "the notables" who are rooted in their

---

12   Pierre-Joseph Proudhon, *Contradictions politiques. Théorie du mouvement constitutionnel au XIXe siècle* (Paris: Librairie internationale, 1870), 89.

natural communities and are *ipso facto* the real bearers of the will of their terms of office.

Nowadays, and everywhere in the world, they are only the registrars of decisions taken elsewhere or the elaboration of decisions that received strong input from elsewhere. Already last century, Cournot noted the innate disposition of the parliamentary system to distance itself from the real: "It carries in itself a principle of degeneration and corruption that develops promptly, even under the oversight of capable men. This principle of corruption consists in an innate tendency to take the sign for the thing that is signified, legal fictions for substantial realities, a vote for a solution." Such a weakness places it under the control of pressure groups whose informers are increasingly the masters. Judicial power in turn submits itself to the direct pressure of information. This has been seen in the Assize Courts for example, and in the famous Softenon (or Thalidomide) trial in Liège in November 1962. It has been seen in direct pressure following the transformation and catalyzation of morals, mentalities, judgments, and in the public opinion on which it operates. Regarding executive power, it is increasingly in the hands of those possessing close knowledge of the democratic "engine room" who are promoted to the highest positions. These people collaborate so closely with the informers that the actions that they exercise over "the people" are rigorously uniform among them. They command while pretending to be commanded.

INFORMATION AND THE SOCIETY OF THE MASSES

Even at the risk of repeating ourselves a bit, it is necessary to prolong our analysis, given that the power of the democratic illusion weighs so heavily on men's minds—because of the information itself that lives from the persistence of this illusion and continuously creates it! The modern democratic regime, born of the French

Revolution and the mutation operated by the intelligence on itself, from all evidence presupposes the ruin, eviction, or, at least, the political sterilization of all natural or semi-natural societies inhabited by man based on destiny of birth or vocation. These societies include the family, professional community, local and regional communities, great or small country, etc. These societies undoubtedly still survive, but very precariously, revocably, inertly, and without the smallest role in the democratic state. Such a situation condemns them to disappear sooner or later. We are in that situation right now. The family is in decline everywhere, not only purely and simply due to the lack of the authority of the father and the mother, but, from all evidence—evidence that few men perceive!—because democratic politics penetrates right into this sanctuary that until recently remained untouched. Democratic politics introduces in the family the ideology of liberation, equality, and mutual indifference, which is disguised as "fraternal" sentimentality, firstly in people's mentalities and then in their conduct. The father, the mother, and the child or adolescent are centered on their own subjectivity, and close themselves into it, only coming out on the occasions when they are pushed to do so by instinct and emotion (always ephemeral with man if he is not settled and fortified by reason). They return as soon as possible to their respective closed worlds. Business is caught in a spiral of business associations and workers' unions, and only accidentally forms a part of the community. The region, suburb, and village are eliminated by the great city and its tentacles and by the capital megapolis—an immense abscess in the heart of the social body. As for homeland, one no longer hears anyone say the sacred name.

Democracy is basically the regime deprived of all skeletal structure or musculature, where the state reigns in solitude through an artificial apparatus whose cancerous metastases proliferate to the very heart of conscience. This reaches its culminating point without being the result of any natural social force. Democracy is uniquely constituted by a state without a society, by a state and a "*dissociety*," by a state and a collectivity that are composed of anonymous, equal, and interchangeable individuals who, being equal and interchangeable, clearly have nothing to exchange among each other and therefore find themselves deprived of communication. In order to have a democracy in the modern sense, what is needed first of all is that the organic and integrated society (where men live among each other in a reciprocal interdependence that forms the same *community of destiny*) disappear to the profit of a mechanical and disintegrated society. In this latter society, individuals, freed from family, village, parish, enterprise, region, etc. and uprooted from living social structures, simply add one to the other in a community of resemblance that forms a collectivity or an indefinitely extendable mass. Democracy is inseparable from individualist "society" and its inevitable direct complement, the "society" of the masses.

Inversely to organic societies, whose members are *present* to one another and share to varying degrees the same sensory, intellectual, and moral experience of beings and things that constitute the solid and unshakable base of their certitudes and capacity for mutual communication, mass society is composed of isolated and impenetrable individuals who are uprooted physically and psychologically from their milieus and who see their experience reduced to a very small radius of their own sensations. This is why the sensibility of a man who is immersed in a society of the masses continuously weakens and requires the support of amplifiers and stimulants that weaken him more in the long run and ensure that this truncated experience does not succeed at being raised to the level of the intelligence. The member of the microgroup is alerted to all that takes place in his community. When one member suffers, all

## Information that Deforms

members suffer! He feels the event in a personal manner and entrusts himself to the other members with whom he is in communion so well that all feel the same ordeal in turn. There is not, properly speaking, an organ of information in this type of society. Personal or interpersonal information is directly weighed down with information. The experienced man distills the sense of this and spreads it. He is more capable than others of feeling the impact of new situations because he has seen such others before. He is more suited to expressing the substance of these new situations in a way that everyone finds in his experience and formulas what they only halfway feel and do.

In mass society, on the contrary, the individual cannot enter into a relationship with someone else without information. Enclosed in his subjectivity, he only knows of the "event" the sensory and emotional shock that the latter provoked in him and that he interprets in projecting onto it the constructions of his imagination and understanding, if he is the direct witness. This mixture of bare fact is apprehended in a way that cannot be communicated and understood in a way that cannot be transmitted. It cannot be communicated by word of mouth except through a system of words whose truth cannot be validated because, in the subjectivist hypothesis on which every democracy is built, the subject defines himself by his liberty with regards to the objective necessities that are solely capable of putting him in relationship with the other. The words thereby chosen must be selected for their shock value and capacity for inspiring imagery. We will return later to this vital aspect that indissolubly links information to the sensational and to fiction by the spectator of the event. Its waves reverberate in concentric circles in passing through those who did not have the immediate perception, with this difference—that their amplitude increases in being deployed instead of weakening. It is a fact that the events about which we are indirectly informed are almost always magnified and distorted all along their diffusion. Information behaves like a magnifying glass combined with a mirror whose convex or concave curvature is determined by the informer's degree of subjectivity. The informer represents the event from outside and transmits it in altered form to another.

The vast majority of men in mass society are faced with an event like the blind man who faces colors without the subterfuge of information. They have no experience. They can only gain knowledge of it with information, that is to say, with the intermediary role of informers who register, collect, sort, configure, express, and diffuse the facts in their place. Without information, mass society would be far inferior to the societies of insects whose members at least have powerful instincts and are capable of immediate reaction when encountering an event. Information is to mass society as automatic reflexes are to animals, so that it requires a mediating central mechanism of news and a fabricator of verbal prosthetics that compensate for the disappearance of experience at the same time as the microgroups where it is deployed vanish. Mr. Sauvy[13] was perfectly right to affirm that information is of fundamental importance in a democracy. It is the sole link that is able to gather together individuals to form "society," the only articulation from one person to another, the only alert to events, the knowledge which is important for the behavior that they must adopt. Information coincides with modern democracy, and it is not extraordinary that little by little it expels the three powers that are attributed to the system, to finally congregate around the power that directs the regime and that is known always to be tyrannical and arbitrary, regardless of the anonymous aspect that it takes on. Democracy and information go together. They are symmetrically unreal.

---

13  Alfred Sauvy (1898–1990), demographer, anthropologist, and historian of the French economy. He coined the term "Third World."

## Information that Deforms

Information is also indispensable for contemporary democratic regimes. Information and democracy are only the obverse and reverse of a medal. It is democracy that sparks the flow of information, and it is information that permits the survival of the system as regards the decorative element of another regime that has not yet received the name. Information infuses it with a semblance of existence because it is perceptible, audible, and visible. The individuals who are immersed in mass "society" that democracy forced from the *ancien régime* in micro-groups henceforth have something in common that resembles them, but due to its precarious nature needs to be renewed at every instant. This renewal includes the contrary of immanent values to both daily life and the final things of life. It also includes novelty, emotional shock dressed up in an imaginary conception of social existence, and the incessant changes that "evolution" brings to the system of laws and regulations that enclose citizens in its nets and that endeavors to channel their subjective conduct by multiplying and tightening the meshes of its net with perpetual "structural reforms."

Information answers to a need that is so strongly felt by our contemporaries that they cannot pass up the "news." The reading of the newspaper is the morning prayer of modern man, Hegel noted. Montherlant evokes somewhere the head of the morning subway rider stuck in the latest edition of his morning read like the snout of a horse in its oats. Dissolved in the mass, the citizen of democracies does not let himself feel, with all the force of his repressed unconscious, the necessity to enter into relationship with his fellows, though this is the nature of the social animal. Sick and weak, this need paradoxically works at him in a more urgent manner than he is capable of satisfying. According to Aristotle, a solitary man is either a beast or a god.[14] If only to fill his solitude, he aspires to

---

14  *Politics*, I, 2, 125 a 27–29.

know what takes place in this collectivity, even though he knows confusedly, despite today's secular and ecclesiastical information that inundates him, that he is neither a beast nor a god, just as he marginally knows that, because of his very isolation, his destiny inextricably depends on the total collectivity into which he is immersed. He searches information for a remedy against individualism and against the mass society that makes him slowly die. And this very remedy confirms him in his bad situation! Cut off from the past, from traditions, objective certitudes, and evidence that natural and semi-natural societies convey, he must give value in his imagination to current events and their promises of a better social future, their promises of a "new man" in a "new society" that he desires, as well as the threats that weigh on their apparition. Information gives a certain body to his aspirations. Without it, and without forgetting as well the accumulated resources from the past that have become dangerously exhausted, humanity would have ended its course.

## MAN DEVOURED BY SIGNS

This unfulfilled social need, now insatiable, had two consequences whose magnitude one can only barely measure: The extraordinary verbal inflation from which we suffer which has turned men into tongues, and the monstrous development of the *Mass Media of Communication*. The first opens the way to the second, and its empire extends to all the domains of knowledge and action. One only has to look into our era to pick out the confirmations. The most remarkable events of our time bear the mark of this.

In breaking with the tradition of scholastic language, in which each term is defined by and refers to determined realities, the recent Council,[15] for example, created a phony quasi-unanimity among its members. In addition, on the pretext of obtaining from the "Christian people"

---

15  Vatican II. [Translator's note]

a better audience, it increased the amount of equivocal language in the Bible that two thousand years of theological effort had instilled with intelligible substance. When an organism as concerned as the Catholic Church is in not sacrificing anything to the seductions of subjectivism and in saving the ontological scope of human intelligence comes to that point, one can say that the evil is universal. The inoculation of the democratic mentality in the most robust societies constrains the members to only agree on words. As everyone puts into these words the little imaginary world that he has constructed and that does not correspond to that of the others, it is always necessary to stretch out to the extreme the signification of the words that are used or to take them in different meanings in the same context, if not in the same phrase. Let us not insist too much on this painful point: The Fathers of the Council made every effort to imitate politics, which is always looking for formulas to try to please and satisfy everyone with misty phrases. The texts on religious liberty[16] or on the Church's relationship with the world[17] can be stretched in every direction. The Conciliar Fathers did not agree on realities, but on a language whose relationship with the realities is indecisive. The proof is that the most opposite interpretations of the texts were made immediately and that a "spirit of Vatican II" appeared. This spirit tried to empty the words that were used of their residual references to the world of grace in order to apply their hollowed forms to a desacralized world. This would have been impossible if the Council had retained the Church's traditional language. The law of the reduction of reality to the common image, and the image to the word, something which takes place in all societies whose members have adopted a subjective view, could not then have worked.

---

16 *Dignitatis Humanae.*
17 *Gaudium et Spes.*

The examples provided by politics are so numerous that it is impossible to list them. The UN collects all of them in its ample and sterile breast. Agreement on words is directly proportional to disagreement on things. It is obvious that humanity is evolving towards Babel. The resounding indication of this is the reduction of culture to the manipulation of the diverse forms of literary or artistic language. The writer or artist no longer communicates with the other through the intermediary of beings and things that this language designates. They make an *impression* on the audience, inform the audience from the *outside*, encapsulate things in the chosen language, and violate this language. As others tire of this and avoid it, writers and artists invent a new language, a new mode which is even more empty of signification, a universe of arbitrary signs that reflect simultaneously the drama of subjectivity that is closed in on itself and its will to power, shock, bewitchment, and magic over other subjectivities that its influence rouses. The exaggerated place that the "philosophies" of language today take in scatterbrained heads is typical of this. The "nouveau roman"[18] is outmoded as pure deciphering of signs and formulas. Man is devoured by signs, and nothing remains for him of culture and humanism except for the formal structures of a language that is methodically and blindly cannibalistic.

Subjectivity dies as soon as it comes true. What remains of it? Unscrupulous spinning wheels, lay or clerical. They lead others with words. They eliminate one another with techniques that vary from a simple verbal or written blow to a shot to the neck. One cannot stop reflecting on the extraordinary and almost unheard of fact in history that the majority of dictators and tyrants of the modern era are writers or artists who substituted for the vain language of esthetic signs a system of signs that spread terror and

---

18 While this is translatable to "new novel," it is mostly known in English by its French term. [Translator's note]

founded the oppression that they employed. From Bonaparte to Hitler, to Mussolini, to Stalin, in passing by so many others who temporarily succeeded or failed in their attempt, *information* hardened and became a sign that absorbed the one who designed it, and made him the slave of the manipulator or destroyed him. In the language of the era, Napoleon observed, "I fulfilled the alliance of philosophy and the sword." His emulators, infinitely less genial and more expert than he on the manipulation of signs, would say today that they achieved the alliance of language and brainwashing.

## SOCIETY AS A SYSTEM OF INFORMATION

The *Mass Media of Communication* which are currently stripping the rational animal of his specific difference do not come from nowhere. Their birth, improvement, and universal expansion accompanied modern democracy and the democratic globalization of mass society everywhere.

In social matters, need begets the organ, and this principle, false from the biological point of view (in which Lamarck introduced it in unconsciously borrowing it from the widespread sociology of his time that was favorable to the progress of the Enlightenment), is one of the fundamental laws of human societies. Man is such a radical social animal, despite his subjectivist follies, that he invents the most complicated and eccentric mechanisms to artificially maintain the life of phony communities. He is forced to ceaselessly make and remake ideas from the spoken and written word, without which he would be dedicated to death or to its equivalent, which is endemic anarchy. A vicious circle, in every sense of the term, is created between the techniques of information and mass society. This is what Teilhard, in caricaturing St. Paul, calls "pleromization."[19] The more mass society annexes

---

[19] Philippe de La Trinité o.c.d., *Teilhard de Chardin, Etude critique*, tome II (Paris: La Table Ronde, 1968), 269–281.

the last debris of exhausted natural societies and extends throughout the world, the more the citizens lose their personal and inaccessible faculty to vitally experience the concrete presence of beings and things, and the more they therefore have to confide the enlightenment and direction of their individual and collective conduct to intermediaries who cannot transmit anything better to them than verbal or pictorial representations of reality. It is a full loop, in which mass society, a society linked by information, a society that is based on words, images, reproductions, simulacra, is built—if it can be called that!—automatically. It is fused in a gigantic collective holding space whose general direction is controlled by the cunning.

At its limit, one encounters a society—if, again, it can be called that!—inserted into a system of information that is composed of symbolic *stimuli*, either audio or visual, that provoke the release of conditioned reflexes by all those who have submitted.

It is inevitable. Here is a bit of reality: the war against communism that the U. S. is waging in Vietnam. The spoken reality is never envisioned, grasped as it is, in its real finality, by employing real means. The poverty of this spoken reality is often to be criticized. The military there is radically submitted to the petitions of democratic politics, the fluctuating demands of opinion, and electoralism. Such an inquiry is difficult to carry out, at least on the instruments that are used and that the mystery that is inherent in every democracy (due to the division between the decorative scene and the hidden machinery backstage) does not stop disturbing.

But this does not matter so much. Reality only serves as the pretext for the exercise of the law of reduction that governs modern societies, clubs, lodges, and medium or large states. Associated to the bare reality of war, which is always horrible, are slogans such as "the dirty war in Vietnam," images of terror which are suitably sorted, an

## Information that Deforms

ideology from which shines a hedonist "peace" or a "justice" for the unfortunate victims of the scourge. In the end, no one can see the reality of it all. Only the repulsion that accompanies it and the cowardly desire to be relieved of it at any price are felt. This is exactly like how Pavlov's dog, salivating before the piece of meat is brought to him through the association of a bell, finishes by salivating only with the ringing of the metal and by sinking in the long run into a sort of neurosis due to the lack of real nutrition.

It is unlikely that the intelligence can resist this treatment. It atrophies and gives way to dread, an obsession, or a complex of resentment against the agents of such an act. The simple mental representation of the United States elicits reflexive animosity, not for its conduct towards a people who want to become free, but for their behavior towards the subject of the reflex himself, which is rooted in the deepest part of his unconscious and programmed by information.

It is often asked why the world press and information, even those who have proven their conservatism and bourgeois mentality, are increasingly hostile towards American politics in Vietnam and, by extension, in the entire world. The secret funding of countries that are interested in subversion has to take some responsibility. But the principal reason for their openness to communist propaganda is simple. It is entirely found in the very system of information. *All information deforms*, and the information that is physically the most powerful (through the words and images with the most stimulating and strongest sensations) ends up deforming all the informers just as it deforms the informed themselves.

The liberal is by definition detached from reality. He is essentially mobile and able to be moved. He tends to accept all forms of fashionable taste. He submits to the strongest information, and spreads it. He confers on the most monstrous tyrannies a label of liberalism. He betrays his own country, if he is a rootless "intellectual" with the noblest and most smug conscience possible. "The effects of weakness are inconceivable, and I maintain that they are more prodigious than the most violent passions," noted Cardinal Retz[20] in a period of struggle analogous to our own. How can the manipulators of public opinion stand up, to correct it, against the stated public opinion that is manipulated by the most powerful themselves? They either have to renounce their roles or become part of the choir. Their very profession obliges them, as they are right in the middle of mass society, where they are always losers unless they imitate their unscrupulous competitors. There are honorable, very honorable, exceptions, but they are rare. They hurt themselves with their concern for objectivity or cede on certain points to the surrounding pressure to better resist on other points.

It is often said that the Mass Media that conveys information is technically neutral. Moreover, the means are neither good nor bad. This is a puzzling attitude, for where are pure means to be found? Pure means are means that would be the means to nothing, means that are not means, that are inert, useless, unused, inexistent, a strange thing Jacques Perret dubbed a "vistemboir" in his admirable novel.[21] A means cannot be taken in this way except in spirit. Only there is it purely "neutral." As soon as one passes to the field of action, where the means reveals what it truly is, one realizes that it gets all of its sense, beneficial or evil, from the end on which it is centered. Now, the Mass Media of Communication, which conveys information, is inseparable from this information. It is destined, as its title indicates, for mass society. Such a society is a pathological phenomenon that stems from the *destruction of the intelligence*. It is the human intelligence, in imbibing from the imagination and in completely fabricating the democracy

---

20  Jean François Paul de Gondi (1613–1679).
21  *Le machin* (Paris: Gallimard, 1955).

of great numbers and vast spaces, that deliberately opted for a politics of the unreal, without social substance and for evil and death, if evil is the absence of a function that is truly required by the human being for him to be who he is. The goal of the Mass Media can only be evil, and its evil can only ring out on the Mass Media themselves.

Isolating information, the Mass Media, mass society, modern democracy, is a totally theoretical enterprise. It doesn't make the least sense to do this because this divorce must be operated in the field of action, where it is impossible. To be effective and beneficial, it supposes man's renunciation of mass society and of democracy. As long as man wishes to retain the one, he will retain the other and, with them, the profound changes to which he subjects human nature. A newspaper, a radio station, or a television station for an elite, for the few, is a round square.

### INFORMATION AS PROPAGANDA

The problem of the good use of information technology is in this regard insoluble. This technology confers on those who have it at their disposal and who wield power such domination over others that it is impossible to renounce this practice without turning to Bergson's "extra touch of soul."[22] This technology ceaselessly dries it up at the source in both the informer and the informed. The informer considers the informed to be like a *thing* that he *informs*. He becomes a *machine* in order to act on a large number of men and inform them one after the other. The informed is, for his part in mass society, pure receptivity, matter that begs for the form that the printing press of information confers on him. The "mysticism" that Bergson

---

22 "Let us not keep simply to saying ... that mysticism invokes themechanical. We add also that an enlarged body expects an extra touch ofsoul, and that themechanical need mysticism." *Les deux sources de la morale et de la religion* (Quadrige / Presses Universitaires de France, 4e édition, 1990), 330.

calls upon to crown the "mechanical" and purge it of its magical spell, can only be a mystification. Mass society can only be prolonged by the abyss, by nothingness. Hobbes could have had his Leviathan overcome with a crown, Robespierre covered him with a red bonnet, Lamennais and his imitators in the contemporary Catholic clergy with a miter or a cascade of episcopal miters. All of this headwear destined to oversee the imaginary must become imaginary in its turn and no longer be anything except unreal.

Jacques Ellul[23] masterfully demonstrates that *information is inseparable from propaganda*.[24] It would be very hard to find a single example in something important that would prove the contrary. The journalist Walter Lippmann, who is a goldsmith, knows it. The American Congress, charged in 1949 with enquiring into the information services of the government of the time, concluded that it was impossible to distinguish information from propaganda. The causes of their reciprocal contamination can roughly be reduced to two categories.

They are first of all *psychological*. In order for a piece of information to reach the public, it must be interesting. This is too obvious. A newspaper that appeared with the headline, "nothing of interest today," and blank pages, would not attract anyone. Specialists in information recognize that, in order to catch the reader's attention, the informer most frequently turns to sensationalist presentations of current affairs that distort the depth of the story. It was therefore in 1952 at the Congress of Zurich that two-hundred and forty-eight directors and editors-in-chief of newspapers from forty-one different countries estimated that the dispatches from news agencies attached an excessive price to *spot news*, to their psychological

---

23  Jacques Ellul (1912–1994), philosopher, Christian anarchist, and long-time professor of history and sociology at the University of Bordeaux.

24  *Propagandes* (Paris: A. Colin, 1962), 129.

## Information that Deforms

shock value, to their spicy or extraordinary details, to the presentation of details not according to their chronological or logical orders, but according to what engages curiosity and provokes disruption, shock, or a "shot" that paralyzes the intelligence and floods the emotions of the conscience.

It is rare that information is repositioned into its context that would give it its real sense. Detached from its historical and sociological environment, it is dismembered and its elements are regrouped in view of influencing the reader or the listener. This manipulation of the news is reinforced by its material presentation. This presentation includes the fonts used by newspapers, the tone on the radio, or the point of view or image presented on the TV. Information is subjected to a great extent to commercial necessities, publicity, and propaganda. Its objective value is of secondary importance.

It gets worse. Whether it concerns the Mass Media held by individuals, groups, or states, the necessity to communicate information to men who belong to mass society and to the democratic regime obliges the informer to take into consideration the psychology of the informed. This latter is, in general, "the average man," who has neither the capacities nor the leisure time to control the information that he receives and criticize it. This is the "man of the masses" who encounters problems whose size, number, and sense infinitely surpass him in the news that surfaces. Assailed by information whose importance or value he cannot measure or prioritize, the informed is handed over to the discretion of the informer.

The temptation then becomes irresistible on the part of the informer to impose his own vision on the news and frame it in a system of interpretation that gives it a sense and makes it coherent. This is what the man of mass society expects and desires. He desires that the information communicates to him the directives of thought and action, an *orthodoxy* and an *orthopraxis*. The man of mass society sees his natural and semi-natural tendencies obstructed. He is incapable of understanding and acting by himself, personally, as his intellectual and voluntary faculties no longer have their normal outcome. The informer knows that he has before him a weak being who is easily fooled. How could he not feel the desire to act upon the informed as a potter does upon the clay? The informer cannot not be tempted to substitute himself for the thought and will of the informed. As soon as he holds any level of position in the Mass Media, his most intense desire pushes him to constrain all those whom he informs to enter in a total and definitive manner into mass society. The informer indefinitely expands his will to power due to this.

This temptation is all the more irresistible because the informed himself wants to be deformed. He becomes the accomplice to his warped information. He himself summons with all his heart the global explanation of propaganda, the framework of a simple ideology, the watchwords that help him avoid reflecting on the situations that he cannot embrace and on the corresponding behaviors that he is incited to adopt. Caught between the desire to be truthful and to exercise his will to power, the informer wavers, *ut in pluribus*, on the side of the mass so as to imprint on it a form that permits him to manipulate it and to exercise over it his appetite for domination.

The example of the Mass Media at the disposal of Catholics is typical in this regard. Almost always, the truth is subtly or cynically sacrificed for efficiency. The exceptions that exist pay dearly for their refusal to adopt these methods.

Besides, the individual who is isolated in mass society feels reassured when he receives from the informer (who substitutes for his intelligence, will, and conscience) the promise to see the problems that his stunted being cannot face by itself resolved without any difficulty. He is invited to choose the framework of solutions that have been proposed to him and to collaborate with the transference of

## Information that Deforms

that framework into fact. Theory and practice are inseparable here, just like in the Marxist system, in which information and propaganda are inseparable. To our knowledge, very little information openly or secretly stimulates action on behalf of the informers of opinion. This is not moral action, but the transformative action of the world. Depending on the information that has deformed him, and with his own consent, the informed individual is therefore almost always called to the socialization and mechanization of his own behaviors by power in order to consolidate democratic, mass society.

The reasons for the drift of information toward ideological propaganda, which is used to mask the will to power, are, secondly, *politics*. There again, we are confronted with evidence that is simply a matter of description.

News stories related to events that erupt around the world are collected by a small number of press agencies, current-event film productions, and television stations that are either state organisms, controlled very closely by the state, or have the greatest interest in secretly retaining intimate links with the state. It is the same situation with national agencies whose information does not go beyond the frontiers of a given country. Contemporary history reveals few examples of a national press agency entering into conflict with the government of the country that it is tasked with informing.

There is more than one example of a government that, in informing the public of its acts, presents this information on the day that is the most favorable or least disfavorable for it. The lies of Paul Reynaud, Churchill, and Count Pierlot concerning the Belgian army's capitulation in 1940, presented to the public as a deliberate betrayal of King Leopold III, is the most striking example. It was a matter for these governments to find a scapegoat.[25]

---

25 Rémy, *Le 18e Jour, La tragédie de Léopold III roi des Belges* (Paris: Editions France-Empire, 1976).

Even supposing that the information disseminated by the State is perfectly truthful, it cannot tolerate being called into question by adverse propaganda. It will therefore clothe its information system in a counter-propaganda that will irrefutably deform the information. A government that would, by some miracle, loathe the association of information with propaganda or pleading *pro domo* would be fatally brought to integrate both of them by the challenges that they would launch. It is enough to read newspapers to be convinced of this. It is not an exaggeration to claim that the psychological war of deformed and warped information did not stop from the moment that the United States realized the vital importance they have, particularly since 1914. A state that is subject to psychological aggression from another state cannot respond to it without adopting the same tactic. If it persists (though there is no example of this) in keeping to the pure and simple information—"Here are the bare facts. It matters less if the other countries wrongly judge me for lying"—it is immediately defeated.

## GOVERNING BY SHAPING THE MIND

The contemporary experience of multi-party or single-party democratic regimes provides more than an abundance of information that the individual, placed before bare information and information interpreted by myth, *always* chooses the latter. The imagination *always* triumphs over the real in the contemporary society of the masses which the democratic regime engenders. It always comes down to the same thing: The sociological conditions that preside over the accession of the masses to power *constrain* the state to deform information in order to govern as it pleases a collectivity of individuals who are docile to its actions. In a democratic mass society, a government that limits itself to informing the citizen without influencing, developing, deforming, or causing him to change direction

*Information that Deforms*

would soon be swept aside, even and above all in Soviet Russia, communist China, and the countries in their orbit.

Here we are touching on the most secret aspect of political and social life. No regime maintains itself without the consent of the governed. As the governments of democratic regimes and mass societies cannot follow the irrational, unstable, and unreal opinion of individuals (most of whom are incompetent), as this would be suicide and lead to the death of the state and nation themselves, the only remaining thing is to fool and persuade opinion that the State is following it, not leading it. Spaak's words concerning socialist voters are typical in this regard: "I am their leader. Therefore I follow them."[26] This implies that he pretends to follow them and that they are led from behind. The way to achieve this is, again, information that is remote-controlled and filled with propaganda. As Ellul writes, "The government cannot isolate itself from the masses, but it can set up between the mass and itself an impalpable curtain on which the mass will see projected an appearance of politics, even though real politics takes place behind it."

At the end of the day, all art of governing boils down to seizing the event that will permit the government to deceive public opinion in its favor. In this way, it obtains the adherence that it needs and without which the regime would crumble. The price that is paid is the permanent deformation of information, deception that insinuates into an event and misrepresents it. There is nothing surprising in that because democracy and mass society are founded on a permanent contradiction, because the former is this society in a permanent state of dissociety, while the latter is the politics that acts, not in function of its being, but in function of its empty being.

It seems to the outside observer that this type of government is difficult and that such politics requires a very

---

26  Paul-Henri Spaak (1899–1972), Belgian politician.

uncommon inventive mind. It is not so. As soon as it is realized that mass-society man, due to his lack of experience, needs information, and that propaganda in favor of democracy (formal or real, liberal or communist) must color this information in order to adapt itself to mass society that is destined for this, governing is a simple act, above all if the monopoly of the mass media is under one's control.

It is enough to get the masses to proclaim what was decreed. The formula, "The people want it," repeated over and over by the minority that possesses the power in the state, has a sort of magical efficacy whose importance it is advisable not to underestimate. In no country of the world do the people admit that they do not exercise power. It takes great intelligence to declare oneself incompetent. Socrates' words, "What I do know, is that I do not know anything," is as little democratic as possible. It is even at the origin of his condemnation to death by the regime he had provoked.

The masses are convinced that they have an opinion on every social or political matter. And in fact, they do have one, determined by the sociological conditions in which they find themselves. But its object is imaginary. It cannot always be this way. One cannot always float in the clouds. One sometimes has to put one's feet on the ground. Opinion sometimes demands a real object. The informers give them one, but clothed in ideology and imagination. Information extended to propaganda thereby gives them the illusion of governing. It is enough to seize hold of an event and present it on a certain day for "the will of the masses" to be activated, thereby "forcing the government into action." Therefore, the monstrous expressions in Beijing in favor of aid to the Vietcong are a response to those in Berlin which "forced" Hitler to invade Czechoslovakia to liberate the "oppressed" Sudenten Germans.

Fear does not put a limit on any of this. The elections at 99.95% in favor of the single party are as authentic as those that take place in the liberal democracies. In both cases, everything is decided by the people, that is, by a few, in an appearance of democracy that information weighs down with the dose of reality that is indispensable to the ascension of the mind into mythical imagination. English film technicians recently declared "that it was easy for them via a careful montage and a skillful use of certain angle shots, to make anyone into a crazy person." An information that is penetrated with propaganda and is a master of its techniques can *invert* the sense of any fact. A man can be made to want what one wants him to want, even his own slavery.

Roger Clausse, director of Belgian radio broadcasts, notes how the conditioning of public opinion in the U. S. A. by the electroshock of information takes place. The operation is carried out in ten acts. 1) Government policymakers have a meeting to orient public opinion in a different direction from the direction that it normally adopts and follows. 2) Involved government workers, particularly those in information, are directed to let some of these new politics filter down into their private conversations. 3) Some "impactful news," related to this subject, accompanied with commentary, is created through a newspaper. 4) This news immediately elicits questions during a press conference made by an "official," and the "new line" is diffused with a great fuss by journalists. 5) Government members and official figures hold talks on "the new line" in different areas of the country. 6) The president of the U. S. himself is asked questions about the matter during a press conference. 7) His declarations appear in the newspapers under large headlines and are the object of multiple commentaries. 8) Politicians and friends of the government commit to the new line and give speeches on this subject throughout the country. 9) All governmental services, from the highest to the lowest, develop "the new line." 10) The public, which has been hammered on this point of view, accepts the change, and the opposition runs for cover. In this way, even before being brought to public consciousness, the event is connected to the trend of a premeditated propaganda. This is how, along with the information that is stretched into propaganda, there is propaganda that precedes it and makes this information acceptable. The two things mix inextricably with each other to the point of becoming indistinguishable. It should be emphasized that public opinion is much more powerfully conditioned in the U. S. S. R.

In the mechanism of democracy and of mass society, it therefore seems impossible to differentiate information from propaganda, the event from the influence that it is given, truth from lie, the real from the imaginary, or data from made-up information. Declared lies and obvious untruths are rarely or rarely-enough the work of propaganda. Ellul rightly notes that modern propaganda prefers silence to lying when it is dangerous to publish information or point out a fact. A good part of Goebbels' instructions to the media were to silence news about an unfortunate event. Khrushchev's famous report to the Twentieth Congress of the Communist Party of the U. S. S. R. in 1956 was not revealed by the communist press until a very long time afterwards. The Egyptian people did not know about the events in Hungary until 1960. In contrast, the authentic fact serves as support for the mechanism of suggestion. It becomes a necessary element in "the smearing technique," for which it becomes useful for mass society and democracy. It is not falsified in the literal sense. It is transposed from the reality of daily occurrence to the mythical unreality of the ideology that interprets it and inserts it into its global representation of politics and society. Even if literally true, the information becomes false regarding its formal signification.

OPINION AND THE LOWEST COMMON DENOMINATOR

How is this denaturation of the event carried out? Always in the same way and with the same procedure that we saw in this book's preceding chapters on intelligence and science: the substitution of the presence of the real by an imaginary representation, creator of a "new world" and a "new man" and—does it need repeating?—creator by essence.

Some say this is incredible! Isn't this an obvious exaggeration? How can the great precision of the majority of information in newspapers and on the radio or TV be denied? Our assertion is not outrageous, and even less is it mistaken. As Cardinal de Retz, a wise analyst of the "information" that circulates in a time as troubled as ours, said, "experience has led us to believe that not everything that is incredible is false." Our minds are so encumbered by mental, verbal, or audiovisual images that information, which continually bombards our psyche, has succeeded in occupying it. Our intelligence no longer exercises its essential functions, which are to *distinguish, critique,* and *judge,* except by fits and starts or by chance. We therefore declare impatiently that everything that does not fit with this system of images goes against common sense. Information has come to be a substitute for the truth, in other words, for the correspondence of the intelligence with the real. Whoever doubts this lacks good sense!

In contrast, good sense reveals to us that, in a political and social system whose members are separated from each other because they are no longer involved in common realities, in common truths, or in the same *common good,* the only opinion that can appear is clearly not real opinion, resulting from agreement on beings and things, an agreement on felt truths, or an action that converges on the good of everyone, which is to say, a social fact that is *prior* to opinion itself. Without this social being, which is a prerequisite to knowledge, there will not be any knowledge, even scientific. This is because there are values and objects that are independent of us on which all of us depend, such as real concordance, harmony, or union among minds and hearts. Knowledge at its humblest level, which is real opinion, is subject to this law. Without this joint, prolonged, conscious or almost-conscious effort of the members of society, on what can their consent be founded? On nothing else but words. That is precisely democratic opinion. This opinion is established on verbal communication and is confused with it. When we are assured that "the Church is a state of dialogue," this firstly means that in the Church the common reality of the believers no longer exists. Second, it means that real opinion no longer has any standing there. Finally, it means that the Church identifies itself more and more with democracy and socialism, which is to say, with a humanity that is composed of free men, who are free of everything and even of God. This logic of error and degradation is unstinting. "Socialism is a grace," wrote Bishop Schmitt without batting an eyelid.[27]

While in a living society, the social being makes real opinion, whereas in a democratic "dissociety," it is opinion that makes social being and builds society. Here it is not the being of truth, goodness, and beauty that gives birth to opinion and its fact of existence. In contrast, it is opinion that generates the values of truth, goodness, and beauty: *Opinion makes being.*

It is necessary ceaselessly to expose and re-expose Augustin Cochin's brilliant analysis related to *societies of thought*. It is entirely valid for our mass society. In a society of thought, the "thought" can only reduce the correspondence of the intelligence and things, which is always personal. The formulation of a common truth always has the effect of an incongruity. The more one hollows out the real, the more one crashes into mystery, transcendence, the ineffable, and the incommunicable. In the society of thought, the real is excluded by definition. The "thought" eliminates the reality in which all would

---

27  De Corte's citation of Bishop Schmitt has "socialization," not "socialism," but the latter seems more appropriate given the context. [Translator's note]

communicate effectively, to the profit of the common mental and imaginative representation and its verbal expression. What the adepts of this society have in common is not the real world, but the internal structure of their minds, the capacity to produce images, forms, patterns, and systems, and to translate them into words.

And they cannot even have in common the very thing which they call "Reason." Their accord results from the adjustment of images, the coherence of ideas, the assembly of forms and patterns, the organization of systems, the connection of discourse—in brief, the adoption of a common ideology and way of speaking. Such an opinion is the result of the extreme impoverishment of the real, if not its depletion pure and simple. Communication is conducted at the level of illusion.

As Grimm already noted, in speaking of the craze to reduce everything to abstractions, which was the rage in 1754, we seem to want to "make everything into the quintessence, put everything into the melting pot." This perfect form, this absolute essence, this *being of reason* deprived of all existence except mental or nominal, not rooted in the exterior world, this world whose presence can no longer be perceived, was a matter then of projecting outside and of thereby creating a brand new world which is perfect and absolute, which would heal men of all propensity for evil because it would only incite them to good.

It is exactly the same in mass society and contemporary democracy.

For the "citizen" to be up to date with what is taking place in the collectivity in which he is an atom, the value of the truth, goodness, and beauty that objectively makes up the fact is automatically put in brackets. This is what is called "tolerance" for the opinion of the other or "respect for the person."

The research of this value would include the remaining time, along with penetration and a sometimes considerable effort, and would have to be done quickly. Without communication, mass society would scatter into what it is, a "dissociety." It is therefore necessary to ceaselessly inform and communicate as rapidly as possible. Successive editions of daily newspapers and the news on the radio or TV contain nothing specifically commercial. They respond to a necessity. This can be seen from the repetition of the news. *Doing* is a matter of making links among men in imprinting in their respective imaginations the same representation of events. This operation needs to be done and re-done continually, with increasing force of impression. This is why we have move from the newspaper on to the audiovisual image of the TV, which outcompetes and eliminates the written news with its increasingly lively images. TV news also makes the audience still more passive than its ancestors who only read newspapers.

Such a revolution is inevitable. The signs of the written word still signify too much and appeal to the intelligence of the real. Their power of bewitchment is imperfect. One can escape their control, make comparisons, take a distance relative to the text, and rediscover oneself. This creates levels among readers. There is a risk that a sort of aristocracy that is still capable of judgment might arise. Despite its tendency towards the sensational, the newspaper, to the rhetoric of shock, is still an instrument of connection that is inadequate for the atoms of mass society. A more fitting tool is necessary.

What Kafka said about the cinema is perfectly applicable to televised information:

> The cinema hinders vision. The rushed rhythm of movements and rapid change of images makes these images inevitably escape the eye. *It is not sight that captures images, but images that capture sight. They submerge the conscience. The cinema* [let's say, the TV] *means putting a uniform on the eye* which until then had been naked... The eye is the window of the soul,

films [filmed current events, audiovisual information][28] are the iron shutters in front of this window.

In other words, TV is the perfect machine that permits the fabrication of the representations that the mass of people without culture absorbs with unanimity. The same image is imposed on each individual, the same *uniform*. The image prevents mass society from dissociating itself from this.

This process of *vulgarization* of the image clearly follows the line of least resistance. It reaches the most malleable part of man, which is his subjectivity. Nothing is softer than the *ego*. It is an amorphous matter that can take on any form. The human being who is cut off from the real and withdrawn into his own insularity has only one appearance. How could it be otherwise since the intelligence that makes him into a human being can only nourish itself henceforth from appearances, dreams, and mirages? All of his being converts into a *look*. Posing as something he is not is his permanent preoccupation. His conduct is commanded by the exterior whose contours he joins.

If the *ego* can entirely and radically be *ego*, it would be the same as a piece of clay on which impressions from outside come to make their mark. Information would have a total hold over it. The ego would be entirely submitted to in-formation. At the end of the day, it would be the pure matter about which the philosophers speak, the pure potentiality to become anything, which philosophers regard as the minutest degree of being, a quasi non-being, a deprivation of form that seeks with unparalleled greed to be informed. Modern man would undoubtedly not degrade until that point, but the fascination for the latest fad, the empire of opinion, the extraordinary conformity of conduct, the vogue for a certain piece of clothing, term, author, actor, etc., demonstrate, with the unequaled prestige that

---

28  These are De Corte's blocked parentheses in both cases.

these things have and the tyranny that they exercise today, and that the degradation is becoming universal.

Information must therefore reach modern man at the lowest point, where he approaches nothingness in his indetermination, in his absence of character and personality, in all of his weaknesses. In that way, it rejoins modern democracy, which is the "leveling down of things"—though there is no need to say so at this point.

At a certain level of technical power of information, *power* cannot not change into a *want*, above all when it is in the hands of the anonymous and radically secularized State. The temptation is immense. One stands looking at a flock that is bleating to be led anyway and anywhere. How can that be resisted? Churchmen holding a spirit-of-Vatican-II mentality do not hesitate for a single instant: God wants it! It is enough to read the progressive newspapers to notice that their allegation of ventriloquism is spot on.

Such a popularization obviously affects the reporting of of fact. And the reporting of fact, popularized in this way, directly reacts on the fact itself and deforms it. Undoubtedly, future historians will have a hard time writing the history of our era, not because of the abundance of documents, but because of the essentially biased character of the information itself.

### CONDITIONING THROUGH INFORMATION: THE HERMENEUTICS OF THE FACTS

This deformation of information obeys laws whose importance we have only now begun to suspect. We have already highlighted the most general, which is that of silence. Everything that is troubling is eliminated. No American newspaper, for example, will admit that its propaganda against the war in Vietnam serves the goals of the enemy and constitutes a felony towards the U. S. By definition, modern democracy authorizes all betrayal except with regards to itself. The "free" man has no obligation towards any thing or person. Modern democracy is founded on this radical autonomy of the individual. Every event or proposal that goes against the opinion that information wants to create is thereby subtracted from the knowledge of the informed. The practice of cutting out information is widespread in newspapers except in the few still-independent ones. Cutting out information is even the rule for TV. We can cite a few indisputable examples.

There is more. Along with the profound, likely made in vain, remark of Jean Madiran:

> The nature of modern information is to *ignore that which is important* or to retain only the outer shell which is foreign to the interior or to historical dimensions... The techniques of modern information demand firstly of the one who controls them that he places himself outside of the human conditions for reflection, meditation, and confrontation that permit an understanding of the meaning of an event.

As well, the information is situated "at the level of sensory activity, but is invasive to the point of suppressing intellectual activity. It is permanently the opposite of an education of the mind," which is carried out through analysis and the gathering together of whatever is essential. "It is an undoing of the healthy mental state. Péguy declared that it is even a *de-creation*, the beginning of the de-creation of the world."[29]

In this way, one winds up where one must wind up when starting from a false principle—with incoherence. As Chesterton, always more penetrating than the majority of sociologists, sarcastically stated, "It is no longer necessary to fight against censorship of the press. We have censorship *by* the press."

The principal law of deformation of information is not always negative as in the preceding case. Just as we

---

29 Jean Madiran, "Après la Révolution de mai 1968," *Itinéraires*, 1968, 19.

see with the preceding, information plays the same role in the political and social domain that *the a priori forms of sensibility* and *the categories of understanding* do in Kant's view of knowledge. Information is almost always an *in-formatio*, a form that is introduced into the matter of events, a manner of conceiving current events, imposed on current events by the informer in a manner to make himself master of the informed. Just as thought, according to Kant, only knows things by what it puts in them, the informed only knows about present, past, or future events that the information traces out for him in the image, which is stamped with the interpretation desired by the informer.

It is too clear that the individual member of mass society cannot get his bearings straight in the maze of facts, beings, and things with which he enters into relationship through the intermediary of information without receiving some light into their signification and without ordering them. To this end, he needs frameworks, labels, and forms.

Political and religious informers (and, of course, their inspirers) are in this regard the virtuosos of the hermeneutic of facts. Examples abound in the newspapers every day. Here are some taken randomly from memory.

It is known that the American agitator Malcolm X was assassinated by a black person according to a whole series of convincing testimony. In fact, a French journalist caught up in black rights and the revolt of the blacks in the United States shamelessly attributes the crime to white people, as being the first to implement segregation.

Precisely four people protested in front of the campaign headquarters of the British Prime Minister against the possible adhesion of the United Kingdom to the European Economic Community. The next day, the television broadcast this same piece of news to the four quarters of the planet and presented it as a popular movement.

At the moment of writing this, the encyclical *Humanae vitae*, which forbids the use of all contraception, is under

## Information that Deforms

attack by all the deformers, whether lay or ecclesiastical, who are passionately ambushing its sense. One newspaper that I have right before my eyes has the headline, "The Pope does not condemn birth control." The reader who is in a hurry will only retain the headline and does not learn that the birth control allowed by the pope is founded strictly on continence and the respect for the natural rhythms of life. Another underscores with gall that the pope tolerates the use of contraceptives because he does not call this a mortal sin. A third announces that under a new papacy an encyclical will soon annul this one since the decisions of Paul VI and any encyclical are not infallible. A fourth argues that the majority of theologians, bishops, and experts on the subject remain opposed to the encyclical. Finally, the television has announced that the pope had declared, after the publication of the encyclical at Castel Gandolfo, that "he is not hostile to a reasonable limitation to births." And as no one told us anything about the adjective *reasonable* being taken in a strictly objective sense by the pope (a *reasonable* limitation is one where reason is conformed to the laws of the real nature of the phenomenon of ovulation), one is free to take the word in its subjective sense: "according to the decision of the individual reason." Clearly, they are making the encyclical say the opposite of what it contains!

The goal pursued by deformed information is clear: It is a matter of molding the event in a way that the event itself appears to say the opposite of what it signifies. The source of the stereotyped representations that come to model the facts of each specific excitation that they provoke is clearly the subjectivity of the informers and those who dictate to them. An objective mind receives the object. In contrast, a subjective mind projects itself into the object that is already brought to a docile and malleable state. The mind thrusts into the mind the ideas and images that *it has made* and that, originating from itself, carry the stamp of this mind. In this way, it constantly finds itself in the beings and things that it informs.

The entire art of information aims to find here a form that is imprinted onto the object in a manner such that the individual of the masses either accepts or rejects it. It is a matter of discovering a way of interpreting the beings and things that in their view trigger positive or negative conduct. Thanks to these *a priori* forms, which are freely provided molds, the individual of mass society becomes convinced that he can easily recognize everything that is favorable or hostile to him. He no longer needs to reason, take a personal position, or have his own opinion that corresponds to reality. He automatically applies the premade models with which propaganda has filled his imagination with the events, people, or situations that he encounters. And as all the other individuals who make up the collectivity of which he is a part have submitted to the same bombardment of information, almost complete unanimity is thereby created. This unanimity marvelously mimics the social cohesion of natural communities. It even outdoes it.

### INFORMATION AS SUBVERSION

The information that comes out of the communist countries is in this regard a masterpiece of simplicity. On the one hand, there are the archetypes of the positive sign that encompass everything that takes place in the Soviet (or Chinese) "paradise," and on the other hand, the archetypes of the negative sign that englobe everything that relates to "capitalism" and "imperialism." This Manichean matrix imposed on history permits an immediate deciphering. The so-called bourgeois democracies have at their disposal a scarcely more complicated arsenal of molds.

These molds, such as people, race, proletariat, work, resistance, collaboration, fascism, liberty, colonialism, etc. (I list these in any order), are not the spontaneous creations of *homo democraticus* nor of mass society which, due to their weight, would tend towards inertia and silence. They were built, experienced, and chosen for their efficacy and capacity to shape minds by informers, formers, and deformers of public opinion (and by those on whom they depend) who, since the eighteenth century, have occupied the commanding positions in Mass Media and fabricate Mass Culture. The technical necessity that is required to rush and push through this information, and the need to present it to the public in a new form, forces the use of these archetypes and molds.

As Jean Madiran, whom we cited just above, notes, information only behaves "with some psychological reality and commercial efficiency in creating a sense of change, permanent mutation, universal cinema, and revolution. What is solid, what is stable, and what remains is not material for information." What remains is that which flows. But to seize that which flows, recipients are needed. Archetypes, molds, and fashionable expressions play this role. And the container counts more than the liquid that it contains and shapes! That is why information is essentially subversive. Every society that has submitted to the regime of information liquifies or becomes "mutant," this admirable contemporary adjective that signifies that the informers (and those who operate them) are occupied with enclosing the stated society into the molds that give them all power over it. The so-called "post-conciliar" Church is an astonishing example of this, invaded as it was from top to bottom by a cancerous modernism compared to which the *Arianism* of the past, occurring in a period of Christian ascension and expansion, is no more than childhood measles.

The subversion that is inherent to information increases from day to day. Just as eroticism has invaded the cinema, art, literature, commercial, political and social marketing, and the liturgy itself, so the revolutionary forms of human life have become increasingly submitted to the information with which the men of the mass society stuff themselves. It is enough to look through the so-called "bourgeois" or "conservative" newspapers, without even paying much attention to them. The war in Vietnam, student incidents, the least political upheaval in South America, and the undernourishment of the peoples of color are so many tests. By a sort of automatic training or sliding down an irreversible slope, information lapses into destructive immoderacy. Still, it cannot be otherwise. As soon as the intelligence refuses to be measured by the real, it cedes its place to the imagination that dismantles the world and commits without limit to fog, working as a demiurge to create from nothing the new human history.

One could see, during the riots at the Sorbonne,[30] the televised information *creating* the event or pushing the revolution out of its nihilist chrysalid. One read and saw every day that the murderous Vietcong are the liberators of their people and that the peoples of the Third World give birth in pain and blood—provoked by their "decolonialization"!—of a civilization that is finally "human" and that conforms to Marxist and Teilhardian prophecies. Everywhere, Europe is invited to resign and be taken over by a sort of primitivist, incoherent, belching "culture," which in a word is idiotic. Information, spread out to all domains because it destroyed everything and has become the educator of the human species, will give a definitive form to this "culture." Information is henceforth proposed to be the energy that is capable of resolving all of humanity's problems. It is the metamorphosis and avatar, in the technical style of the twentieth century, of the Enlightenment's *Reason*, a creative and imperative force that was deployed, as we know, in the Revolution and its aftermath. Tocqueville stated, "The French Revolution

---

30  In May 1968.

continues, and is always the same." Information wants to be the conscience of the collective.

This is visible in the Church, where a clergy that has been captured by the most intemperate wordiness persists in bringing out of the souls of the faithful the interior sentiment of humanity's supreme value. "God is dead" in the eyes of this impious clergy. The function of mediator between man and God is therefore useless. How, then, to remain at the head of the flock and operate a will to power on it that increases with the dissatisfaction of the appetite, if not in replacing God with man? The rage that the postconciliar clergy has in raising the awareness of the faithful of current political and social problems is the stunning proof. It is no longer the Good News or the *Credo* that it spreads, but information that arouses subversive events. It aspires to be the commander of this information. The call to revolutionary violence launched by the clergy in South America—exemplified by the Cuban episcopacy giving its benediction to Fidel Castro's work—signifies that the "new priests" insistently offer their candidacy to the totalitarian information of humanity. The Legend of the Grand Inquisitor becomes clear reality under our bewildered eyes.

This is equally visible in all the secular enterprises of information. Informers are persuaded that they have a mission to accomplish, which is to guide men and, to this end, to make them docile to the prefabricated solutions that they bring in creating from nothing the event or the situation that "will make" the problem for them. Undoubtedly, the bare fact is always there, controllable, such as the Parisian riots of May 1968, for example. But it serves as a pretext to the information for a development that it is not involved in itself. Information inoculates fact from the exterior with the methodological monotony that we have already outlined. This monotony is the character of the modern revolution.

For example, here is the motion voted on the fourth of June, 1968 by the "general assembly"—they won't say how many members there were!—of the "workers of the production center of Belgian Radio-Télévision of Liège": "Radio and television are major instruments of information, culture, and entertainment. Information must be understood *in a dynamic sense,* that is to say, *it must aim for the awareness of the problems that are characteristic of the community.* To that end, there must exist among the workers of radio and television, and the concerned populations, *the most direct contact.*" The management and direction of the R. T. B.[31] must therefore be autonomous and entrusted only to the workers of the R. T. B. Are we wrong when we affirm that information, the informers, those who pull the strings, claim to be *the form* whose bare fact, communicated in this distortion to the poor "concerned" consumer of information, is nothing but matter? It is the mold of opinion, impressed on the exterior of the soul, that makes the being.

SUBVERSION AND THE EGO

The procedure is simple, and all the agents of subversion employ it, as well as those who want to maintain and extend their empire over men. The point of departure is always the *ego.* The rupture of its links with the real engenders in it an unconscious malaise. The nature of the *ego* is to always be malcontent and persist in the ignorance of the *real cause* of its inner difficulties. If it knew the cause of these, it would have already escaped in some way from its insularity. It is therefore a matter of making the conscience aware of the deprivation that torments it *in assigning an imaginary cause* to its latent worry and resentment. As the *ego* is deprived of everything except itself at the political and social levels under a democratic regime, it is not difficult to find a point of

---

31   Radio-Télévision belge.

## Information that Deforms

support to maneuver the control of awareness. The social instinct suffers from dissatisfaction. The bare facts that the thereby aroused "conscience" will mask in an imaginary representation are therefore not lacking. Moreover, the conscience that is withdrawn into itself is incapable of being confronted with the real. The imagination invades, and swells to infinity everything that is offered to it. The accident becomes essence. Everyone knows that the jealous, the envious, and the pretentious amplify, by a new awareness, the parts of reality that they distort and from which they draw nourishment. Helping and exciting them to this awareness is child's play.

With his customary acuity, Sainte-Beuve[32] even noted that the conscience that deludes itself in this way creates its own object. He even gives a date for the event. It is from Descartes that the conscience withdraws into itself and reconstructs the world far from reality.

> Descartes killed philosophy at school, but he established the philosophy of the study, not that of life... The man he describes is the man of the study, the man who is found and formed (*fingere*) by cogitating all winter, wrapped up by the wood-burning stove. This is the man whom modern neo-Cartesians believed that they found in their psychological armchair. In the study of anatomy, when one is working on nerves cut off from the brain, one has to carefully create with the instrument of dissection the appearance of an organ, which one then portrays as real and found. *In the same way, with psychological anatomy, one creates in a flash of wit the division that one imagines right at the very moment of observation.* It is said that the human mind has the marvelous capacity to aim its telescope everywhere it wishes to, and to create worlds there. *But that is so much easier when the telescope only turns within!*

---

32  Charles Augustin Sainte-Beuve (1804–1869), French literary critic.

It is the same way in the social organism whose anatomy offers matter for the imagination as soon as it is moved outside of its natural environment, which is *others* with whom we are really in relationship. Instead, it is wrongfully hoisted into the conscience *separated from others*, where it loses its own character. Any difficulty or obstacle is generated from almost nothing in order to provoke awareness in the conscience.

This is why the adolescent who is separated from the social world of infancy, and who gains entrance to man's social world, is an easy prey for the troublemaker or informer who profits from the inevitable moment of awareness produced by the disturbances that are provoked by this passage. The adolescent is maintained in this withdrawal into himself and in this awareness of deprivation in order to introduce into his soul imaginary evils and imaginary remedies whose efficacy he is incapable of recognizing due to his lack of experience and maturity. The entire art of television-related information is to enclose the human in his crisis of puberty until his death and to "dope him up" with chimeras. The citizen of modern democracies is particularly exposed to definitive imprisonment. Separated from his natural communities, he vainly attempts to join a "new society" whose edification is ceaselessly postponed into the future. Democracy is a *perpetual* crisis of political puberty.

It is in inciting the *ego* to distance itself more from others and be collectively isolated in a pure and simple juxtaposition with those who are in the same situation as he is, like the grain of sand next to another grain of sand, that awareness operates in the handiest way. The ego and its imitators suffer from this separation. They do not delay in becoming clearly aware of things. This is profitable, as an imaginary object can be assigned to this awareness. "The cause of all your troubles is other people. They cause you to suffer. It is they who are not like you. Oppose them.

Fight them. Get them out of political and social life, out of life itself. Having gotten rid of your ills, you can build with those like you a society that is henceforth peaceful, a collective without any cracks, a community that is exempt from all tribulations and weakness."

In other words, the *ego* and its imitators, amputated from the natural or semi-natural communities where they live in interdependence with others in the organic hierarchy and solidarity that is implied in every living society, become conscious of their solitude and are incited to place the blame on those whom they had previously opposed. For this imaginary ailment, there is only one imaginary remedy, which is the construction of a community that appears to be egalitarian and where everyone is in the same situation. This artificial collectivity is built around entities that are imaginatively provided with social value by themselves. These values include language (which can separate as much as unite), race (whose tribal or clannish breakdown can be seen), class (which ceaselessly crumbles and is impossible to mark out), the people (which has no precise signification), and the nation (which is constituted by dogmatic decree, outside of history, on paper with pen and ink).

### THE AUTONOMOUS EGO AND HUMANITY

As soon as one avoids naturally diverse communities, one falls into the uniformity of the collective. Unity in diversity yields to identity in separation, which is the fate of democratic regimes. Ultimately one is faced with a sole concept, the emptiest, *the most asocial that there is*, in the name of which men rise against men and become divided unto death. This is *humanity*, the "big animal" about which Plato speaks, the Leviathan of Hobbes, "the Church" of modernists and their acolytes, *whose nature is to exist only in the imagination*.

The informers and their machinists, who "aim for the awareness of problems inherent to the community," have at that stage reached their goals. They have created their object. They have created out of nothing an imaginary community populated with imaginary citizens who are confused real individuals intoxicated by information. Nothing is simpler than to lead these pseudo-citizens in a state of sleepwalking. As with morphine, the dose needs to be increased to the final explosion in the nihilist and revolutionary folly. Contemporary youth who have submitted to the bombardment of information and trendy education are one example of this. The "permanent struggle" that youth call for is the logical conclusion of the "permanent mutation" to which revolutionary (or "liberal") information and education drives them. The whole world today is in an adolescent situation.

Monotony now and forever. Napoleon, who pushed the revolutionary and democratic adventure as far as trying to conjure it up, had already used this procedure and defined its status: "I act only on the imaginations of a nation. When I no longer have this means, I shall be nothing, and another will take my place. The nose of a population is its imagination. It is by the nose that it can easily be led." The emperor did nothing there except sharply and cynically bring about Rousseau's dream which haunted the minds of his time: "I felt contempt for my century and my contemporaries and, feeling that I would not find among them a situation that could bring contentment to my heart, I slowly became more and more detached from the society of men, *and I made another in my imagination*, one which was so much more charming since I could easily cultivate it, without risk, and always find it safe and such as I needed it."[33] As a good disciple of *The Social Contract*, Napoleon only tolerated the appearance of an imaginary society whose machinery he operated. Every real society

---

33 Jean-Jacques Rousseau, Deuxième lettre à M le Président de Malesherbes. A Montmorency le 12 janvier 1762, *Oeuvres complètes*, volume I (Paris: Bibliothèque de La Pléiade, 1959), 1135. De Corte's italics.

was an obstacle for him. He stated, "My soldiers would be perfect if they had neither family nor country."

All of this heavy romantic heritage still weighs on us, the difference now being that its implacable force of inertia is crushing us. André Charlier[34] notes,

> If one wanted to carefully research the deep reason for the apparently more and more abnormal demonstrations of our time, one would find it in the fact that the "exterior world" to which natural communities accustom us is no longer felt to be real... It follows that once the object is dissolved, nothing remains except the subject. Far from being relieved of the subjectivism of the romantics, we get deeper into it every day.... Denying the reality of creation [and natural communities, we would add] is also a way to deny God. It is a form of blasphemy.[35]

It is not by chance that Victor Hugo placed in *William Shakespeare* the equation: "Romanticism = Socialism." Marx, Teilhard, and the disciples of Lamennais, Sangnier, and Bishop Schmitt, founder of the religion of Saint-Avold, are so much evidence. We always arrive at this inevitable denouement: Without a real society, the democratic regime's autonomous *ego* must be constructed by the information of an imaginary society, a City in the Clouds, "the alliance of sword and philosophy."

This dream has today reached its technical point of perfection and fullness thanks to the *Mass Media of Communication. The illusion* of "living" in society with the powerful of the moment (celebrities, stars, champions, famous singers, kings, queens, clergy of every religion and of atheism, "sacred monsters," the princes of this world) and of participating in universal politics from the U. N.

---

34  André Charlier (1895–1971), was a professor and director at École des Roches, author of several pedagogical books, and co-author with his brother, Henri Charlier, of a book on Gregorian chant.
35  The square brackets are De Corte's. [Translator's note]

and the Council to the Israeli-Arab War, Asian and South American guerillas, riots, conflagrations, and explosions everywhere, has never been more endemic. To borrow Sainte-Beuve's expression, it reaches us as we are esconced in our psychological armchair and, simply, in our armchair.

As Edgar Morin[36] saw very well, we are witnessing a second colonization, that of the soul, and a second industrialization, that of the mind, brought about by the sellers of information, knowledge, and new education, by the peddlers of social and political merchandise, by the manufacturers of culture, and by the Sophists in appearance, beside whom Protagoras and Gorgias are mere infants.

The industry that shapes minds is not, as is often thought, a twentieth century invention. The eighteenth preceded it in this way but, lacking technology, deforming information only reached a minority, the liveliest, it is true, in the aristocracy, clergy and Third Estate. It spread from there into a population that still had immense social resources in reserve and resisted it one way or another.

It is no longer the same today. Deforming information penetrates everywhere by forcing itself in. Thanks to public schooling and the "education" of which it is the principle, it shapes all men from their youngest age. One needs a foolproof intellectual and moral health which is undoubtedly accorded as a "divine gift," as Plato had already said,[37] to defend oneself and keep this principle harmless.

Without exception, the intellectual "elites" have won, as we saw in the previous chapter, by deformation. They are even the most active agents of propaganda. In refusing to submit their science to the corrective illumination of metaphysics, scientists have chosen immoderacy and a romanticism of Promethean information and transformation of the world that is then extended to the ignorant.

---

36 Edgar Morin (b. 1921), French philosopher and theoretician on the nature of information.
37 Meno.

## Information that Deforms

As for the "clerical caste," it has hardly stood out in its opposition to the mass pressures commanded by the users and profiteers of the regime. From Cardinal Innitzer, blessing Hitler's invasion of Austria from the height of the balcony of his episcopal palace in Vienna, to the Cuban bishops celebrating in Fidel Castro "the liberator of the country," and to innumerable prelates who have hastened to pick up the slack for Communism even as its power declines, the clergy threw itself, and throws itself, wholeheartedly into the unmaking of the Gospel. Montherlant's bitter formula is verified in our era's extravagant *aggiornamento*: "The clergy, always hungrily clinging to the powers that be, in the hope of merging with them."[38] It is enough to read the information spread by the religious press, from the *Osservatore Romano* sometimes to *La Croix*, and right to the diocesan or parish bulletins, not to mention *Informations Catholiques Internationales* (specialized, as Cardinal Wyszyński knows all too well, in the propagation of Catholic-communist progressivism), to notice that the apparatus for modeling, making impressions, and conditioning minds and souls is handled with an unparalleled virtuosity by the "new priests" who are dead-set on power.

All of the dykes collapse under the pressure of deforming information.

### THE RELIGION OF HUMANITY

Illiteracy, lack of culture, and ignorance (in the modern senses of the words) were once the reservoirs of virgin intelligence uncontaminated by the illusion of knowledge and ordered to the protection of life from the harsh imperatives of reality. The introduction of the radio and television into this world of "traditional civilizations" decimated its beneficiaries more quickly than smallpox, tuberculosis, and

---

[38] Henri de Montherlant, "Les zanfandeyzecols," in *Textes sous une occupation, Essais* (Paris, Bibliothèque de La Pléiade, 1963), 1451.

alcoholism. The diffusion of public schooling sped up the process of the breakdown of eternal values everywhere. Victor Hugo, who was, the well-known pope of democracy and of the religion of the masses, naively believed that all it took to close a prison was to open a school. Despite our disappointments in this respect, teaching men to read is more than ever the peak of progress for us. We glory in our statistics in this regard. But, as Fichte had already noted in his time, the majority of those who learn to read "hardly read books, but read instead what the newspapers say about books. This narcotic reading ends up with their losing all their will, intelligence, thought, and capacity to understand." Rare are those minds who see that reading (listening to the radio and watching the TV as well) is a technique that fits in a mass society and that henceforth it is rigorously finalized by it. Reading is therefore conditioned by the imperatives of this society, by deforming information, by socialization in everything against which Pius XII called Christians to rise up "with their vast energy." One only reads what mass society produces or tolerates and what its enormous anonymous stomach has predigested.

Reading only makes sense if the reader is *first* equipped with judgment, if he is capable, to the extent that he is organically connected to the real, of discerning true from false and reality from illusion. The *Mass Media of Communication* excludes this type of man *preemptively*. The man to whom these means of information are addressed is disposed to believe everything that is written, everything that he is told or made to see. It is enough to observe a newspaper reader, a radio listener, or a television viewer. Skeptics are rare. Everything is accepted as the Gospel truth. Never was Hugo more right:

*For the word is the Word, and the Word is God.*[39]

---

[39] Victor Hugo, "Suite," in *Les Contemplations*, livre premier, VIII, *Oeuvres complètes*, II (Paris: Bibliothèque de La Pléiade, 1967), 503.

*Information that Deforms*

Through the information that supplies his vanished social vitality, modern man has entered into the kingdom of the Imagination, with no way back. No longer having any effective contact with beings and things, he no longer *knows*. He is forced to *believe*.

Bernard de Jouvenal[40] writes,

> Our world is characterized by our mind's extreme receptivity for affirmations over which we find ourselves unable to exercise personal control and that we accept due to the certification of their origins... The progress of 'individual free choice,' to which our ancestors attached so much importance, is found to be incompatible with the expansion of human knowledge... We can only live on the faith and word of others. But then the choice of the authorities to whom we accord our confidence appears as the supreme importance.

When it is a matter of building a "new society" on the ruins of vanished natural communities, with "autonomous" human atoms separated from each other, the *faith* in this society-to-be-born must be literally made *red hot*. This is why our era is one of secular religions whose common denominator is socialism and the cement of information, propaganda, and publicity. The pontiffs of this religion are Marx, Lenin, Stalin, Mao, Teilhard, and their imitators. The best minds end up sinking down into *the idolatry of the social* that is spread and popularized by incessant information. We won't cite names here. That would be too cruel. Dead social reality has ceded its place to social imagination, and social imagination is supported by an act of faith in the "future City," by the religion of humanity finally reconciled with itself and equipped with its definitive cohesion.

Let's read a passage from *Les Miserables*, in which this act of faith in the saving information that leads humanity towards the new Promised Land, pours out for us its promise:

---

40  Bernard de Jouvenal (1903–1978), French philosopher and political economist.

Citizens, can you picture the future? The streets of our cities are flooded with light, green branches on the doorsteps, sister nations, just men, the old giving their blessings to infants, the past loving the present, totally free thinkers, believers in all faiths fully equal, heaven alone for religion, God for only priest, and the human conscience before the altar. No more hate... Citizens! Where are we going? *To science made into government* [we say: to information that shapes, molds, polishes, cultivates the "citizen" of mass society!], to the force of things [i.e., the tide of history!] having become public force..., to a rising of the truth that corresponds to the rising of the sun. We are moving towards the union of peoples. We are moving towards the unity of man. No more make-believe, no more parasites. This is the goal: the real, governed by the true... The nineteenth century is great, but the twentieth century will be happy. So nothing will resemble the old history. We will no longer fear conquest, invasion, usurpation as we do today... We can almost say that there will hardly be any events. We will be happy.[41]

The world that the poet's imagination glimpsed, and the mass society and the society of the information that regulates it are at the moment tirelessly *constructing* it despite all of the refutations arising from experience, all the accumulated failures, wars, and ruins .

## FROM ORGANIC CIVILIZATION TO THE SOCIETY OF THE MASSES

We are daily informed that we have entered a new civilization. We build it without submitting ourselves to the natural laws that are claimed. We are under the single direction of "dynamic information" under the devices of triumphant technology. We express in reality all that the imaginations of our fathers dreamed about. The City of the Clouds has become a city in concrete. The passage

---

41  The square parentheses are De Corte's.

from the imaginary to the real is being accomplished before our eyes. The future has already begun. Jean-Jacques Servan-Schreiber[42] has announced it to us. The civilization of the second half of the twentieth century will be *of a different nature* than all of the civilizations that preceded it. Besides the wealth and superior standard of living, its characteristics will be:

> The unprecedented freedom of man regarding physical, economic, and biological constraints; the near-disappearance of manual work; more free time than work time; the abolition of distances; the spectacular development of the means of culture and information; and power uncoupled from nature and life.[43]

Unique to this civilization, as to information and propaganda (and to publicity) which together make a unity, is the subordination of thought and action to *doing*, in destroying everything that remains of ancient European civilization and other civilizations. It follows that a single and same mass civilization based on the means of the masses is covering the entire planet. "*A single world or nothing*," pompously forecast Roosevelt, together with Stalin. And there are the exultations of Teilhard de Chardin when he sees the "*noosphere*" weave the network of its messages around the world and orienting itself towards the Omega Point, like a rocket.

The ancient world was not ignorant of art, gadgetry, technology, or artificial constructions, but it submitted these to contemplation, wisdom, and science, as well as to the divine, moral, and human laws that govern the world and men. The expression *ars addita naturae* admirably sums up this attitude. For example, the traditional institution of marriage as elaborated by jurists and priests

---

42   Jean-Jacques Servan-Schreiber (1924–2006), French journalist and politician, and co-founder of the magazine, *L'Express*, in 1953.
43   J. J. Servan-Schreiber, *Le défi americain* (Paris: Editions Denoël, 1968), 57. This book was an international best-seller and translated into over 15 languages.

rationally extends the natural tendency of life to multiply itself. It is not founded on the shaky feeling of love, which has been established as the absolute criterion of family *planning*. In this civilization, all means depend on the *real* ends of man, which are the knowledge of being, the good and the sovereign Good, and beauty. But the *homo democraticus* of mass society, both in his individualism and collectivism, broke his links to being. He is without the world of values that surrounds and surpasses him.

He cannot, however, live without a world. He needs to build another out of thin air to replace the older world that was totally destroyed, and chase away its last vestiges. The privilege that information technology and all the other technologies have in the contemporary world derives from it. The world is henceforth no longer the creation of God. In other words, the world is no longer Nature. It is the creation of man. In other words, it is Machine. The new culture ceaselessly builds informing signals that incite contemporary man to project into the crowd the facts that stimulate him *a priori* in his sensibility and understanding, exactly like the mold in an assembly line of standardized objects, in such a way that artifice continually supplants the natural. *Another* world, which informs contemporary man, is built in place of the one that our fathers knew, and loved or feared.

### IMAGES, OPINIONS, ILLUSIONS

It is a matter in this case of an imaginary world that rolls out all of its very real—too real—consequences under our eyes according to the very well-understood condition that we keep them open. There is nothing strange with this assertion. Does not each loss of the sense of the real ring out in reality? Mass civilization can only be a civilization of the image due to its source.

In mass society, an incident, if it were by chance presented in its bare objectivity, would be reported to many people lacking in even the slightest experience of it. This

## Information that Deforms

would risk their interpreting the event according to their individual patterns of thought. In such a case, the *Mass Media* would have to use thousands of different languages to express itself. This is why opinion about a given subject cannot be formed except through information imbibed through abstract symbols. These symbols are able to be imprinted on a great number of minds that are ready to accept them. Let us think of a pure and simple fact that would be colored by the adjectives "democratic" or "fascist." The man of mass society has a way of being in the world and a manner of thinking about facts which are both determined by his ideology, by words, formulas, slogans, and stereotypes that stand between him and the facts. What he learns is not the event, but the event that is molded in an abstract symbol. The African views and understands the events in the Belgian Congo, for example, not objectively, but in the symbolic form whose subjectivity is impressed onto him in the schema of "colonialism."

It follows that the opinion thereby informed and formed becomes increasingly unreal. In a mass society, information forms an opinion that does not bear on the object itself, but on the symbolic image that has formed the opinion. The information centers on the imaginary representations that it contributes as reinforcement. In this way, a genuine screen of unreality is woven between the intelligence and being. Contemporary man no longer perceives and conceives the world of daily experience, but the world of illusion. There is nothing strange in that because democracy is not a political regime, and mass society a society, except by illusions of our mind.

And so, the crafting of illusions that deform the perception and conception of the real is one of the most flourishing industries on the planet. Its revenues, including monetary profits and psycho-sociological investments, increase in proportion to the decline of humanity's intelligence and adaptation to the real.

Every activity in every domain in contemporary civilization consists of replacing reality with images and the presence of beings and things with representations. In this regard, the American sociologist D. J. Boorstin[44] recalls a meaningful dialogue between two women of his country. On seeing the baby of the second, the first one cries out, "My God! What a splendid baby you have!" The mother replies, "Oh! This is nothing, if you have seen his photos!" We can increasingly define information as the art of not saying the truth without outright lying. The difference between the lie and the truth blurs. What's more, the man of the street tends to prefer the pseudo-event to the authentic event because the first better responds to the subjectivity of his desires or aversions. Along with Gresham's law that bad money chases out good, the world of the image chases out the world of the real. Today the *appearance* of false events, reputations, celebrities, and a whole political and social universe, is created with disconcerting ease. We no longer speak of things, but of their images that are imposed by publicity and propaganda that is then transplanted onto information.

This civilization of the image increasingly incorporates science and technology that, with their close and indissoluble association, construct in turn a new artificial human environment that exiles nature. The man of mass society who lives in the metropolis no longer has any lived experience of nature. There are remarkable analogies between these two worlds, between the world of the imagination and that of precision. They are both built according to preconceived schemas. The world of the imagination considers the human mind to be a sort of plastic substance that is fundamentally suitable for being informed, for receiving a form. The world of precision considers matter

---

44  Daniel Joseph Boorstin (1914–2004), American historian at the University of Chicago, author of over 20 books, and the 12th Librarian of Congress.

in the same way. Both are worlds of imagination. We also see their connection is paradoxically operated in all mass societies and all democracies.

We are so habituated to this civilization of the image and of information that we have come to think and live as if the imagination were the real and information were experience. This is noticeable just as much in liberal democracies as in communist democracies. It is not class warfare, materialism, ignorance, tyranny, or anarchy that threaten us, but *the loss of the sense of the real*. The world of information is the world of Narcissus. Man only encounters his own image there. It is a world of mirrors that merely refers us back to ourselves. It shrinks the field of experience to the *ego*, to the sole idol that, with the collective on which it is projected in an outrageously aggrandized form, is substituted for God. Born of individualism, this world returns to it. It does not leave it for a single instant.

In this way, the deception produced by our *fin de siècle* surpasses all that previous eras could have produced. The technology of *information*[45] has reached such a point of perfection that it prompts man to substitute an imaginary world for the real one. It does so first of all to ruin the real world, and, with an art that I do not hesitate to call diabolical, it then makes the imaginary world the sole true real world. This is what our era cynically calls "authenticity." Authenticity is no longer that which is assured by a competent authority that certifies it, but, in the pseudo-world, that which corresponds to the imaginative representation of man and the world that the ego builds and that it most often receives already-made as *information*. "Authenticity" is the subjectivity that is affirmed as objectivity and that is thereby found in the objects it made itself and whose successive sedimentations constitute the modern world.

---

45  De Corte often spells "information" as "in-formation" to highlight the "formative" role of information. Information forms or molds who we are. [Translator's note]

This is a false, artificial, and fake world founded on the *negation of the principle of identity*.

When one successfully persuades men that the unreal is the real, phenomena is being, appearance is truth, existentialism or communism is full humanism, socialism is a grace (as stated by Bishop Schmitt), or revolutionary Christianity is the religion of salvation preached by Our Savior Jesus Christ, the only way to escape the guilt of this trickery is to double down on it. To hollow out the doubt, worry, and skepticism that such a position could trigger, this position needs to be strengthened and consolidated. It needs to give humans the assurance they lack despite their outward confidence. Those who submit to this position are greedy for this assurance. And so, both in the case of the informer and that of the informed, information tends to be endlessly reinforced, to be more dream and lie, to become, as in *Alice's Adventures in Wonderland*, "the cat's grin when there is no cat." In other words, it is to change into a hallucination directed by the wills to power that govern a world abandoned to the ravages of the democratic disease.

We have already said that information is inseparable from publicity, propaganda, and brainwashing. The hammering of minds has become stronger in recent decades. Nevertheless, it needs to be stated, and this is done too rarely, that *information* tends already to be the substitute for sensation, and that it has become universal. The importance of this double transformation cannot be emphasized enough, given that the repercussions on human intelligence are deadly.

Information has not just become "sensational." It occupies not only the place that is allotted to our personal perception of beings and things, but also tends, either by hypertrophy or atrophy, to dry up the source of our objective knowledge in us. This source is sensation. *Nihil in intellectu quod non prius in sensu*: there is nothing in the intelligence—no true judgment—that was not firstly in the senses. The scholastics expressed this evidence by declaring that if the intelligence is itself founded on *being*, the human intelligence is itself based *on the being of sensible reality*. On the day when man can no longer sense things, he will no longer be able to think. He will be separated from the true, the good, and the beautiful. This day has arrived. Are we even at the twenty-fifth hour?

At the same time, by means of the image, information becomes universal and generic, and is addressed to the entire human species, which is to say to man's *animal* character. This universalization is intensified by the confusion of the imagination with the real, which is unique to information itself. The intelligence is persuaded by information that deprives humans of their specific difference, that makes fiction into reality, and that asserts that the moon is made of green cheese. Our contemporaries want to be sure that their sickness *is* health. This is why they are contagious; they even want to be. They believe that their aberrations have become universal. All of their aspirations are condensed in Roosevelt's well-known formula, "*to make the world safe for democracy.*" We understand them: the ecumenical expansion of their distractions transforms their errors into truths. Propaganda provides them with the means to fix their attention on the image of reality, and not on reality—on the soap brand that renders it irresistible for all women to use it in the same way that the movie star uses it, and not on the soap itself. In associating the image of the soap with that of the actress who is a global celebrity, the soap is endowed with a universal reputation. Anything can thereby be enlarged to the dimensions of the universe. This is necessary. The image needs to coat the unique attribute of the truth that it supplants. That coating is universality. When fiction is universal, it is true.

How can man's intelligence still survive?

# Conclusion

### MENTAL REPRESENTATION AND TRANSFORMATION OF THE WORLD

If one tries to gather together our conclusions and formulate our diagnosis of the sickness of which contemporary intelligence is suffering, one easily sees that the analyses that we have carried out all converge onto a unique center: *Intelligence is inverted.* Instead of conforming itself to the real, it wants the real to conform to its own injunctions. But because it violates nature in order to achieve this, it was necessary for intelligence to be altered to the point of completely submitting to the powers of the imagination. This is our only faculty able to construct *another* world that can supplant the real world and that, being the work of man, will be totally submitted to him.

Intelligence, therefore, is made anemic and stunted. It is cut off from its roots and emptied of its substance. It has become the slave to what only a short time ago was its servant. At present only functioning against its own constitution, like a motor whose gears are in reverse, it progressively dies. The natural reserves that it still possesses are almost exhausted. It no longer has any power to resist this *other* world that it built when it submitted to the imagination. It has become incapable of recognizing the artificial character of this situation. It has become absorbed and harmed in its own productions. It has formed one body with this *other* world that it produces. It has lost itself in it, and materializes in it. Modern man is similar to the ant whose entire being is immersed in its work. His

## Conclusion

intelligence has become the prisoner of "the perfect and definitive anthill" that it constructed but no longer knows about because this intelligence has become so weak that it is captive to the matter over which it desires to wield transformative and demiurgic power.

In a word as in a hundred, the modern intelligence no longer *knows*, it *makes*.

There are three functions that philosophy always recognized intelligence as having: 1) the function of *knowledge* (θεωρία) in which the intelligence attempts to discover the beings and things of a universe that does not depend on it, but on which it depends; 2) the function of *action* (πρᾶξις) in which the intelligence attempts to achieve the end that man does not cease to pursue and that does not depend on his will, which is the fulfillment of his being and happiness; 3) the function of *fiction* (ποίησις) in which it produces the works that depend entirely on it regarding their objectives. The only one of these three functions that remains with us today is the third one, and it is the smallest of all our knowledge. St. Thomas justly notes, *Procedere per similitudines varias et repraesentationes, est proprium poeticae, quae est infima inter omnes doctrinas.*[1] Technology, which depends on the image and representation of the things it aims to comprehend, is unique to the poetic activity of the human mind. It is lower than knowledge. This is unsurprising since technology refers to representation, that is to say, to the mimicry and simulation of reality, and not to reality itself.

Such is the triumphant ransom of poetic intelligence, which is the maker of artificial objects. The knowledge that it has, which is total and exhaustive, does not leave the tiniest place for mystery or the obstacles that we face in nature. The world that it constructs has no more secrets for the intelligence, but this is not the real world into

---

1 *Summa theologica*, Ia, q.1, a.9, arg. 1. "Proceeding by various resemblances and representations, which is the characteristic of poetry, is the lowest of all teaching."

which the destiny of our birth casts us. It is only the film that we add over the real world. This film remains ridiculously thin in comparison with the immensity of creation and infinite number of inert or living creatures that do not depend on it. The intelligence dominates the world, and only measures the world's work if it can do so according to its own determinations, that is to say, look at itself in it. At this level of poetic activity, man does not even know himself. He recognizes himself in his work. He identifies himself as the author of his work because he projects himself into it entirely and finds himself there. That's all. The work of man perpetually returns man to his ego, as this work is the extension of man.

If knowledge is defined by the correspondence of the mind to reality, reality being independent of the mind, it needs to be affirmed, though our pride and self-love suffer as a result, that the field of human knowledge has shrunk terribly since antiquity and the Middle Ages. Now we only know what we make and what we introduce into reality in order to make it knowable, such as quantitative measurement. Metaphysical measurement has all but disappeared, and with this disappearance, all knowledge that relates to the contemplation of the universe, the essential principles that rule over the nature of beings and things that it contains, the supreme Principle to which the universe's existence is linked, has also disappeared. We have even reached the point at which we give a negative sense to the word θεωρία. This term signified for the ancients the highest activity of the intelligence. The translation of θεωρία, *speculation*, also has a negative connotation at present. The positive sense of theory is no longer used to denote this vision of the universe and its laws and Cause. In this denotation of theory, light spreads out to particular pieces of knowledge in order to situate them in the totality of knowledge. At present, theory is scientific hypothesis dependent on experiment, and subject to verification.

## Conclusion

The sense of morals and good conduct have evaporated in turn after a brief attempt that action took at replacing ostracized contemplation. Their disappearance was inevitable. When metaphysical laws and the cause of being were eliminated, the discarding of the nature of man and of his end had to follow. The moral code was no longer established on man's being and his destiny, but was suspended in emptiness, at the very moment when it was given the inherited burden of dead metaphysics. It only took two generations for Kant's *categorical imperative* and the *postulates of practical reason* to rise like balloons. It was the same with Blondel's *L'Action*. Called to give to Christian philosophy the base that it lacked, the consequence of *L'Action* was Action Catholique. This latter excluded the moral code and religion from any role. They were replaced by "elaboration on the new man and the new world" and by participation in "the construction of socialism." In other words, the *poetic* activity of the mind took over.

This is why our era is ignorant of poetry and art. The reason for the exile of these two is clear: Both have gone beyond their limits. Instead of producing beautiful works, subordinated to deep laws existing independently of the poet and artist in the same way that the laws of being and the good exist independently of man's arbitrariness, poetry and art claimed a radical and promethean autonomy. This was the same autonomy that modern intelligence claimed. The result is very obvious. These works have degenerated into pure and simple gimmicks, which is to say, into procedures implemented to achieve nothing that is independent of the author. The poet and artist wanted to be creators like God, but their works vanished into the abyss. They joined the technologies and technocrats in the exclusive cult of the artificial and of fiction, in the mystique and mystification of *making* that substituted for all other activities of the mind.

*Making* has invaded all things! As Gilbert Tournier[2] recently wrote, "We no longer savor or discover things. We *make*. We *make* Italian lakes. We *make* boats. We *make* speed." This "obsessional mark" of production in leisure appears to the point, never before achieved, that our era is fascinated by the conviction of knowing only what it has made. Such is the implicit postulate around which all the aspects of our time operate their revolution, in all the senses of the word. The human mind can only know what it has made! Leisure itself, only recently still a condition of contemplation and knowledge, has become work. The evolution of the Greek word σχολή, which signified *idleness* and that nonetheless gave us the word *school*[3], shows very well the radical subversion to which the human intelligence has submitted. And today, school itself is no longer the place where "theoretical" knowledge is dispensed, but a place where we are prepared to produce. All modern pedagogy bears witness to this. The universities have been carried along by the current. They are already advanced professional schools.

It is therefore easy to understand why our era made *work* the unique value to which all others refer, and the *worker* the very exemplar of "the new man" who, creating the world according to the new forms that come from his brilliant creativity, transforms the world and also transforms the worker himself. The worker is the demiurge of nature, society, and himself. In *making*, he *makes himself*. Henceforth, he only depends on himself for being. He is no longer subject to any transcendence. He is no longer under a claimed "nature of things" that might resist his ascendency, or under a reality that would be distinct from him. This is because he is joined to this

---

2   Gilbert Édouard Tournier (1901–1982), was director of Compagnie nationale du Rhône from 1950–1966, and author of several books, including a critique of technocracy, *Babel ou le vertige technique*, 1959, with a preface by Gustave Thibon.
3   *École* in French.

reality in transforming it, and to an eternal law because he ceaselessly modifies everything, even himself, by his work. Our era is the only one in human history that made work into a religion and the worker into a sort of divinity who creates the world and himself. Work is the modern substitute for the Absolute. Underestimating the pre-eminent dignity of work amounts to committing a sacrilege. Such a superstition could only be born into a type of civilization where the highest human activity is fiction, *making*, production, the incessant transformation of the world and of man.

Our study comes to its end in the highlighting of this *poetic* activity of the mind. The object of intelligence is no longer the real; it is the idea that intelligence *makes* by resorting to the powers of the imagination. The intellectual is a producer of ideas. He transforms the world according to the mental representation that he has formed of it. In this he is assimilated to the manual worker, a producer of objects, and transformer of matter according to a pre-existing model. The candidate for the *intelligentsia* is increasingly recognized as a worker whom society prepares for his function as a producer and who, from that time onwards, has the right to a "pre-employment wage."

## MODERN SCIENCE AND THE TRANSFORMATION OF NATURE

No longer wearing the crown of metaphysics, the sciences have increasingly become the technologies of the transformation of nature. They approach the real with the aid of instruments that man *made* to apprehend the quantitative aspect to such an extent that one many wonder whether they relate only to the schemas of the mind that thought up these instruments and forced nature to submit itself to the conditions of experimentation.

Simone Weil reckoned that "something strange happened to us westerners at the turn of the century. We lost science without realizing it, or at least that which for four centuries went by that name. What we now possess under this name is a different thing, a radically different thing, and we don't know why. Perhaps no one knows why."[4] Hannah Arendt thought that "it was not reason that really changed the vision of the physical world. It was an instrument made by the hands of man, the telescope. It was not contemplation or observation, nor speculation that led to the new knowledge. It was the active intervention of *homo faber*, of *making*, of manufacturing."[5] The strict alliance between the new type of knowledge and the mathematical and experimental technologies therefore placed man in the presence of a world that, at the end of the day, is his own work. Science went beyond the limits within which contemplative intelligence had situated it. Science has become the temptation to modify nature, to bewitch it in some way, and to achieve its ultimate domains and arrange them in a way to make a miraculous world and a superhuman man.

As for information, it *makes* opinion.

In the three cases that we have analyzed and that are like sections that are operated in the contemporary "*dissociety*," we saw that the ailment stems from the rupture of the relationship that the intelligence forms with reality and from its withdrawal into itself. In this interior world, it grants to leisure the largest independence possible from the real and its principle, with the debris of the dislocated world, an ideological and imaginary universe. It is then constrained to superimpose around itself this world that comes from nowhere. It could not live in its stifling solitude without this replacement world. The exterior world becomes for the intelligence nothing more than an immense demolition and construction site for which it is the sole architect.

---

4  "La science et nous," *Sur la science* (Paris: Gallimard, 1966), 121.
5  *Condition de l'homme moderne* (Paris: Calmann-Levy, 2009), 345.

## Conclusion

To this end, intelligence is constrained to appeal to the imagination, which is the sole faculty in us that is capable of representing the forms that matter must take. Intelligence brings matter under submission, though without admitting it is doing so. All the aspirations of man's inferior powers that are deprived of their regulation still converge towards the intelligence. The withdrawal of intelligence into itself cut these powers off from their human finality, leaving them with nothing more than their animal impulses. They blindly search for an outlet for their appetites. The now-anemic intelligence places itself in the service of the passions and instincts which move towards whatever can satisfy them in the world. The intelligence, with its capacity to calculate, deceive, and even use logic, supports this concupiscence and these dreams which all emerge from the lower parts of human nature. This unformulated greed is still linked to the real. The modern intelligence grafts itself onto this greed to confer on it its own determinations which it elaborates in its own retreat. The intelligence thereby reconstitutes its own world.

Without this stunning, explosive, and inhuman mixture of rationalism and irrationalism, modern man would be stripped of the world around him. He must *make* this "new world." He can only construct it if the intelligence in him lets itself be led towards this world of heaviness and the fall in order to find there an existing matter on which is imprinted the dominating form of dreams and lies. These dreams and lies accumulate in the recesses of the independent "conscience." Modern man forbids the intelligence this act of humility before the object that defines true knowledge. The result is that *rationalism is dedicated to irrationalism*. The more reason wants to be rational by being a faculty that is independent of the limited human condition, the more it must make a large part of itself irrational. Reason needs this in order to exercise over pre-existing matter its will to power and to autonomous determination. At the end of the process, the intelligence destroys itself and makes way for the imagination and the forces of the unconscious. In this way, what is born is a world torn between logic, whose empty form it receives, and folly, which grants it a shadow-filled existence. This is what our era calls the dialectical activity of the mind.

This is similar to how Simone Weil noted that "Descartes' adventure did not go well."[6] This adventure is based on thought which, deprived of its constitutive relationship to being, tries to find being. We are contemplating the final and gigantic efforts of this *poetic* activity in which the father of the modern world misdirected man's intelligence while preventing him from giving this direction its benefits. Auguste Comte had already seen this: "In its current vain supremacy, the mind is, all things considered, our main disruptor." He forcefully stigmatized "the current craze for the poetic pride" and "the vicious political pretensions of artists and poets." He notes that from the eighteenth century, "doctors, in the proper sense of that term, were increasingly replaced, in the spiritual presidency of the movement of decomposition, by pure literary men who were poets, not philosophers, but deprived of all vocation. The arrival of the great political crisis naturally gave this equivocal class the political benefits of its revolutionary supremacy." Contrary to popular belief, Descartes is much less a philosopher and a scientist than a *failed poet* for whom "the ideas of all things can be imagined" (*rerum omnium ideae fingi possunt*[7]) and then projected onto an exterior matter so as to construct a rational world as an artist or artisan would.

As soon as a human activity supplants another and imposes its unique functioning on another faculty, we find ourselves in the presence of a sickness that is the more serious that it reaches man's higher powers. If it is a matter

---

6 "Réponse à une lettre d'Alain," *Sur la science, op. cit.*, III.
7 René Descartes, *Regulae ad directionem ingenii*, XIV (Paris: Librairie philosophique Vrin, 1965), 129.

of the intelligence, the danger is mortal. Substituting the *poetic* activity of the mind for the practical (or moral) activity and the contemplative activity, amounts purely and simply (as we have said many times) to substituting *homo faber* for *homo sapiens*, technology for intelligence, and, in the democratic, or, more exactly, pseudo-democractic, *"dissociety"* of today, the tyranny of the technocratic state over natural communities as well as over the information that is directed at living and true knowledge.

Such a substitution takes place under our eyes with this aggravating double circumstance, on the one hand, that we are the benevolent accomplices and, on the other, that the techniques of persuasion, thaumaturgy, and mind-conditioning that are at the disposal of the technocratic state and the workers of the machine-filled factories, are such that utopia has become achievable. The stupefaction of our contemporaries comes from this omen. We do not even see ourselves any more because of how subjugated we are by the poetic perversion and by fictions that history has become prophecy, economics a prediction of a new terrestrial paradise, sociology an oracle, psychology a horoscope, and technology magic, while theology announces the definitive death of God and the introduction of humanity into a new Covenant under the world government of entirely secularized priests.

*Lacking intelligence*, we do not even see ourselves any more and therefore go ever further away from reality. Capable of knowing only this world that we build through our work, even in our leisure time, we are unaware that from that moment on our intelligence collaborates in its own disappearance.

### THE MODERN INTELLECTUAL AS REVOLUTIONARY

The time is coming, if it has not already arrived, when the most massive unintelligence will coincide with the freest and most devious technology. Know-how will come to eliminate knowledge and perpetual fiction, like a permanent movie, will do so to wisdom. Everything will contribute to this, including the technological *intelligentsia*, science, and information. It is the triumph of *poetic* activity over everything, as Victor Hugo had foreseen: "The modern ideal has its type in art and its means in science. It is through science that this august vision of poets, the good society, will be achieved. Eden will be remade through rational methods."[8] Or again: "Every civilization begins with theocracy and ends with democracy... At the moment when the eighteenth century came to an end, [the press] destroyed everything. In the nineteenth century, it is going to be remade... The great poem, the great structure, the great work of humanity will no longer be built. It will be printed."[9]

> Yes, thanks to these supreme men,
> Thanks to these victorious poets,
> Building altars of poems
> And taking hearts for stones,
> Like a common river of the soul,
> From the white tower to the bitter ruin,
> From the brahman to the Roman flamen,[10]
> From the hierophant to the druid
> A sort of fluid God
> Runs through the veins of the human species.[11]

Chateaubriand was more laconic: "The poet is always the man of excellence." And Shelley said it another way:

> According to the circumstances of the period or the nation where they have support, in the first ages of the world poets are called legislators or prophets. A poet

---

8  *Les Misérables* (Paris: Bibliothèque de La Pléiade, 1951), 1265.
9  *Notre-Dame de Paris* (P\Paris: Bibliothèque de La Pléiade, 1975), 177.
10  A *flamen* was a priest in ancient Rome.
11  Victor Hugo, "Les Mages," *Les Contemplations, Oeuvres poétiques* (Paris: Bibliothèque de La Pléiade), 791.

basically reunites these two characters at once. For not only does he strongly perceive the present as it is and discovers the laws according to which the present things must be ordered, but he sees the future in the present. His thoughts are the seeds of the blossom and fruit of the time to come. I do not want to say that the poets are prophets in the popular sense of the word or that they can foresee the form of events to come as surely as they know the mind. I leave this pretension to the superstition that would make poetry an attribute of prophecy instead of making prophecy an attribute of poetry. The poet participates in the eternal, the infinite, the one. In relation to its conceptions, there is neither time nor space nor number... The poets are the hierophants of an instinctive inspiration; the mirrors of the gigantic shadows that the future throws onto the present; the trumpets that sound the battle and do not feel what they inspire; the influence that is not touched and that touches. Poets are the unrecognized legislators of the world.

They are the demiurges of the divinity and, when God dies after the bitter rivalry that they deliver Him to, they are the poets, the makers, the creators of the world and of humanity:

> It is in their transparent and limpid thought
> That the infinite image is best traced
> And that the vast idea where the Eternal is painted
> With ineffable colors is illuminated and vivid.

sings Lamartine[12] in *La Chute d'un Ange*. This idea does not have to be pushed for long to discover that the poet is the true Word who is made flesh in Jesus Christ.

Deviating from reality was inevitable. When the real world vanishes and only the knowing subject remains, like the Spirit hovering over the waters, it is necessary to believe

---

12 Alphonse Marie Louis de Prat de Lamartine (1790–1869), poet and author, and influential figure in the founding of the Second Republic.

and *make* entirely anew, based on an image that is carried in the mind and that comes from the ancient, dislocated reality. As Novalis said in a few words, "*the world becomes a dream and the dream becomes the world.*" But as there is no possible passage from the concept of being to being, and the ontological proof of existence of reality and its Principle is invalid, the intelligence is misdirected into an unreal universe, a world of appearances, and a society of phantoms, in a dream that degenerates into a nightmare.

So there it is: the poet has been debased into a technocrat of science, information, and the intelligence. In a pseudo-democratic society in which the ego only encounters its similars, the fall is foreseeable. Instead of a universe of words, it is a universe of stereotyped things put together on an assembly line (in which man himself is a thing of the assembly line) that is henceforth our world. It is a world where the will to power has completely chased out the intelligence.

Marx sensed it in a way. His system, far from explaining modern "society," is itself only explicable by it. This system is entirely founded on the absolute primacy of *poetic* activity and the equally radical abolition of the other activities of the human mind. It is what he called *praxis*, but whose rigorously unique name is *poetry*. He wrote, "the issue of knowing whether human thought can achieve an objective truth is not a theoretical issue, but a practical one. It is in *praxis* that man must demonstrate the truth, that is to say, reality, power, and the precision of his thought. The controversy about the reality or non-reality of thought—isolated from *praxis*—is a purely scholastic question."[13] It cannot be said more clearly that the thought of man *makes* the truth because it *makes* the reality of things, nor that knowing is *making* a work or giving a human form to matter. Marx's philosophy is perfectly adapted to the situation of man which stems from the

---

13  Karl Marx, *Thèses sur Feuerbach*.

Conclusion

inversion that was operated on the human mind by the eighteenth century and the French Revolution. This is what explains its prodigious success, especially with the intellectuals whose class claims to combine the two heritages of the aristocracy and the clergy of the *ancien régime*.

Again, it cannot be otherwise. We have seen that the modern intellectual, having lost everything except reason, is constrained to follow the path of the sole poetic activity of the mind and build a new world and new man according to the image that he has devised. Thanks to this "mutation" of human intelligence, and to science and information, utopia has become achievable. It takes the name of terror.

Lenin artlessly admitted,

> As for socialist doctrine, it was born from philosophical, historical, and economic theories that were elaborated by its representatives. They were instructed by the classes that owned things and by the intellectuals. The founders of contemporary scientific socialism, Marx and Engels, were themselves, given their social situation, bourgeois intellectuals. It was the same in Russia, where the theoretical doctrine of social democracy emerged in a way that was totally independent of the spontaneous growth of the worker movement. This doctrine was the natural and inescapable result of the development of thought by the revolutionary socialist intellectuals.[14]

As Kostas Papaioannou[15] noted in a text whose significance is amplified in light of our analyses:

> one sees here an unexpected reversal [we would rather say, expected][16] of one of Marxism's fundamental propositions: It is not being that determines conscience. Ideas are no longer the 'reflections' of the

---

14 *Que faire? Les questions brûlantes de notre mouvement* (Moscou: Editions en langues étrangères, 1954), 35.
15 Kostas Papaioannou (1925–1981), philosopher who specialized in the thought of Hegel.
16 De Corte's square brackets. [Translator's note]

social situation, but develop spontaneously, and follow their own logic independently of every class or other situation. These ideas end up determining being. There is more: The being of the proletariat is finally determined by the conscience of the intellectuals... By their social position, they belong to the lower bourgeoisie, the bête noire of Marxism. And nevertheless, they alone are able to think of the social totality according to a revolutionary perspective. Meanwhile, 'left to its own devices, the working class can only reach trade-unionist consciousness.' And because the workers, abandoned to themselves, can only think obscurely and inadequately about their own historic situation, the lower bourgeois intellectuals who have become professional revolutionaries must, according to Lenin, form the core of the party and take on the mission of bringing consciousness and 'proletarian science' to the proletariat.[17]

What a display of victorious joy, what doubling of the will to power in the soul of the intellectual who finally discovers malleable matter and obedience to his dreams in a proletariat that submits to him like clay to the sculptor's hand!

Communism is very simply the modern "intellectual" in power. This intellectual is even convinced of the ability to convert into reality the myth that his brain, uprooted from the real, made into a world with himself as the sole author. As soon as the intellectual takes power, he broadens the scope and penetration of this world to infinity. The order that the intellectual imagines and imposes, which is artificial at its very origin, has to substitute for the living complexity of beings and things. These beings and things adjust in the universe and in society. This order is a mechanical device that is composed of ever-growing administrative machinery. It can take hold of life at a very close distance and insinuate itself into the most intimate parts of souls. Setting this immense machine in motion requires

---

17    Kostas Papaioannou, *L'Ideologie froide* (Paris, 1967), 40.

a very powerful will, and only one such will. The spread of the poetic activity of the mind to politics and social life inevitably leads to the reinforcement of the central power and of the state. This poetic activity is fundamentally totalitarian and, as such, arouses an implacable fight for the possession of power.

Every kind of work wants one author, and one alone. Alain[18] notes,

> Every multi-person operation—and political power operates constantly in 'democracy'—desires a leader, and this leader is absolute. Saying that he is absolute is saying that he is a leader... When twenty men lift a length of rail, they follow a leader. If they discuss the action, they will have their fingers crushed. An intersection jammed with cars wants an absolute monarch.

## THE DESACRALIZATION OF MAN AND THE WORLD

What shall we say about uniform mental representations and of the ideology to imprint onto souls and behavior? Such a colossal power moves wills to action and leaves only one survivor, the strongest and greediest. Divine omnipotence stops before everyone who loathes the essence of being: *solum id a Dei potentia excluditur quod repugnat rationi entis*, wrote St. Thomas.[19] God cannot make man into *another* being besides man. The intellectual who holds power can do this, or at least attempt to. He has in his

---

18  Émile-Auguste Chartier (1868–1951), French philosopher and journalist.

19  *Quodl.* V, q.2, a.1, resp. The entire Latin quote is as follows along with its English translation: *Potentia enim Dei se extendit ad totum ens, unde solum id a Dei potentia excluditur quod repugnat rationi entis; et hoc est simul esse et non esse, et eiusdem rationis est quod fuit non fuisse.* "For the power of God extends itself unto the whole of being, whence that only is excluded from the power of God which is repugnant to the ratio of being; and this is simultaneously to be and not to be, and of this same ratio is that that which was should not have been." (English translation taken from the Aquinas Institute —Ed.)

mind the new form that he wants to impose on man. He has before him an amorphous, prostrate, and submissive humanity. He possesses the technological means to permit him to *mutate* man. How can this temptation be resisted when one possesses leadership positions, technology, the means to spread information, and propaganda?

Intellectuals, theologians, and even bishops with a "preconciliar mentality" and whose "Christian" regard for man should have inspired them to turn away from this ambition, did not hesitate a single instant. They subjected the Christian people to the arbitrary whims of an immoderate will to power. It is in the service of humanity and as a witness to their love for all men without exception that they subjected the Christian community to intensive brainwashing and unheard-of information-based conditioning.

Who is more powerful than God? The response is straightforward—whoever makes man into a "mutant." The "mutation" in which Bishop Schmitt and the partisans of the religion of Saint-Avold indulge themselves merely consists of pathetically repeating a duly-orchestrated theme, created a half-century ago by Marxist propaganda. It is not only the radical transformations that they introduced into the history of Christianity that testify to the extraordinary virulence of their will to power. Their falsification of the original sense of the Gospel would have inspired Napoleon to dream, he who shamelessly declared, "The spirit in which history must be written must be assured before all... The important thing is to direct the energy of memories as a monarch."

Their "pastoral orientations" are nothing but a poor imitation of Marxist *poetry* camouflaged as *praxis*. It is for them a kneading of souls in order to conform them to something new, to *inform* them, and, when all is said and done, to treat them like a soft matter that they subject to their empire.

Intellectuals, whether atheist or more generally nonchristian, persist in desacralizing the world and man. Their devotion to Darwin, Marx, and Freud alongside their exploitation of the myth of evolution, socialism, and the unconscious, signify that the world and man are purely and simply understandable in terms of immanence and that nothing in them is related to any sort of transcendence that would make them sacred in some way. The world and man perceived in this way due to propaganda *are prey* that can no longer defend themselves against their projects and domination. The sacred, an obstacle that breaks the will to power, needs to be destroyed in order to allow for the extension of the empire of *poetic* intelligence over the world, including over man.

The establishment of positive science (which concerns only the perceptible and measurable) as the only knowledge there is will come to destroy the sacred in the world. The sacred will be destroyed in man by exhausting the metaphysical value of the intelligence and of common sense. It will be destroyed in the priest by "declergifying" him, according to the barbaric expression of a certain clergyman. We see this paraded in all the theaters of this world. Its practice began even before it was given its name. In this way, all things and humans find themselves reduced to a wretched state, ready to take on the form that would give them the lay and ecclesiastical wills to power that were provoked by a long impatience, because these wills still found themselves in a society that was taking forever to die.

Our diagnostic would be incomplete if it did not underline striking analogies, which are comical and tragic at the same time, that bring together the *mutants* of the contemporary "dissociety" (whose intellectuals, scientists, and informers are "the dynamic conscience") with adolescents who wallow in a dead-end crisis of puberty and who, instead of joining the world of adults, create an imaginary world where they are its victims. At the same time, today one understands romanticism. Intelligence, science, and information overflow with romanticism, though we no longer even perceive that we are imbibed with it. There is also the mortal danger to the intelligence of this sickness known to the Greeks as *excess*.

## THE IMAGINATION OF THE ADOLESCENT

Chateaubriand's account of an experience from his youth contains the elements that correspond, individually and as an entirety, with the points that we have provided. A neighbor from the region of Combourg had come to stay a few days at the château with his wife. The latter, while looking outside, pushed the young François between herself and the window.

> I no longer knew what was happening around me. From this moment, I saw that loving, and being loved in a manner that had been unknown to me until then, had to be the highest happiness. If I had done what other men do, I would soon have learned the sorrows and pleasures of passion whose seed I possessed. But everything took on an extraordinary character in myself. *The ardor of my imagination, my timidity, and my solitude prompted my withdrawal instead of my stepping out of myself;* lacking a real object, *I evoked through the power of my vague desires a phantom that would never leave me... I made for myself a woman of all the women that I had ever seen...* This charmer followed me everywhere invisibly. I conversed with her, *as with a real being...* She often became a fairy, *who submitted nature to me.* I ceaselessly *re-touched my canvas...* Pygmalion was less in love of his *statue.* My shame was to please mine... Heroes of a novel or story, *what make-believe adventures did I pile onto fiction.* When I exited these *dreams ...* I no longer dared raise my eyes to *the dazzling image that I had attached to my steps.* This fantasy lasted for two whole years, during which *the faculties of my soul reached the highest point of exaltation...* I climbed with my *magician* onto the *clouds....* Diving in space, descending from the throne of *God* to the doors of the abyss, *the*

*worlds were handed over to the power of my love*... I found simultaneously *in my marvelous creation* all the allurements of the senses and the pleasures of the soul.

Crushed and as if submerged in these double delights, *I no longer knew what my true existence was. I was a man and wasn't a man. I became the clouds, the wind, noise. I was a pure spirit*, a being of the air, singing of *sovereign happiness. I* got rid of my nature so as to fuse with the daughter of my desires, *to transform myself in her*, to contact beauty more intimately, *to be at the same time the passion that is given and received, love and the object of love*. Suddenly, struck by my *foolishness*, I rushed onto my couch, rolled around in my pain, watered my bed with bitter tears... *For nothingness*. Increasingly tied up in my phantom, no longer able to enjoy *that which did not exist*, I was like *mutilated* men who dream of bliss that for them is elusive, and *who create a dream for themselves* whose pleasures equal the tortures of *hell*.[20]

This prodigious text, incomparably more beautiful than all the ramblings of the modern intellectual, than the entire works of Marx and Lenin which are the transpositions and hardened caricatures in the social domain, than all the rhapsody of Teilhard (who displaces the theme in a pseudo-biological universe that is confused with a "mother goddess" whose son and lover is this new theologian), than all the geometric delirium of the technocrats, than all the fantasizing of the new world and the man. This incredible text, a translation of a lived experience, condenses all our long and patient analysis.

In this text we find the solitude of the *ego* cut off from its attachments to reality, the intelligence submerged by the imagination, the withdrawal of the conscience into itself with the creation of a pseudo-reality of substitution, the projection of this mental representation onto

---

20 René de Chateaubriand, *Mémoires d'Outre-Tombe* (Paris: Classiques Garnier, 1989–1998), 209–217.

the universe, the intoxication of the will to power that transforms fiction into a "reality" that it directs and dominates as it pleases, the conviction of replacing God and being as the Creator of these worlds, the certitude of no longer being what one is, of becoming all things, of being superhuman, of changing at the same time as the universe. There we find the subject who makes an object and finds himself identified with his work and the multiple facets of his creation. It is not until the death itself of the intelligence that the brilliant Chateaubriand (unlike our runts who are persuaded of their gigantic height and "historic mission") insists that the world of poetic activity, when it leaves the path of artistic or literary creation, is foolishness and nothingness. It mutilates its author and imprisons him with his fools in hell.

The author of *Mémoires d'Outre-Tombe* nevertheless asks "whether the history of the human heart offers another example of this nature."[21] The admirable naïveté of a genius! Chateaubriand's adventure is that of all adolescents. Ortega y Gasset[22] correctly writes,

> Perhaps what most differentiates the childish mind from the mature one is that the former does not admit the laws of reality. It substitutes for things the image that is formed from its desire. For it, reality is like a soft and magical substance, docile to the calculations of our ambition. Maturity commences for us when we discover that the world is solid, that the leeway offered to our desires is weak, and that, encountering this, a resistant, rigid, and inevitable matter emerges. It is at that point that we disdain the pure ideal and value the archetype. In other words, we begin to consider reality itself as ideal in what is profound and essential. It is nature that provides us with these new ideals, no longer our heads. These ideals are much richer in content and fantasy than all of our desires.

---

21 *Ibid.*, 209.
22 Ortega y Gasset (1883–1953), Spanish philosopher and essayist.

## Conclusion

The majority of our contemporaries who have deliberately broken with the real and with their own reality are delayed adolescents who did not psychologically settle their crisis of puberty and, if we are to judge according to their words and acts, will never settle it. These perpetual ephebes[23] are therefore restricted to constructing a world of dreams with the hopeless monotony just described.

In the sexual order, their incomplete instinct is incapable of moving on to the concrete. They cannot love a specific woman, but desperately exalt the generic woman with a capital W whose abstract form they have sculpted in their imaginations and that is nothing other than their disguised *ego*. They project this onto an indefinite series of real-life women who refuse to let themselves be absorbed into this image.

In the intellectual and moral order, they are given over to the same thing. They do not support reality. Their weak intelligences cannot succeed in piercing the hard and tough bark. They deny reality. They want to destroy it because its mere presence denounces their weakness. An act of humility before reality or an admission of its mystery would at least recognize its existence. The delayed adolescent refuses to do so. At whatever age, he is no longer even capable of exiting his *ego*, which is the site of the permanent crisis of his imprisonment. His constitutional narcissism forces him to be satisfied with mental representations that come from his own substance. He imposes this model on all things in order to create a world that is accessible to him and that he accesses, and will only ever access, from himself! He builds this new world, this new man, this new society, because he adores himself.

This is why a pervasive or shameless eroticism permeates all of the subversive, *poetic*, and creative activity of

---

23  Between 18 and 20 years.

the universe of this new man, who is the measure of this world. As Gregorio Marañon[24] reckons, "self-love is in principle loving one's own sex" in terms of the undetermined, the general, the powerless, and the incapacity to focus on one individual of the opposite sex. Is it necessary to conclude that the abstract love of humanity, which rages among young and old adolescents, is in this regard a latent form of homosexuality? It is likely. To be convinced that the shaping of the masses by politics, socialization, and even sermons is a derivation and sublimation of a rogue sexual instinct, one only needs to observe a rabble-rouser, government agency, or preacher who needs to *possess* the crowd. The only way to discipline this instinct, which is deeply buried in the darkness of our animal nature, is to bring it to the light of our specific distinctive nature that purifies it, compels it to obedience, and places it under the service of the transcendent end of the *ego* and its will to power. This way is the transmission of life and the fertilization of souls.

Sexuality can only invade and flood the *ego* in an insidious or violent manner which is separated from the real and from human nature. At this point, human nature can only become confused with the *poetic* activity of the imagination that generates a new world and new man. Sainte-Beuve writes somewhere, "Voltaire's libertine noted that *making* ideas, for someone who thinks, gives a bit of the same pleasure as *making* babies for someone who does that."[25] The adolescent peoples the universe of representation in which he is enclosed with dreams generated by his uncertain sexuality. The intellectual who refuses the human condition, the scientist who finds escape in going outside the limits of his science, and the informer who rejects the real are

---

24 Gregorio Marañón y Posadillo (1887–1960), Spanish physician, writer, historian, philosopher, and author of over 80 books.
25 *Pensées et maximes* (Paris: Grasset, 1955), 111. De Corte's italics.

## Conclusion

unwitting adolescents. *This is why they ceaselessly claim to be "adults" and imperiously demand that everyone recognize this quality.*

Such is the scheme of the will to power that they obey. They submit to its implacable determinism. They baptized this determinism as "the movement of history." The adolescent who normally settles his crisis never has such requirements. These requests and pretensions are on the contrary *the clear sign of his immaturity*. These requests and pretensions have at their end the confirmation of the adolescent who utters them, who is assured that the imaginary world where he has cloistered himself is the "true" world and must therefore be recognized as such. He therefore expands his empire over this world that is accorded him without it being possible for him to dispute it otherwise than by a redoubling of the imagination. The mature man, who knows the solidity of the real and his own limits, is defeated ahead of time at this level. Only the immoderate wills to power are in the race. Whoever arms himself with the most mystifying illusion and the most blinding smoke and mirrors will triumph over the others. Some religious, either Jesuits or Dominicans, declare themselves to be more communist than any communist and more materialist than any atheist. They know very well that they are unbeatable on this road towards utopia because their competitors must deal with orders coming from Moscow, Beijing, or Cuba. The more the adolescent, young or old, is confirmed in his crisis of puberty by another adolescent, young or old, who persuades him that "they" want to prevent him from becoming an adult, the more he becomes the prey of this other who imposes on him his own immoderate imagination and limitless will to power.

When one observes adolescents, one sees that their leader is always the one whose imagination is the best producer of illusions. It is the inverse order of reality: In the balance of weights, the lightest, the emptiest, the most conceited, the most extravagant, and the silliest prevail *automatically*. Look at newspapers or images offered to the Catholic youth of today by the Eliakims of Subversion.[26] The hierarchy doesn't even see it! Does it also remain backward in the same endless crisis?

The denial of the past, the morbid hatred for tradition, and the ease with which the members of the contemporary *intelligentsia* are closed to the lessons of the present and only see in current events a matter that is suitable for receiving the form of their dreams are the many traits that still characterize persistent adolescence. These traits all come down to the "mutation" with which the intelligentsia are all afflicted. The capacity to put themselves into the future, which is an appropriate place for mirages, the frenzy of the new, the satiety with the new that only recently appeared, and the delusion of change are other such traits. What never changes in all of this is permanent revolution, continuous subversion, and mutation that does not grow tired. The adolescent only raises questions through his opposition. He is a dialectician of the situation. He expresses his antagonism with regards to everything that reconnects him to his past by the love of negation, that is to say, of himself. Rediscovering his universe of birth and raising it to the level of the intelligence would imply that he becomes man, that he manfully accepts the human condition, and that he matures. In refusing to obey this harsh law of ascension, he goes on and on inside his narcissism. He can only exit this narcissism through artificial means, by creating an image of the world and of himself according to which he then wants to shape reality.

Among "intellectuals," the priest without a strong vocation, deprived of humility and respect towards creation

---

26  See Isaiah 22:20–25.

## Conclusion

and the Creator, is undoubtedly a perfect representation of the aging adolescent. His prevailing hypocrisy, which he proclaims in all his interactions, is to be "a man like all others." He rebels against the "tutelage" of the Church of which he is a member. He also rebels against the "paternal" authority of the hierarchy and pope. He encourages subversion and nihilism. He is part of the conveyor belt that transmits the revolutionary mythology that he embraces. He claims the dignity of "the assassin of the faith" in the name of Christ. These are all aspects of his "mutation." They show us that he is more than anyone else a slave to the psyche of adolescence that has fallen into the grip of the kaleidoscope of enchanting images. His aversion to the Church's "Constantinian" past and to the dogmas that are qualified as "static" have the same effect.

The resemblance would not be complete if we did not mention the powers with which he is invested and that, in his particular case, make him a singularly dangerous adolescent. They enrage him and make him into a kind of maniac who is capable of putting the planet to fire and the sword in order to introduce his dreams to it. Every adolescent aspires for his dream to become reality. Given a lack of means, this desire is almost always unsuccessful. This is not the case with the priest who is confined to imagination, whose lack of realism tends to relegate God to the role of constitutional monarch who reigns but does not govern. Such a priest even proclaims "the death of God" and his resurrection in humanity. However, regarding what must be called his apostasy, this priest carefully preserves the power with which he is invested to bind and unbind. When such a priest is able to substitute himself for God, to believe himself to be penetrated with the Holy Spirit and the worst extravagances, to support in the name of his prophetic charism his insane visions of the future and his loss of common sense, when he refuses to leave the Church with which he clashes, when he no longer fears anathemas and expulsion for heresy, *his will to power increases tenfold.* His unbalanced imagination wields an unbalanced power to make the world and man according to the absolute forms that every frozen adolescent carries in himself.

Such is the tragedy of our time, and it spares no country. All the elites, or those called such, are consumed with a lack of realism, by nihilism, by the forgetting of and scorn for *what is* and, at the same time, of *what must be*. They have allowed the intelligence in themselves to be extinguished. Intelligence is the faculty of adaptation to the real. They have replaced it with the imagination, which is the faculty of adaptation to chimera. The formal intelligence is left, but emptied of its natural content: the truth. It has become method and technology in the service of the most extraordinary adventure in human history, which is the incarnation of the dream in reality, of nothingness in being. The *poetic* activity of the human mind, abandoned to itself, does not *make* anything, but *unmakes*, does not build anything, but *destroys*.

The ringleaders of the contemporary *intelligentsia* announce to us, with the supreme refinement of intelligence, the death of man, the reasonable animal. Lévi-Strauss[27] writes, "The final goal of the human sciences is not to build man, but to dissolve him."[28] And Michel Foucault[29] trumpets the feeling of "consolation" and "appeasement" that he experiences in "thinking that man is only a recent invention, a figure who is not two centuries old, a simple fold in our knowledge, and that he will disappear as soon as this figure has found a new form."[30]

---

27  Claude Lévi-Strauss (1908–2009), French anthropologist and ethnologist.
28  *La pensée sauvage* (Paris: Plon, 1962), 326.
29  Paul-Michel Foucault (1926–1984), French public intellectual, philosopher, and historian of ideas.
30  *Les mots et les choses* (Paris: Gallimard, 1966), 15.

*Conclusion*

There is no need to search for this new form of knowledge that kills man in his specific difference. It is the child of the lay and ecclesiastical *intelligentsia* who possesses this. The rogue intelligence that accepts neither its limited human condition nor the limits that the real and its Principle impose on it, generates an intellectual plebeian who attacks the planet under the leadership of the princes of this world and the Prince of this world. This rogue no longer knows any brakes. Provided with all of the bursting appetites of the beast, equipped with a hypertrophied technical power, it has every license (in the good conscience that it creates) to transform men according to his own image.

We already hear his roaring like the clashing of gunfire: "Join us or die!

# INDEX OF NAMES

Aesop, 9
Alain, 224, 231
Anaxagoras, 72
Arendt, Hannah, 222
Aristotle, xx, xxii, xxiv, xxxvii, 5, 18, 22, 54, 68, 72, 73, 96, 126, 142, 167
Bacon, Francis, 104
Balzac, Honoré de, 137
Baudelaire, Charles, 37
Beauvoir, Simone de, 6
Bergier, Jacques, 121
Bergson, Henri, xxii, xxxviii, 71, 106, 175
Bernard, Claude, 97, 98
Bernanos, Georges, 57, 154
Berthelot, Marcellin, 109
Binet, Alfred, 90
Blondel, Maurice, 219
Bloy, Léon, 128
Boorstin, D.J., 212
Boucheix, Mgr. Raymond, lvi
Bounoure, Louis, 135
Bridgman, P.W., 90
Broglie, Louis de, 87, 88, 95, 99, 106, 113, 114
Brunschvicg, Léon, 100–102
Calvet, Dom Gérard, OSB, lv
Cassirer, Ernst, 133
Castro, Fidel, xxii, xxiii
Cato the Elder, 3
Caullery, Maurice, 134
Charlier, André, 203
Chateaubriand, François-René de, 226, 234
Chesterton, Gilbert Keith, xxiv, xlii, 137, 191
Churchill, Winston, 179
Clarke, Arthur C., 128
Clausse, Roger, 183
Clémenceau, Georges, 7
Cleopatra, 21
Cochin, Augustin, 21, 150, 155–157, 186
Comte, Auguste, 20, 117, 224
Compton, Arthur Holly, 87
Confucius, 128
Cournot, Antoine Augustin, 162
Dartan, Jacques, 121
Darwin, Charles, 135, 233
Decourtray, Cardinal Albert, lvii
De Gaulle, Charles, 151
Delage, Yves, 135
Descartes, René, 23, 32, 38, 41, 78, 80, 86, 117, 199, 224
Diderot, Denis, 7, 67, 133
Duhem, Pierre, 99, 113
Eddington, Arthur, 39, 84, 89, 92, 98
Einstein, Albert, 90, 93, 95, 100, 101
Ellul, Jacques, 176, 181, 184
Engels, Friedrich, 229
Feuerbach, Ludwig, 26–28, 42, 228
Fichte, Johann Gottlieb, 206
Filippi, Ulysse, 87
Foucault, Michel, 242
Fourier, Joseph, 115
Frank, Philip, 95
Freud, Sigmund, 233

Galileo, 39, 78, 86, 97, 126
Gauss, Carl Friedrich, 101
Gilson, Étienne, xxiii, 125–127
Goblot, Edmond, 113
Goebbels, Joseph, 142, 184
Goethe, Johann Wolfgang von, 54, 119
Gorgias, 76, 204
Gresham, Thomas, 212
Grimm, Friedrich Melchior, 187
Günther, Gotthard, 128
Haeckel, Ernst, 135
Haldane, J. B. S., 121, 129
Hazard, Paul, 6
Hegel, Friedrich, 26, 28, 167, 229
Heisenberg, Werner, 39, 87, 88, 114
Herder, Johann Gottfried, 133
Hildebrand, Dietrich von, xliv
Hitler, Adolf, 171, 182, 205
Hobbes, Thomas, 176, 201
Homer, 54, 107
Hugo, Victor, 119, 203, 206, 226
Huxley, Aldous, xlv
Huxley, Julian, 121, 139–141
Infeld, Leopold, 93
Innitzer, Cardinal Theodor, 205
Janssens, Père, S.J., 142
John of St. Thomas, 96
John Paul II, lvii, lviii
John XXIII, xxxix
Jesus Christ, xxxiii, 128, 132, 214, 227
Joubert, Joseph, 10
Jouvenel, Bertrand de, 207
Jugnet, Louis, 138
Juvenal, 33

Kafka, Franz, 188
Kant, Immanuel, 24–26, 28, 100, 112, 133, 192
Khrushchev, Nikita, 184
Kosygin, Alexis, 126
Koyré, Alexandre, 39
Laborit, Henri, 121
La Bruyère, Jean de, 131
La Fontaine, Jean de, 33
Lamarck, Jean-Baptiste de, 134, 171
Lamartine, Alphonse de, 47, 227
Lamennais, Félicité de, 176, 203
Leibniz, Gottfried Wilhelm, 133
Lenin, Vladimir, 142, 207, 229, 230, 235
Leo XIII, xvii
Leopold III, 179
Leprince-Riguet, Louis, 121–127
Le Roy, Édouard, 101, 102
Lessing, Gotthold Ephraim, 133, 134
Lévi-Strauss, Claude, 242
Lippmann, Walter, 176
Littré, Émile, 147, 148
Lubac, Cardinal Henri de, 139
Madiran, Jean, xxiii, xxx, xxxiii, xliii, lviii, 65, 191, 195
Malcolm X, 192
Mao Tse Toung, 126, 207
Marañon, Gregorio, 238
Maritain, Jacques, xxii, 64, 65, 97
Marx, Karl, 8, 26, 28, 38, 42, 51, 128, 203, 207, 228, 229, 233, 235
Maurras, Charles, xxx, xxxiii, 7–9, 16, 44, 57, 66, 153

## Index of Names

McLuhan, Marshall, xv
Meyerson, Émile, 136
Mohammed, 128
Molière, Jean-Baptiste, 37, 67, 121
Montaigne, 5, 37, 105
Montherlant, Henry de, 167
Morand, 128
Morin, Edgar, 204
Mounier, Emmanuel, 51, 128
Mussolini, Benito, 171
Napoleon I, Bonaparte, 171, 202, 232
Newton, Isaac, 78, 86
Novalis, 228
Ortega y Gasset, José, 236
Orwell, George, xlv
Papaioannou, Kostas, 229, 230
Parkinson, 59
Pascal, Blaise, 21, 116
Paul, St., 142, 171
Paul VI, xli, lviii, 193,
Pauwels, Louis, 121
Péguy, Charles, 6, 59, 121, 191
Perret, Jacques, 174
Pic de la Mirandola, 78, 149
Pius X, lviii
Pius XII, xxxvii, li, 150, 206
Philippe de la Trinité, O.C.D., 171
Pierlot, Hubert, 179
Pindare, 77
Planck, Max, 40, 92
Plato, xxxii, 75
Poincaré, Henri, 97, 98, 136
Pressey, Sidney, 120
Protagoras, 75, 100, 204,
Proudhon, Pierre-Joseph, 161

Rambaud, Henri, 139
Ramuz, Charles-Ferdinand, 57, 104
Ratzinger, Cardinal Joseph, xli
Regnault, 99
Rémy, 179
Renan, Ernest, 110, 111
Retz, Cardinal de, 174, 185
Reynaud, Paul, 179
Rideau, Émile, S.J., 98
Riemann, Bernhard, 101
Robespierre, Maximilien de, 176
Roosevelt, Franklin D., 150, 209, 215
Rousseau, Jean-Jacques, 9, 202
Sainte-Beuve, 199, 204, 238
Sangnier, Marc, 203
Sartre, Jean-Paul, 34, 35
Sauvy, Alfred, 166
Schmitt, Msgr. Paul-Joseph, xliii, 186, 203, 214, 232
Schrödinger, Erwin, 41
Seneca, 3
Servan-Schreiber, Jean-Jacques, 209
Shakespeare, 19, 203
Shaw, Bernard, 129
Shelley, Percy, 226
Socrates, 182
Spaak, Paul-Henri, 181
Stalin, Joseph, 31, 171, 207, 209
Taine, Hippolyte, 21
Teilhard de Chardin, 43, 105, 120, 130, 139, 142, 171, 209
Thatcher, xvi
Thibaudet, Albert, 6
Thomas Aquinas, xx, xxii, xli, 85, 117, 126, 142, 217

247

Tilgher, Adriano, 25
Tocqueville, Alexis de, 21, 59, 60, 196
Tournier, Gilbert, 220
Valéry, Paul, xxxvi, xxxvii, 37, 48, 122, 147
Vigny, Alfred de, 7
Vinci, Leonardo de, 78
Virchow, 135
Virgil, 22
Voltaire, 9, 238
Weil, Simone, 221, 224
Wyszyński, Cardinal Stefan, 205

## ABOUT THE AUTHOR

MARCEL DE CORTE was born in Belgium in 1905 and died in 1994. Philosopher, heir to the great Aristotelian tradition, contemporary of Jacques Maritain, Etienne Gilson, Gabriel Marcel, and Gustave Thibon, he taught at the University of Liège until 1975. Author of more than twenty works on philosophical reflection, he is notably interested in social evolutions that stem from the French and Industrial Revolutions, principally regarding the moral and social disintegration of modern man.

www.ingramcontent.com/pod-product-compliance
Lightning Source LLC
Chambersburg PA
CBHW020242010526
44107CB00038B/1447/J